THE BLUE GUIDES

Austria
Belgium and Luxembourg
China
Cyprus
Czechoslovakia
Denmark
Egypt

FRANCE
France
Paris and Versailles
Burgundy
Normandy
Corsica

GREECE
Greece
Athens
Crete

HOLLAND
Holland
Amsterdam

Hungary

ITALY
Northern Italy
Southern Italy
Florence
Rome and environs
Venice
Tuscany
Umbria
Sicily

Jerusalem
Malta and Gozo

Morocco
Moscow and Leningrad
Portugal

SPAIN
Spain
Barcelona

Switzerland

TURKEY
Turkey: the Aegean
   and Mediterranean Coasts
Istanbul

UK
England
Ireland
Scotland
Wales
London
Museums and Galleries
   of London
Oxford and Cambridge
Gardens of England
Literary Britain and Ireland
Victorian Architecture
   in Britain
Churches and Chapels
   of Northern England
Churches and Chapels
   of Southern England
Channel Islands
USA
New York
Boston and Cambridge

Yugoslavia

D0273003

Mosaic of Leda and the Swan, from Palea Paphos

BLUE GUIDE

CYPRUS

Ian Robertson

Maps and plans by Doug London

A & C Black
London

W W Norton
New York

Third edition 1990
Second impression 1993

Published by A & C Black (Publishers) Limited
35 Bedford Row, London WC1R 4JH

© A & C Black (Publishers) Limited 1990

ISBN   0–7136–3274–7

A CIP catalogue record for this book
is available from the British Library

Apart from any fair dealing for the purposes of research or private study, or criticism or review, as permitted under the Copyright, Designs and Patents Act, 1988, this publication may be reproduced, stored or transmitted, in any forms or by any means, only with the prior permission in writing of the publishers, or in the case of reprographic reproduction in accordance with the terms of licences issued by the Copyright Licensing Agency. Inquiries concerning reproduction outside those terms should be sent to the publishers at the above address.

Published in the United States of America by
WW Norton & Company, Inc
500 Fifth Avenue, New York NY 10110

Published simultaneously in Canada by
Penguin Books Canada Limited
2801 John Street, Markham, Ontario L3R 1B4

ISBN   0–393–30730–1   USA

The rights of Ian Robertson to be identified as the author of this work have been asserted by him in accordance with the Copyright, Designs and Patents Act, 1988.

The publishers and the author have done their best to ensure the accuracy of all the information in Blue Guide Cyprus; however, they can accept no responsibility for any loss, injury or inconvenience sustained by any traveller as a result of information or advice contained in the guide.

Please write in with your comments, suggestions and corrections. Writers of the best letters will be awarded a free Blue Guide of their choice.

Ian Robertson was born in Tokyo in 1928; and educated at Stowe. He is the author of a number of Blue Guides, having been commissioned to re-write that to Spain, his first, in 1970. Since 1978 he has made several extended visits to Cyprus, and compiled the first three editions of the Blue Guide to the island.

Typeset by First Page Ltd, Watford
Reproduced, printed and bound in Great Britain by
BPCC Hazell Books Ltd,
Aylesbury, Bucks, England
Member of BPCC Ltd.

PREFACE

This third edition of *Blue Guide Cyprus* follows the successful pattern set by the previous editions, the continuing demand for which confirmed the revival of interest in that island in spite of its still-divided state. It had been hoped, by the time this revision was called for, that the Gordian knot in which Cyprus had become almost inextricably entangled would have been unravelled, if not cut, but the persuasive powers of diplomats had by late 1989 proved unavailing.

Nevertheless, its fine climate and the range and beauty of its landscape, its archaeological and historical sites, and its individual character—understandably—continue to lure travellers to its shores, even if it is not quite the same island it was four decades ago, when so evocatively described by Lawrence Durrell in 'Bitter Lemons'.

Its first tenuous association with England was when, on his way to join the Third Crusade, Richard I, 'Coeur de Lion', seized the island in 1191, and at Limassol married Berengaria of Navarre; but the following year it passed to Guy de Lusignan, and remained with that dynasty until 1489, when it was occupied by the Venetians. From 1571 until 1878 Cyprus was an Ottoman province. It was then administered by the British under the suzerainty of Turkish sultans until 1914, when it was annexed to the British Crown. It became a Crown Colony in 1925 and remained so until 1960, when the Republic of Cyprus was set up. The island's unhappy history since its independence is outlined in the latter pages of the Historical Introduction, which has been corrected and updated. In July 1974 much of the north and north east of the island was occupied by forces from the Turkish mainland, and a partition of Cyprus was effected. Until the complex problems thus posed are resolved, foreign visitors will find it difficult to explore the whole island without restrictions being imposed by one side or other, an unfortunate situation which it is hoped will be soon regularised.

This third edition, as did the previous two, perforce describes the island in two sections, still concentrating on the Government-controlled part, although the main monuments and sites in the North are likewise treated, even if in some cases they are covered in less detail. The island is described in a series of routes and sub-routes, the conventional formula for the Blue Guides, although the order of several have been changed, for with the recent and continuing improvements of roads, the visitor can now follow less exacting routes from one centre to another, but he will not necessarily see more in the time at his disposal. Unless he deliberately intends to break away from the beaten track onto rougher winding hill-roads, he will miss much of that enjoyment which the exploration of less frequented districts can give. He will too often miss those frescoed churches, those uncluttered vistas, and the simplicity of a village meal; and where else will he capture that peculiar 'spirit of place', the idea of landscape being—to quote Durrell—'the important determinant of any culture'?

The archaeological sites of Kition, Khirokitia, Tamassos, Kourion (Curium), Palea Paphos (Kouklia), and Kato Paphos, among others, well deserve exploration, while the museums of Nicosia, Larnaca, Limassol, and Paphos display the majority of finds from these sites; of no less interest are the early Byzantine churches and chapels to be found throughout the Troödos range, among them those at Galata and

Kakopetria, Asinou, Moutoullas, Kalapanayiotis, Lagoudhera, and Stavros tou Ayiasmati. The monasteries of Stavrovouni, Kykko, Khrysorroyiatissa, and Ayia Napa, among others, should certainly be visited, while individual monuments such as the castle of Kolossi or the church at Kiti should on no account be overlooked. It is sincerely hoped that the ancient sites of Salamis, Enkomi-Alasia, Soli, and Vouni; the castles of St. Hilarion, Kyrenia, Buffavento, and Kantara; walled Famagusta, the abbey of Ballapais, and other churches and monasteries of the northern range will be easily accessible by the time a fourth edition of this Guide is called for.

As the traveller from northern climes passes through the towns and villages of Cyprus he cannot fail to notice with interest the ubiquitous solar-heating panels on the flat roofed houses, above which are perched the water-tanks, together with television aerials; he will also observe, regrettably too often, that the old-world harmony of brown-stone bungalows with their flower-festooned verandahs has been irrevocably destroyed by the erection of a brash new block, which has been left standing in a sea of dust and rubble, and from the roof of which reinforcing rods still protrude....It is only too easy to criticise this apparently uncontrolled speculative building, let alone the lack of civic pride, but in extenuation it must be emphasised that only 16 years have passed since the island was convulsed by a major demographic revolution. That the government has been able to grapple with the problems of resettlement with as much success as it has, is very remarkable, and a special note of admiration must be recorded.

It is hoped, nevertheless, that those with a spirit of conservation are equally successful, and that the natural beauties of the island's shores and forests will be as protected from the encroachments of a materialistic age as are the many ancient monuments which are its cultural heritage, for there are ominous signs—east of Limassol, east of Larnaca, and even at Paphos—in marked contrast to extensive underdeveloped areas in the north of the island, one of their most valuable assets. Much work of conservation and restoration is constantly being carried out by the Department of Antiquities, and by some Municipalities (the restoration of the *Famagusta Gate* and *Laiki Yitonia* in Nicosia spring to mind), and every encouragement should be given to those entrusted with the task, which might still save Cyprus from the ravages of 'development' which have already wrought havoc on other Mediterranean shores. It has not *yet* suffered too much from the insidious blighting effects of mass tourism as have some other countries where the foreigner (no longer 'the stranger as guest' and who must be rich to have travelled so far) is welcomed only for being another 'invisible export': the sacred cows of Tourism, even in herds, should not be lured abroad by specious brochures merely to be milked....

While the island is described from the point of view of the traveller by road, having hired his car, its towns are described for sightseeing on foot, almost always the most convenient and enjoyable way of getting about. It is hoped that the visitor to Cyprus will be able to wander at will before long. On his recent tour, the author was able to traverse certain areas of the occupied North which were 'out of bounds' to him previously, due to the Turkish presence, but even so, several restrictions are still in force, particularly—as is understandable—where military forces are in evidence. While invading Turkish troops inevitably caused damage and indulged in desecration, it now seems more likely that much of the subsequent depredations—the theft of icons and removal of murals, etc.—was the direct result of art thieves most of whom were no amateurs and who had access to international markets; those at present responsible for the protection and restoration of antiquities in the north are attempting to preserve that part of the island's heritage, although their means are limited. See p 60.

Unfortunately the author was still unable to explore and research to the extent he would have wished in the service of this third edition, but many of the revisions—the amount of alterations varying from very minor corrections to the addition of considerable new matter—have been made from personal observation on the spot; nevertheless, he would appreciate receiving any detailed *factual* information about minor sites and monuments in the north.

He has been to some pains to remain impartial—although attempts have been made to use the Guide as a vehicle of political expediency—and it is sincerely hoped that, in spite of the occasional errors of omission, commission, or interpretation, it will provide–in the continuing extenuating circumstances—a reasonably balanced account of most aspects of Cyprus without intentionally neglecting any which might appeal to the traveller, and without being so exhaustive as to leave him no opportunities of discovering additional pleasures for himself.

It must be reiterated that the Government of the Republic of Cyprus will not allow travellers to cross into the unoccupied part of the island if they have entered by a port or airport in the Turkish-occupied sector, these being considered illegal ports of entry. The Government will, however, in most circumstances, allow visitors to cross into the occupied zone at the Ledra Palace checkpoint (Nicosia) for day trips, but for longer visits official permission is required.

The reader's attention is drawn to the permanent exhibition of Cypriot antiquities in the British Museum known as the A.G. Leventis Gallery, established in 1987. This is one of the largest such collections outside Cyprus and will be of considerable interest to the visitor either before or after having travelled to the island.

The Author alone is (as he has been held!) responsible for all inexactitudes, inconsistencies, solecisms, and shortcomings. Any constructive suggestions for the improvement of future editions will always be most gratefully welcomed, and acknowledged.

In addition to those who offered every assistance to the author in the compilation of the previous editions of this Guide, and which where there listed, he must likewise express his obligation to the following: *Orestis Rosides*, director of the C.T.O., London, and *Lillian Panayi*; and *Panos Economides* and *Maria Georgiades* at Nicosia. Others who have offered advice or facilities, or who have corrected errors of fact or interpretation, are *Michael Loulloupis*; *Humphrey Maud*; *Christopher Breeze*; *Clive Mogford*; *Nicos Karanikis*; *Fenella Cracroft*; *Demetrios Michaelides*; *Lellos Demetriades*, *Michael* and *Maroula Prodromos*; *Tonia Georghiou-Loizou*; *Mrs Theodora Pierides*; *Vassos Ioannou* at Paphos, and *Savvas Ioannou* at Larnaca; *Andreas Savva*; *Frosso Egoumenidou*; *Michael Santamas*; *Dominique Collon*; *Konstantin Sakkas*; *Constantin Leventis*; *Agni Petridou*; *Kemal Aksay*; *Robin Barber*; *Rosamond Hanworth*; *Robin Cormack* (whose report to the Council of Europe on the cultural heritage of Cyprus was helpful); *Johanna Olby*, and *Tessa Henderson*.

The introductions to the Monuments and Early History, and to the

Later History of the island, by *Nicolas Coldstream* and *Douglas Dakin* respectively, have been revised and updated; *David* and *Iro Hunt's* article on the Food and Wine of Cyprus has been extended: and *Doug London's* maps and plans have been corrected.

Among recent books to which I would like to draw the reader's attention are: *Early Society in Cyprus*, ed. by Edgar Peltenburg (1989), Peter W. Edbury's *The Kingdom of Cyprus and the Crusades, 1191–1374*, and *The Infidel Sea: travels in North Cyprus* (1990), by Oliver Burch.

This third edition will be the last revised by the original author, who would like to take the opportunity to thank again those many Cypriots who have extended their hospitality to him over the years. Several of them, both in the north and south of the island, have gone out of their way (during the very difficult period of almost 20 years of partial military occupation and re-settlement of their homeland) to facilitate his work of compilation, and have contributed to make it as comprehensive and as accurate a guide as possible to the island while still in its divided state.

A NOTE ON BLUE GUIDES

The Blue Guides series began in 1918 when Muirhead Guide-Books Limited published 'Blue Guide London and its Environs'. Finlay and James Muirhead already had extensive experience of guide-book publishing: before the First World War they had been the editors of the English editions of the German Baedekers, and by 1915 they had acquired the copyright of most of the famous 'Red' handbooks from John Murray.

An agreement made with the French publishing house Hachette et Cie in 1917 led to the translation of Muirhead's London Guide, which became the first 'Guide Bleu'—Hachette had previously published the blue-covered 'Guides Joanne'. Subsequently, Hachette's 'Guide Bleu Paris et ses Environs' was adapted and published in London by Muirhead. The collaboration between the two publishing houses continued until 1933.

In 1931 Ernest Benn Limited took over the Blue Guides, appointing Russell Muirhead, Finlay Muirhead's son, editor in 1934. The Muirheads' connection with Blue Guides ended in 1963 when Stuart Rossiter, who had been working on the Guides since 1954, became house editor, revising and compiling several of the books himself.

The Blue Guides are now published by A & C Black, who acquired Ernest Benn in 1984, so continuing the tradition of guide-book publishing which began in 1826 with 'Black's Economical Tourist of Scotland'. The Blue Guide series continues to grow: there are now more than 40 titles in print, with revised editions appearing regularly and many new Blue Guides in preparation.

'Blue Guides' is a registered trade mark.

CONTENTS

MAPS, TOWN AND SITE PLANS

EXPLANATIONS

Type. The main routes are described in large type. Small type is used for sub-routes, excursions or detours, and for historical and prelimi-nary paragraphs, and (generally speaking) for descriptions of greater detail or minor importance.

Asterisks, although perhaps subjective and inconsistent, may help the hurried traveller to pick out those things which the general consensus of opinion (modified occasionally by the Author's personal prejudice, admittedly) considers he should not miss.

Total and intermediate **Distances**, measured in kilometres, are given at the commencement of each route, together with the total distance in miles, and the total length in kilometres is given at the beginning of each sub-route. Road distances along the routes themselves record the approx. distance between villages, etc. described, but it is very likely that these will vary slightly from those measured by a motorist's milometer, while it has not always been possible to give more than very approximate distances along forest tracks.

Since January 1986 road distances, at least in the south of the island, have been changed from miles to kilometres; and as no maps specifying such distances were then available, those indicated in this edition of the Guide are merely conversions from miles, and are not exact. To avoid further confusion it was also thought best to show distances in kilometres throughout the island.

Heights, and the measurements of buildings and archaeological sites have been expressed in metres (m).

Place-names are given in their English version as printed on the *Survey of Cyprus Administration and Road Map* (revised 1984) in the form recommended by the Social Research Centre of the Government of Cyprus, occasionally supplemented by material in J.C. Goodwin's *Toponymy of Cyprus*, but several new transliterations have very recently been agreed, though phonetically similar, which will be in-corporated in the next edition.

Although in 1976 the self-proclaimed Turkish Federal State of Cyprus (as it was then known) chose to change the names of over 200 villages in the zone occupied by the Turkish army, it has been decided, until there is an entente, to ignore these changes, which are both illegal and unofficial as far as the Government of the Republic of Cyprus is concerned, and their inclusion would be additionally confusing, as they do not appear on any easily available map, even if about 75 of them were *old* Turkish alternative names revived and another 15 are not substantially different from their earlier and mostly non-Greek versions.

Only in certain cases, with the larger towns, has the Turkish equivalent been indicated. Travellers to the occupied part of the island are advised to equip themselves in advance with a general map of the island (see p 49) in addition to the one available in the North giving Turkish place-names only. Armed with both, they should have no difficulty in verifying their position.

The same applies to street names in the larger towns. No attempt has been made to make changes in the town plans for Famagusta,

Kyrenia, and North Nicosia. These changes include the conversion of streets named after Gladstone and Shakespeare to Gündogdu, and Mehmet Akif. The traveller should be able to find his way about without too much difficulty, even if every minor street and alley is not shown.

Some place-names have been included twice in the index: i.e., for (modern) *Curium*, see (ancient) *Kourion*, the latter being that by which it is usually referred to by archaeologists. Similarly, although *Ktima* is now generally known as *Paphos*, it is also cross-indexed.

Populations. Provisional figures, applicable in late 1988, have been given for towns and villages having over 1000 inhabitants in the Government-controlled area. Figures for the Northern zone are not so easily available, and in view of the considerable demographic displacements which have taken place, both after 1964 and subsequent to the Turkish occupation of July 1974, to print a figure would be misleading.

In 1960 there were only about 20 villages of over 600 throughout the island with a population between 2000 and 4000. Most of them are still very small.

A map published by the Department of Lands and Surveys, Nicosia (Series D.L.S.19; 2nd ed. 1986) indicated the distribution of population by ethnic groups as at the census of 1960, but in this guide no indication of race or religion of the villagers is given. It may be assumed that the great majority of those in the south are Greek Cypriots ostensibly belonging to the Orthodox Church; elsewhere they will be Turkish Cypriots and ostensibly Moslem. All population figures exclude members of the British, UNFICYP, and Turkish forces.

Abbreviations. In addition to the generally accepted and self explanatory abbreviations, the following occur in the Guide:

C   Century
C.T.O.   Cyprus Tourism Organisation
EOKA   Ethniki Organosis Kyprion Agoniston, the National Organisation of Cypriot Fighters
Pl.   Plan
Rte   Route
UNFICYP   United Nations Forces in Cyprus

Ayios Lazaros, Larnaca, by Tessa Henderson

INTRODUCTION TO THE MONUMENTS AND EARLY HISTORY OF CYPRUS

by NICOLAS COLDSTREAM

Prehistoric Cyprus: Neolithic period to Middle Bronze Age; c 8000–1600 BC. Although claims have been made for earlier human occupation in a rock shelter on the *Akrotiri* peninsula, the earliest Cypriots of whom we know for certain lived during the eighth millenium BC. The first Cypriots of whom we know lived during the eighth millennium BC. They dwelt in circular huts, built of rubble, wood, and mud-brick. The largest and best-preserved of their settlements is at *Khirokitia*, on a hillock overlooking the modern Nicosia–Limassol motorway. There one can obtain a surprisingly complete impression of a closely-knit farming community of early Neolithic times. Pottery as yet was unknown, but vessels and figurines were fashioned out of the local andesitic stone. At *Kalavassos (Tenta)*, another Early Neolithic site, a fragmentary wall-painting of a human figure has been found.

After the desertion of these Aceramic Neolithic sites during the sixth millennium BC there follows a long period for which the record remains a blank. A Late Neolithic phase, however (c 4500–3500 BC), is well represented by excavated settlements: the most illuminating are *Ayios Epiktitos* on the north coast near Kyrenia and, in the south, *Sotira (Teppes)* and *Kalavassos (Kokkinoyi)*. By now the potter's art had been well established, the most distinctive types being red jugs and bowls lightly scored with combed patterns. Both shapes have rounded bases recalling the gourd, that favourite vessel of the Cypriot villager from time immemorial.

The CHALCOLITHIC PERIOD (c 3500–2500/2300 BC) saw the first appearance of copper tools alongside the traditional stone implements. Our information now comes mainly from the south and west. *Erimi*, near Episkopi, affords evidence of round houses with hearths and wattle-and-daub superstructure, and also a new pottery type with bright red designs painted on a white ground. From burials in the Paphos region come the remarkable Chalcolithic human figurines in steatite; the finest have a slender cruciform shape with backward-tilted head, recalling the Cycladic marble idols of the Aegean. An ample enlargement of this form in limestone, evidently representing a fertility goddess, has been found in the earliest known Cypriot sanctuary at *Lemba (Lakkous)*, another settlement of circular houses. The neighbouring Chalcolithic settlement of *Kissonerga (Mosphilia)* has produced a clay model of a circular house containing figurines in stone and clay, some portraying women in childbirth.

For an island so rich in copper ores, the transition to a fully bronze-using culture came surprisingly late. The EARLY BRONZE AGE (c 2500/2300–1900 BC), not yet represented by any excavated settlement, is known only through the rich contents of family chamber-tombs. Two northern cemeteries are especially informative, *Philia (Vasiliko)* for the change from Chalcolithic, and *Bellapais (Vounous)* for the full sequence of its Red Polished pottery, a ware first evolved in the north and eventually accepted all over the island. Apart from some Anatolian influence at the outset, Red Polished ware developed along its own lines with a typically Cypriot exuberance of spirit, seen especially in the vast composite vessels, and in the modelled figures of animals and humans sometimes applied to the surface. More usually, decoration consists of carefully incised rectilinear patterns filled with white paste; on the plank-shaped female idols in the same fabric, these patterns suggest the dress of the day. Further vignettes of daily life appear in the scenes modelled on the vessels, and also in independent models; among the latter, the most elaborate shows a circular open-air shrine where 19 worshippers go about their business of sacrificing bulls to a trinity of plank-like deities.

Cyprus enters the MIDDLE BRONZE AGE (c 1900– 1600 BC) without experiencing any great change; but now there are more signs of regional diversity. At the southern site of *Episkopi (Phaneromeni)*, where rectangular houses and chamber tombs of this period may be seen, the contemporary pottery is still Red Polished, sometimes with a mottled surface, and sometimes bearing decoration in punctured dots. A copper-working hamlet of this period is known at *Ambelikou (Aletri)* in the Troödos foothills. Meanwhile, among the tomb offerings at *Lapithos* on the north coast, there arises a new ceramic tradition in White Painted ware, bearing geometric patterns on a pale matt ground. This tradition spreads to the centre and the east, each district evolving its own style. At *Alambra (Moutes)* near Dali, a settlement of large rectangular rooms, the Red Polished ware predominates over White Painted. The Karpas peninsula, meanwhile, evolved its own individual Red-on-Black ware. By the end of this period the eastern Mesaoria plain, with its chief settlement at *Kalopsidha*, was attaining to greater importance within the island; thence, too, came the first mass exports of pottery to Syria and Palestine. At the same time the building of numerous forts, notably in the inland Dali region, suggests a degree of internal unrest which continued some way into the Late Bronze Age.

The Late Bronze Age: c 1600–1050 BC. Hitherto, Cypriot civilisation had a homespun character, showing little sign of foreign influence or interference. Now, at last, the island emerged from its long isolation. Commercial exchanges were intensified with Egypt (XVII–XVIII Dynasties) and the Levant, especially with the emporium of Ugarit on the north Syrian coast; it is generally thought that the copper-bearing land of Alashiya, often mentioned in Ugaritic, Hittite, and Egyptian documents, is no other than Cyprus. Apart from copper, Cypriot pottery now enjoyed a wide circulation overseas. The two leading wares, still handmade, were Base Ring and White Slip. Base ring is thin-walled, and coated in a dark lustrous slip; small juglets in this ware, shaped like poppy-heads, found special favour in Egypt and may have contained opium. Typical of White Slip ware is the 'milk-bowl' of traditional half-gourd shape, now painted with light and delicate patterns.

Commercial enterprise encouraged the growth of large mercantile cities on the east and south coasts. At *Kalavassos (Ayios Dimitrios)* and *Maroni (Vournes)* foundations of public buildings datable to the 13C BC have recently come to light, constructed of huge ashlar blocks dressed in the finest Near Eastern traditions. The most extensively excavated site, however, is *Enkomi*, near Famagusta. Founded around 1600 BC and twice destroyed amid the recurrent unrest of the next two centuries, Enkomi was eventually to enjoy an age of untroubled prosperity from 1400 to 1250 BC. Copper, the chief source of wealth, was worked there and at *Kition*, founded in the 13C BC. It was during this tranquil period that Mycenaean Greek merchants first became frequent visitors, in search of copper. In return, among other goods, they traded painted pottery of surpassing quality, including many vessels bearing figured scenes. The sophisticated wheelmade technique of these Mycenaean imports had its effect on Cypriot potters; and indeed almost every other form of art—seal engraving, gold jewellery and other metalwork, work in ivory and faience—now displays a blend of Aegean and oriental elements. Literacy, too, may have come to Cyprus through her westward contacts: the Cypro-Minoan syllabic script, named after its supposed derivation from the Linear A system of Crete, was employed from the 15–11C. It still awaits decipherment.

From 1250 BC onwards, Cyprus became embroiled in the general collapse of Bronze Age civilisations in the eastern Mediterranean. Peaceful commerce was interrupted by piracy; among the Mycenaean visitors, the merchant was replaced by the soldier of fortune. Enkomi and Kition were hastily fortified, only to suffer wholesale destruction in c 1220 BC by attackers as yet unknown. Both sites were then rebuilt on a quite different plan.

The new city of Enkomi, largely that which the visitor sees today, by far eclipses the old in architectural sophistication. The rambling rubble edifices of the preceding period are succeeded by an orderly grid plan, the more important buildings being faced with huge ashlar masonry. Nevertheless the new residents, to judge from their local painted pottery, included a fair proportion of Mycenaean immigrants, seeking their fortunes in Cyprus during the collapse of civilisation in their Aegean homeland. They brought with them various technical and artistic skills. Under their stimulus, the Cypriot bronze industry flourished as never before. Of outstanding interest and quality are the four-sided bronze stands bearing Aegeo-oriental figured scenes in openwork or relief, and the large statuette of the Horned God from one of the sanctuaries at Enkomi. Another Enkomi bronze, portraying an armed god standing upon an ingot, attests the divine patronage of the copper industry; similarly, at Kition, the smithies were immediately adjacent to a vast new open-air temple in the finest ashlar masonry, with a triple holy-of-holies in the Near Eastern tradition. Contemporaneous, and equally impressive, are the monumental remains of the oldest open-air temple within the sanctuary of Aphrodite at Old (or Palea) Paphos. Minor arts which flourished especially at this time are ivory carving in relief, and gold jewellery, sometimes with cloisonné inlays of enamel.

These splendours, however, were short-lived. In c 1190 BC the coastal cities were devastated by marauders known from Egyptian sources as the 'Peoples of the Sea'. Further disruption was caused by the steady incursion of Aegean refugees. Initial resistance to them is suggested by the fortified native settlements at Idalion and Episkopi (Bamboula). Eventually, after a huge new influx in the 11C, the Mycenaean element prevailed, and homogeneity was restored: a new wheelmade pottery type, Proto White Painted, is closely akin to Aegean Submycenaean, and was manufactured throughout the island. Henceforth Cyprus was to be a predominantly Greek-speaking land. By the end of the Bronze Age the Aegean newcomers had established themselves at the sites of all the historical Greek-Cypriot kingdoms: Salamis (replacing Enkomi), Lapithos, Marion, Soli, Old Paphos, Kourion, and Tamassos. The oldest Greek inscription from Cyprus (c 1000 BC), written in a syllabic script, is an Arcadian personal name engraved on a bronze spit from a tomb at Old Paphos (Skales).

The Cypriot kingdoms of the Iron Age: c 1050–300 BC. After the turmoil at the end of the Bronze Age, the next two centuries were comparatively uneventful. Written sources are silent, and the archaeological record is virtually confined to the family chamber-tombs. Their contents show that the Greeks of Cyprus soon lost touch with their homeland, though not with the Near East. The tomb offerings from *Old Paphos* are especially rich and varied at this time.

During the 9C Phoenicians from Tyre founded a colony at Kition, where they refurbished the grandest of the Bronze Age temples in honour of their fertility goddess Astarte. Meanwhile the indigenous Cypriots (Eteocypriots) had their main settlement at *Amathus*. The lively interplay of influences between Greeks, Phoenicians, and Eteocypriots accounts for much of the artistic vitality of the island at the dawn of its recorded history. Yet the very remoteness of the Cypriot Greeks from their Aegean kinsmen made for extreme conservatism in their ways: they were never to know any constitution other than despotic monarchy in the seven independent Greek states; and their archaic dialect of Greek, akin to Arcadian, continued to be written even as late as the 3C in a syllabic script (Classical Cypriot) inherited from Bronze Age tradition—a deliberate rejection of the more practical alphabetic system which Aegean Greeks had learned from the Phoenicians well before 700 BC.

The 8C, as in Greece, was a time of recovery and rapidly widening horizons. Contact with the Aegean was restored, and eastward trade flourished once again. The royal tombs of *Salamis* (c 800–600 BC) illustrate one of the most brilliant phases of Cypriot civilisation, richly compounded of Greek, native, and eastern elements. It may have been pride in their Mycenaean ancestry that inclined the Salaminians to bury their princes in a manner recalling Homeric epic, sending chariots with sacrificed horse teams to accompany their dead masters. Nevertheless the finery from these tombs is almost wholly oriental: the horse trappings are of Assyrian type, while the tomb furniture was fitted with delicate ivory plaques of Phoenician workmanship. Elsewhere in Cyprus, another notable Cypro-Phoenician art-form of this time is the shallow metal bowl embossed inside with scenes of cult, warfare, or animal life.

From 708 until 663 BC the Cypriot kingdoms came under the sway of the Assyrian empire, but retained their local autonomy; Assyrian rule left hardly any trace on the island's material record except perhaps to encourage the spread of Phoenician influence. From the 6C the most remarkable monuments are the royal chamber-tombs of *Tamassos*, careful copies in stone of domestic dwellings roofed with wooden rafters, and decorated in relief with volute capitals of 'Protoaeolic' type. A brief period of Egyptian rule (c 560–540 BC) encouraged Cypriot commerce in Egypt. Thereafter the Cypriots transferred their allegiance to the rising Persian empire, while still enjoying a large measure of independence; king *Evelthon* of Salamis, for example, was able at this time to mint in his own name the first coinage of Cyprus.

In 500 BC, however, relations with the Persian overlord suddenly deteriorated when the Cypriot Greeks joined the abortive Ionian revolt against the Great King. A poignant memorial to their valour can be seen in the Persian siege mound at Old Paphos, riddled with ingenious devices of the defenders to undermine it. After the failure of the revolt, and during the 5C, the islanders showed little enthusiasm for various Athenian attempts to detach them from the Persian empire; the Phoenicians of Kition, meanwhile, annexed Idalion with Persian support. The finest architectural monument of this period is the palace of *Vouni* (c 500–380 BC), a spacious building of predominantly oriental character.

Rivalries between the Cypriot states prevented any more general uprising against Persia, until king *Evagoras I* of Salamis (411–374 BC) succeeded for a very brief interlude in ousting the Persians altogether, and uniting the island by force rather than by consent. Cyprus was finally freed from Persian domination around 330 BC through the victories of *Alexander the Great*, but after his death became a battleground between his successors *Antigonus* and *Ptolemy I* of Egypt; during their wars Kition, Lapithos, Marion, and Cerynia were destroyed, never to be resettled in antiquity. *Nicocreon*, the last king of Salamis, was killed in 310 BC; a large tumulus just outside Enkomi village has been identified as the cenotaph built in his honour. Subsequently the island was annexed by Ptolemaic Egypt, and we hear no more of any Cypriot kingdoms.

Pottery. The Cypro-Geometric wares (c 1050–750 BC), named after their simple linear decoration, continued the tradition of the wheelmade Proto White Painted pottery made at the end of the Bronze Age. At first they bore a family resemblance to contemporary Greek pottery, but new impulses tended to come from the Levant rather than from the Aegean. The chief types at first were White Painted (with the ornament painted on a light ground) and Bichrome, where red was added as a second colour after the Levantine fashion. From the 10C BC onwards these were joined by Black-on-Red and Red Slip, two wares with Phoenician associations; ornament on Black-on-Red vessels consisted chiefly of concentric circles. Figured decoration, never common, occured mainly near the beginning and end of this period; the Hubbard amphora (c 800 BC), showing an oriental scene of libation and ritual dancing, is a typical work of its time.

During the first Archaic phase (c 750–600 BC) Cypriot pottery reached its most creative and imaginative stage. Regional distinctions are now noticeable: circles still proliferated in the conservative western style, while the potters of eastern Cyprus introduced oriental rosettes, cables, and lotus flowers. The best and most ambitious work was now in Bichrome Ware, including the Free Field style where single but elaborately drawn birds or animals spread themselves expansively over the flanks of baggy jugs.

The same wares persist into later Archaic (c 600–475 BC) and Classical times (c 475–325 BC), showing a steady deterioration in quality and invention. Any new inspiration now came from Greece, seen especially in the finely modelled female heads attached to some large pouring vessels.

Sanctuaries and Sculpture. Most Cypriot temples were small and unpretentious rectangular buildings, without any of the architectural refinement associated with the Greek orders. Worship was conducted around altars in rustic open-air enclosures, which might often have been crowded with a veritable forest of statues representing the votaries rather than the deity. A vivid impression of such a sanctuary is conveyed by the thick concentration of figurines from *Ayia Irini* displayed in the Cyprus Museum, Nicosia.

From its beginnings in the 7C Cypriot sculpture often attained life size, and employed either limestone or terracotta. Both male and female figures are almost invariably draped; facial expression always held more interest for the Cypriot sculptor than body anatomy. The earliest Proto-Cypriot statues, of indigenous inspiration, have vivacious and over-large features, often verging on the farouche. During the 6C the milder Neo-Cypriot style borrowed freely from Egyptian and Archaic Greek sources; Egyptian sculpture was imported and imitated during the brief period of Egyptian domination. In the first phase of Persian rule (c 540–500 BC) there flourished a lively and distinguished Cypro-Archaic school owing much to Ionian sculpture of the eastern Aegean. But with the failure of the Ionian revolt this Greek connection lapsed, and stagnation set in. A Sub-Archaic tradition in limestone sculpture persisted throughout the Classical period, soon losing its vitality; meanwhile, local work in a Classical Greek style was virtually limited to a few grave reliefs, some large terracottas from Greek moulds, and the fine limestone head of a youth from *Arsos* (c 400 BC) which combines a Classical face with an Archaic hairstyle. At the end of the 4C the expressive terracotta heads from Nicocreon's cenotaph recall the manner of the Greek sculptor Lysippus.

Hellenistic and Roman Cyprus: c 300 BC–AD 330. When Cyprus became part of the large Hellenistic state of Egypt, the island's aristocracy was replaced by a Ptolemaic elite. Consequently, the material record lost its characteristically Cypriot flavour and became merely provincial. In inscriptions, the local syllabary finally gave way to the Greek alphabet; the local dialect was superceded by the common idiom of Hellenistic Greek; and the coins began to bear the heads of the ruling Ptolemies. The new city of *Paphos* (or *Nea Paphos*), which replaced the old *(Kouklia)* around 310 BC, became in the 2C BC the island's capital, and the seat of the Egyptian governor *(strategos)*. Of its Hellenistic monuments little survives apart from the subterranean rock tombs arranged round peristyle courts in the Doric order, perhaps imitating the current fashion of Alexandria. Their use continued into Roman times.

With the decline of the Ptolemaic kingdom, Cyprus was first annexed by ROME in 58 BC. Although it twice reverted to Egypt during the civil wars of the Republic, Roman control of the island was finally consolidated with the establishment of the Empire. There followed a long and prosperous period of *pax romana* when Cyprus was administered through a proconsul as a senatorial province, with its capital still at New Paphos. One such governor, *Sergius Paulus*, was an early convert to Christianity when *St. Paul* visited the island in AD 45 in company with a citizen of Salamis, *St. Barnabas*.

One symptom of the general prosperity of these times was the construction of spacious public buildings, many of which replaced older structures after the earthquakes of 15 BC and AD 76. Thus, after the earlier upheaval, a fine colonnaded gymnasium was built at *Salamis*, with a bath complex attached to its eastern portico (the existing remains, however, belong chiefly to repairs in later antiquity). The theatre of Salamis formed part of the same building programme; other well-preserved Roman theatres, of later date, can be seen at *Soli* and *Kourion*, the latter being converted in the 3C AD for spectacles of hunters fighting wild animals. Also at Kourion is the sanctuary of Apollo Hylates, where the existing layout belongs to a reconstruction after the second earthquake. The same is true of the Roman courtyard buildings in the sanctuary of Aphrodite at Old Paphos; their juxtaposition with the Late Bronze Age shrine argues an astonishing continuity of worship. Roman domestic architecture on a lavish scale is preserved at New Paphos, where the 3C House of Dionysus with its 70-odd rooms is named after the chief subject of its exceptionally fine mosaics. There, too, are the sumptuous mosaics of the even larger 'Villa of Theseus', now identified as the Roman proconsul's palace. The 4C mosaics in the House of Aion, which include the portrayal of a beauty contest between Cassiopeia and the Nereids, are thought to reflect the concepts of Neoplatonist philosophy.

Early Christian and Byzantine Cyprus: 330–1192. The 4C saw the triumph of Christianity and the gradual elimination of pagan worship; and with the final division of the Empire into two halves, Cyprus was allotted to the province of Oriens, ruled from Constantinople. Within the island, Salamis became the capital once again, now rebuilt and renamed *Constantia* after two terrible earthquakes which ravaged the whole island in 332 and 342.

Lying far away from the ceaseless wars on the Empire's frontiers, Cyprus enjoyed an Indian summer of peace and prosperity during the next two centuries. The Cypriot church, at first controlled from the see of Antioch, won its independence in 478 thanks to *Abp Anthemios'* timely discovery of St. Barnabas' tomb at Salamis. City life, meanwhile, continued on a luxurious scale. In the baths of Eustolios at Kourion, built around 400, a mosaic inscription could still refer to both Apollo and Christ as the city's protectors. Nevertheless the rapid advance of Christianity, and the growing power of the bishops, are attested by the numerous basilica churches erected throughout the island during the 5–6C. Among the excavated remains, exceptionally fine is the so-called *Kampanopetra* basilica at Salamis, lavishly adorned with carved marble capitals and extensive floor mosaics; along its flanks are long corridors where, according to the Syrian rite, converted catechumens assembled for baptism. A fine wall mosaic, showing the Virgin and Child between Archangels, survives in the apse of a basilica at *Kiti*, near Larnaca, incorporated in a later church. A similar apse mosaic, in the monastic church of *Kanakaria* at *Lythrangomi* in the Karpas, was recently destroyed, but parts of it are now housed in the Byzantine Museum in the Archbishopric of Nicosia. The small churches at *Aphendrika* in the Karpas, now in ruins, date from the 7C, shortly before the Arab invasions. Outstanding among early Byzantine artefacts are the early 7C silver dishes from the treasure of the bishops of Lapithos *(Lambousa)*, chased with scenes from the life of David; but these may well be metropolitan work from Constantinople.

Life on the island was severely disrupted soon after the advent of Islam. Already masters of Egypt and the Levant, the ARABS invaded Cyprus first in 647; Salamis-Constantia was sacked, and never recovered. Once again Cyprus found itself on a frontier, a bone of contention between two warring empires. Within the next three centuries the island changed hands at least eleven times, sometimes a no-man's land between the two powers, and sometimes even paying tribute simultaneously to Byzantine emperor and Umayyad caliph: according to the English pilgrim Willibald, who visited Paphos in 723, 'Cyprus lived between the Greeks and the Saracens'. During these troubled times many Cypriots were slaughtered, or captured and deported to Arab lands as slaves. A pointless attempt by *Justinian II* to resettle the survivors by the sea of Marmara in 692 was abandoned six years later, but not without provoking yet another Arab invasion of Cyprus—an invasion which gave rise to the only significant memorial of the Arabs on the island: the shrine of *Hala Sultan Tékké*, near the salt lake outside Larnaca, where a much later mosque commemorates the spot where the Umm Harām, a kinswoman of the Prophet Mohammed, fell off a mule and died.

Exhausted by war and pillage, and also afflicted by drought and plague, the ancient coastal cities withered away, as the survivors moved to more defensible sites. Thus refugees from Kourion transferred themselves inland to the new seat of their bishop, *Episkopi*. Paphos became the headquarters of the Arabs, while many Cypriots retired to the inland stronghold of *Ktima*.

Relief eventually came with the reviving fortunes of the Byzantine empire, and the Arabs were finally ousted from Cyprus in 963 by the emperor *Nicephorus Phocas*. Secure at last from any further Islamic attack, and largely by-passed by the Crusaders, Cyprus now became a peaceful backwater for the next two centuries under the firm rule of a Byzantine *katapan* or governor. As the island recovered some measure of its commercial prosperity, new towns grew up in the neighbourhoods of the old: *Ammochostos* (Famagusta) became the successor to Salamis, *Lemesos* (Limassol) to Amathus; *Leucosia* (Nicosia) was founded, perhaps on the site of the elusive ancient city of Ledra. Apart from the original structures of *St. Hilarion's castle*, very little secular architecture survives from this period; its chief glory is to be seen in the churches of the 11–12C and their frescoed decoration. Their plans are simple versions of the basilica with apse, sometimes with transepts added. From an architectural point of view the multi-domed village churches of *Peristerona* and *Yeroskipos* have a special attraction as examples of a local Cypriot style. Churches in the Troödos mountains, protected against snow and rain by wooden gabled roofs above their interior domes, also contain the finest and best-preserved of the fresco paintings. Lively works of provincial character can be seen in *Ayios Nikolaos* at *Kakopetria* (11C) and at *Asinou* (1105), while the frescoes at *Lagoudhera* (1192) display a finesse reflecting the style of Constantinople.

As the Byzantine empire began to crumble in the later 12C, it was inevitable that Cyprus should eventually fall into the hands of the Crusaders, who had become fully aware of its strategic importance. After a brief spell of independence (1184–1191) under the unstable and unpopular tyrant *Isaac Comnenos*, the island was overrun by *Richard I* of England on his way to the Third Crusade, sold at first to the Knights Templar, and then presented in 1192 to *Guy de Lusignan* who established a dynasty with a long future. The castle of *Saranda Colonnes* (Forty Columns) at Paphos, destroyed in 1222, is an early monument of the Lusignan kingdom.

The Lusignans in Cyprus: 1192–1489. Under Lusignan rule Cyprus became closely involved in the fortunes of the later Crusades. From 1197 onwards the king of Cyprus was also king of Jerusalem—a hollow title after the final loss of that city in 1244. Distinguished visitors to the island included the emperor *Frederick II Hohenstaufen*, and also *Louis IX* of France, whom the king of Cyprus joined in the disastrous Seventh Crusade against Egypt (1248–1250). When Acre, the last Crusader outpost in the Holy Land, eventually fell to the Mamelukes of Egypt in 1291, Cyprus provided a haven for the Christian refugees. In the 14C the island enjoyed a golden age as the last bastion of Christendom in the eastern Mediterranean, and the natural centre of seaborne commerce; *Famagusta*, in particular, gained a reputation for its luxurious living. Outwardly, the Lusignan kingdom reached the height of its power under the energetic king *Peter I* (1359–1369), who won temporary footholds on the Anatolian coast at Corycus and at Antalya, and then mounted the final crusade against the Mamelukes which achieved the sack of Alexandria.

Within the island, however, all was far from well for the Greek Cypriots. They had become a subject population under alien rulers, from whom they were divided by ethnic background, language, and religion. Their island was appropriated, and awarded on a western feudal system to Latin nobles. A Latin archbishopric was established at Nicosia, with suffragans at Famagusta, Limassol, and Paphos. According to the *Bulla Cypria* of Pope Alexander IV (1260) the Latin Archbishop became Metropolitan of both churches, but the Greek Orthodox Church kept its own cathedrals and retained some measure of independence.

Thanks to the Lusignans, Cyprus abounds in western medieval architecture—although it is a curious irony of history that virtually all such monuments are situated in what is now the Turkish-occupied zone. For the Gothic cathedrals and churches, France appears to have been the chief source of inspiration throughout; but a distinction can be drawn between a somewhat provincial manner in the 13C, and the sophisticated *rayonnant* style of later French Gothic reproduced in the finest buildings of the 14C. To the former stage belongs the main body of *St. Sophia's* cathedral in Nicosia. Its west front, however, was completed in 1326 in the latter style, seen at its finest in the abbey at *Bellapais*, the Latin cathedral of *St. Nicolas* at Famagusta, and (mixed with Byzantine elements) the small Orthodox cathedral of *St. George* in the same city. Secular monuments of this age include the three castles of the Kyrenia mountains—*Hilarion, Buffavento,* and *Kantara*—in their final forms; the square keep at *Kolossi*, housing the Knights of St. John; and part of a manor-house at *Kouklia* (Old Paphos).

After the ambitious adventures of Peter I, the decline of the Lusignans was swift. A riot at his successor's coronation led eventually to the seizure of Famagusta by the GENOESE. Worse still, a devastating invasion of MAMELUKES in 1426 was bought off only by a ruinous indemnity, an oath of allegiance, and an annual tribute to their sultan in Cairo. In the 1450s Queen *Helena Palaeologa*, herself a Byzantine princess, tried to alleviate the lot of the Greek Cypriots. Her illegitimate stepson, who became king *James I* (1458–1474), ousted the Genoese from Famagusta with aid from the Venetians, who then astutely provided him with a Venetian queen, *Caterina Cornaro.* Inheriting the throne on his death, Caterina assigned all important posts to her countrymen, and in 1489 was persuaded to hand over the island to the Venetian Republic.

The Venetians in Cyprus: 1489–1571. For the Venetians, Cyprus was a forward base against a rapidly expanding Ottoman empire, and a source of revenue through trade and taxation. The sugar industry, for example, flourished greatly under Venetian rule, but its profits went to Venice rather than to the Cypriots. Levantine commerce, however, declined sharply after the opening of more profitable trade routes across the Atlantic and around the Cape of Good Hope; thus Famagusta, once a flourishing emporium, became little more than a naval station. The new administrators, closely watched from Venice and relieved every two years, developed no interest in the island's

Map illustrating the Turkish invasion of 1571, based on that of
Hans Rogel (Augsburg, 1570)

A· Ierusalem im ẅubel

welfare and soon alienated all sections of the population. The Lusignan nobles kept their estates but were excluded from political power. Although the Orthodox Church was allowed its independence (its 16C cathedral in Nicosia is the so-called *Bedestan*, a curious blend of Gothic, Byzantine, and Renaissance elements), the Greek Cypriot peasantry were impoverished by heavy taxation under a regime which became increasingly corrupt and ineffectual. The scene was set for the inevitable attack by the Turks.

Venetian Lion in Jeffery's Museum, Nicosia

To meet this menace, the Venetians concentrated their energies in the construction of massive and handsome defence works. The castles of the Kyrenia mountains, rendered obsolete by the invention of artillery, were dismantled. An older fort guarding Kyrenia harbour was remodelled and enclosed within an immense stone-faced earthwork, to resist bombardment. Famagusta received a complete circuit; its rectangular citadel (romantically called 'Othello's tower' under the British Protectorate) was drastically redesigned. At Nicosia, only three years before the Turkish invasion, the peripheral districts were demolished to make way for a grandiose circular defence wall with eleven heart-shaped bastions.

All these precautions, however, were fruitless. When a vast Turkish armament landed at Larnaca in July 1570, the island waited in vain for a relieving force from the west, and resistance was confined to the fortified cities of Nicosia and Famagusta. The new defences could not withstand the combination of heavy bombardment and vast hordes of irregular attacking troops. Nicosia was stormed in September 1570; Famagusta, after a valiant resistance of ten months against overwhelming odds, capitulated to the Turks in August 1571.

THE HISTORY OF CYPRUS FROM THE TURKISH CONQUEST

by DOUGLAS DAKIN and IAN ROBERTSON

The Turkish Conquest. When in 1441 *Helena Palaeologina* married the Lusignan king *John II* there was some prospect, so great was her influence, that Cyprus would be united to Byzantium. But that prospect vanished when in 1453 the Ottoman Turks captured Constantinople. It was not, however, until 1571 that they seized Cyprus, from 1489 a Venetian possession. Venice and her allies had been ill-prepared and although Famagusta held out until August 1571 there was really no hope for the island, which lost thousands of its inhabitants and most of its wealth.

In March 1573 Venice renounced all claims to Cyprus, whose four-century connection with Western civilisation came to an end. The Latin Church there was destroyed, the Latin community was reduced to insignificance, and the island became a poverty-stricken province of the Ottoman Empire. That vast Empire covered a part of the world already in relative economic decline, the centres of trade being in the process of shifting to the Atlantic. This decline the Ottoman Turks, an 'army without a state', and only two centuries away from their nomadic past, were to hasten. They lived on tribute: assimilating what they found (institutions, castles, churches, houses and landed estates), they did nothing to improve their heritage or arrest its decline. However, their saving grace was that, being short of manpower, they made no systematic attempt to uproot the conquered populations, and they tolerated others' religious beliefs. In Cyprus, as elsewhere, the Turks recognised the Orthodox Church and re-established the Orthodox Archbishopric, which had been in abeyance for some 300 years. They allowed the Orthodox Church to resume possession of the monasteries and church buildings, being content to take the Latin churches for conversion into mosques.

In driving out the Latins, the Turks swept away western feudalism, and although they allotted the best land to some 20,000 Turkish settlers, chiefly soldiers, the agricultural Cypriot population (Greeks, Armenians, and Maronites), numbering some 85,000 taxable persons, became peasant proprietors or free tenants. These peasants enjoyed limited self-government. No wonder then that, like their clergy, they had welcomed the invader who promised to be less oppressive than the detested Latins.

Although the Sultan and the high officials around him had the welfare of their Christian subjects at heart, at the provincial level Turkish governors and their agents were capricious and tyrannical: peasants, artisans, and small traders were mulcted mercilessly. These local authorities were devoid of all sense of decency: they (and the inhabitants, too) allowed the monuments of antiquity, defaced at the time of the conquest, to fall into decay. They made little effort to maintain the roads, bridges, castles and fortresses. Under their rapacious rule the indigenous inhabitants suffered all sorts of privations. To make matters worse, locusts and droughts ruined the crops. Frequent famine and epidemics further reduced the population already reduced by emigration. By 1641 the number of taxable persons had already fallen to 25,000. The Sultan, hearing of the island's plight, would sometimes alter the administrative arrangements and replace the higher functionaries, rarely however to any lasting effect.

One change was nevertheless important for the future: in 1660 the Sultan recognised the Greek Archbishop and the three other bishops as spokesmen of the Orthodox population, with the right to send petitions directly, or even to proceed in person, to Constantinople. Making frequent use of this privilege, the Archbishop established a close relationship with the *dragoman* (or interpreter) to the Porte, who was a Greek exercising considerable influence on Turkish policy. In 1754 the Sultan recognised the Archbishop as head of the autocephalous Church of Cyprus, in other words as *Ethnarch* or leader of the Greek Cypriot nation. To him and his bishops was entrusted the allocation of a fixed sum of taxation. In many ways this was a doubtful blessing, for the ecclesiastical officials were often as ruthless as the Turkish, and it is not surprising that in occasional revolts against financial oppression the poorer Greeks and Turks were to be found in alliance against what was becoming a Turko-Greek condominium. It was at this period that the Church acquired much of its land, in lieu of the payment of taxes. Out of this popular unrest a succession of Turkish adventurers endeavoured to make political capital and encouraged rebellion against the authorities. During all these conflicts the Archbishop increased his ascendency, his arm being strengthened by the institution (c 1779) of a Greek dragoman in Cyprus, who in effect replaced the Turkish governor as the civil power.

None of these disturbances in Cyprus had yet had the character of a national revolt. But in the years 1818–21 many of the Greek intelligensia, clergy, and traders became implicated in the widespread Greek conspiracy of the *Filiki Eteria* to dismantle, even to take over, the Ottoman Empire. This led to a fiasco: as in several other Greek regions within range of the Turkish military machine, the Turks struck first, massacring Archbishop Kyprianos, several of his clergy, and many of the wealthier Cypriots; and subjected the island to a decade of terror.

The **Greek War of Liberation**, and the Russo-Turkish War of 1828–29 had thrown the Ottoman Empire into disarray, and *Mohamet Ali* of Egypt, an overmighty vassal, seized the opportunity to assert his independence, to overrun Syria and to demand the cession of Crete (which he occupied) and Cyprus, which he was likely to invade at any moment. The Sultan's fate largely depended on the British, who, once the Greek question had been settled to their satisfaction, had decided to protect the Turkish Empire from the threats of both Mohamet Ali and Russia. In return for that protection the Sultan had necessarily to display clemency to his subject peoples, and to attempt to reform the administration. For Cyprus this meant happier days, especially as western traders were returning to the Eastern Mediterranean, bringing a degree of economic prosperity which led to slight improvements in the standard of living among the poorer classes. Concurrently, educational facilities were improved, largely under the auspices of the Church, with the result that a growing number of young Cypriots went to Athens to continue their studies. But although the Greek Cypriot community was now in the ascendant on the island, the Archbishop's role was not so important as in an earlier age: finding himself in conflict with a new generation of educated Cypriots, he tamely co-operated with the ruling Turks. When in 1853 the Russians annihilated the Turkish fleet at Sinope, causing the nationalist Cypriots to think that their hour of deliverance was near, he sided with the Turks, who, as the price of British support in their war against Russia, refrained from their threats to exterminate the Greek Cypriot population. But although the Turks avoided the worst malpractices, their administration remained chaotic. Very little was spent on improvements: out of a total revenue of £230,000, at least £200,000 went to Constantinople or into private pockets.

The British Occupation. In June 1878, in order yet again to protect the Ottoman Empire from Russian encroachment, the British Government, following a virtual ultimatum, took over the control and administration of Cyprus, promising to pay the Sultan the excess of revenue over expenditure—a burden, known as 'the tribute', which was widely condemned throughout Cyprus and in many quarters in England. As the strategic importance of the Eastern Mediterranean developed, the idea of obtaining a base in Cyprus had also been under discussion not only in England but also in French official circles. Many doubted whether Cyprus was in fact a suitable base, however, and in the event the British, who were shortly to obtain Alexandria, made no attempt to develop the island for military purposes, being content to deny its possession by another power.

The Greek Cypriots, mindful that in 1864 the British Government had ceded the Ionian Islands to Greece, welcomed the newcomers, hoping for better government and further prosperity. They were not altogether disappointed. Under a succession of High Commissioners beginning with *Lt-Gen. Sir Garnet Wolseley*, and of Secretaries for the Colonies beginning with *Lord Kimberley*, the British introduced a new legal system and English legal procedure; they set up a rudimentary parliament in the form of a legislative council; they abolished certain taxes and swept away the age-old malpractices of tax collection; they reduced the ravages of locusts, epidemics, and crime; they improved educational facilities; they constructed (by 1930) 3000 miles of roads; they provided water supplies and irrigation systems; and progress was made in the work of afforestation. Nevertheless, having to pay the annual tribute and having many other calls on the home revenues, Britains's expenditure on Cyprus was parsimonious, and the promise to make the island productive and highly prosperous was never fulfilled, although there was indeed a marked improvement in trade and agriculture. The population increased threefold, by 1921 reaching 310,700, of which 246,500 were Greek Cypriots (there were 470 English); and the per capita income rose appreciably. But although this improvement owed something to the presence of the British administration and the British connection, in the main it was a reflection of the general economic expansion of Europe.

Meanwhile, in the immediate wake of the military forces and civilian administrators, a number of authors and artists visited Cyprus and described the island to a larger public. Among the former were R. Hamilton Lang, W. Hepworth Dixon, and Sir Samuel Baker, while the etchings of Views by Tristram Ellis, and the photographs of John Thomson, both published in 1879, illustrated aspects of Cyprus. Noteworthy in the next few decades were Camille Enlart's study of the island's Gothic architecture and C.D. Cobham's compilation, 'Excerpta Cypria', issued in 1899 and 1908 respectively: see Bibliography pp 46; 48.

Despite the improvement in social conditions, the Greek Cypriots were far from satisfied with British rule, so firmly maintained by High Commissioners (and from 1925, Governors) like *Sir Malcolm Stevenson* and *Sir Ronald Storrs*. Although the only serious disturbances were those of 1931, they had always deeply resented the British failure to develop the institutions of self-government. Moreover, there was a growing desire for union *(enosis)* with Greece. It is difficult to say how steadfast this feeling really was. There were certainly many who wanted to maintain the British connection, and others who would have preferred autonomy. But in 1915, when Great Britain offered Cyprus to Greece as the price of entry into the Great War on the side of the Western Allies, or again in 1919–20, when there was some chance that Cyprus would be ceded to a Greater Greece, the majority of Greek Cypriots would gladly have accepted *enosis*.

Enosis. After World War II the Greek Cypriots' demand for self-determination became more fervent. In 1947 (the year in which the island of Rhodes became part of Greece) the Cypriots rejected British offers of a Constitution. Three years later the young Bishop of Kitium, *Makarios*—soon to become Archbishop and Ethnarch— organized a plebiscite which produced a 96 per cent majority in favour of *enosis*. But it is doubtful whether the implications of *enosis* were fully appreciated, and it might have been wiser in the first instance to have worked out an acceptable constitution. Makarios had, however, great determination and a firm grip upon his people. He also had a large following in Greece, which kept up constant pressure on the government. Against the advice of their Ambassador in London and the more cautious politicians, Field Marshal *Papagos's* cabinet took up the cause of Cyprus, instituted vicious anti-British radio broadcasts (which estranged many Philhellenes), and somewhat naïvely threatened to arraign Great Britain in the United Nations, where it was most unlikely that they would receive any tangible support: they failed to see that Great Britain, despite the *Treaty of Lausanne* (1923), whereby the Turks had recognised Cyprus as British territory, might call upon the Turks for support against the Greeks, and they completely ignored the warning of the Americans, whose blessing was essential if they were to browbeat the British. Mindful of the instability in Greece itself, and doubtful whether Cyprus would be better off under Greek rule, the British Conservative Government was determined to hold Cyprus, which had by then become of greater strategic importance than ever before.

In June 1955 the British Government, having previously refused to discuss the Cyprus question, invited Greece and Turkey to a tripartite conference, which invitation the Greek Government—much to the annoyance of Makarios—unwisely accepted, not realising that acceptance was a tacit recognition that the Turkish Government had rights in Cyprus. At all events the conference failed, as did subsequent negotiations. In February 1957 discussions were transferred to the United Nations, where, after two years of waiting, Greece had managed to get the issue included in the agenda of the Political Committee. The outcome was Resolution 1013, which, although not of immediate application, nevertheless announced the principle of establishing an independent Cypriot State.

Meanwhile, in Cyprus, Makarios had encouraged the activities of the Freedom Organisation of Cypriot Fighters (EOKA), led by a former Cypriot in the Greek army, *Colonel Grivas Dhigenis*. This guerrilla force, small though it was, carried on a relentless struggle against the British forces under the command of the Governor, *F.M. Sir John Harding.* It has been estimated that 500–600 were killed during the period of emergency, Grivas's terrorists being responsible for the deaths of 142 British, 84 Turkish Cypriots, and over 200 Greek Cypriots, as against 166 at the hands of the security forces.

The End of British Rule. In 1958 the Greek delegation to the United Nations obtained support in the Political Committee for a resolution recognising the right of the Cypriots to self-determination, and although the resolution failed to obtain the necessary two-thirds majority in the Plenary Assembly, it enabled Greece in the protracted negotiations that followed to combat the Turkish design for 'double *enosis*' or partition. During these negotiations the Turks claimed 30 per cent of the soil for a Turkish Cypriot population which was only 17 per cent of the total, and they spoke of the compulsory movement of the population to overcome the problem of the scattered nature of the Turkish Cypriot settlements. Eventually the Greek Government, instead of working for the self-determination of Cyprus, concentrated on obtaining the creation of an independent Cypriot state. Out of their negotiations there emerged a Greco-Turkish agreement, which lead to the *Treaty of Zürich.* This tripartite treaty, which gave Great Britain sovereign rights in respect of her military bases, envisaged Cyprus as a unitary state, with a unitary House of Representatives, two Communal Chambers, a Greek Cypriot President, and a Turkish Cypriot Vice-President with a veto on issues of security and external policy. Moreover, it provided for a treaty of alliance to bind the new state to Britain, Greece, and Turkey. Only with the greatest reluctance did Makarios accept these terms.

The Republic came into being on 16 August 1960, and as an independent state Cyprus made considerable economic progress; but a political settlement was long delayed. Whereas Makarios, who had been elected President, wanted to unify the administration, *Fazil Küchük*, the Vice-President, worked for the segregation of the two communities. In December 1963 the Turkish Government rejected Makarios's proposals for constitutional amendments which would have given the Greek Cypriots a greater control of the government of the Republic, and threatened military intervention if these were introduced unilaterally. Following the intercommunal incidents precipitated by a gratuitous policy of intimidation of Turkish Cypriots sanctioned by Makarios, the Turks concentrated strong military forces opposite the island; but under pressure from the United States, Britain, and Russia, refrained from aggressive action. The continuing intercommunal violence, however, was such that in February 1964 the United Nations sent a peace-keeping force to Cyprus (UNFICYP), and a mediator. The mediator achieved nothing.

For a decade the island, still progressing economically and becoming an ever-increasing tourist attraction, remained politically highly unstable; various demarcation lines—notably in Nicosia, but also elsewhere—were set restricting the movements of Turkish Cypriots, who also suffered an economic blockade. They retaliated by keeping Greek Cypriots out of their enclaves. Throughout this period both the Turkish and the Greek governments acted with circumspection, but in July 1974 the Greek military junta, in attempting a *coup d'état* to get rid of Makarios, goaded the Turkish government into taking the offensive. Claiming that they had an obligation as a guarantor power to protect the threatened Turkish Cypriot minority, they invaded and occupied the northern part of the island. Neither Britain, which as a guarantor, had an obligation to intervene, nor the United States—which wanted to keep Turkey within the NATO alliance—took any effective steps to check these reactionary measures, while the Greek armed forces were deterred from interfering. The Turks were therefore able to establish a *de facto* partition, even if under international pressure they were compelled to resume negotiations. Nevertheless the invasion resulted in the displacement of c 210,000 people, c 180,000 of whom were Greek Cypriots, forced to flee in the face of rapidly advancing Turkish armed forces, and on whose lands several thousands of Asiatic Turks were later settled.

Although the Greek Cypriots were prepared to accept a bi-regional federation, the Turks showed no inclination to renounce their partitionist policy. Makarios died on 3 August 1978. Fruitless intercommunal negotiations continued sporadically until 15 November 1983, when, after continued Greek refusal of Turkish demands, the Turks unilaterally declared an independent Turkish state under military control, within the territory of the Cyprus Republic. This declaration was recognised only by Turkey, and was condemned in repeated resolutions by the United Nations calling for Turkish withdrawal. These actions served only to complicate and to frustrate the efforts of the UN Secretary-General to find a solution to the Cyprus question.

In June 1984 the UN Secretary-General renewed his initiative and arranged a series of proximity talks and high level meetings. These resulted in him presenting a draft frame-work agreement to both sides in April 1986. The draft was acceptable to *Rauf Denktash*, the Turkish-Cypriot leader. However, *Spyros Kyprianou*, the Greek-Cypriot president, felt unable to commit his side without securing agreement in advance on certain fundamental points which the Secretary-General's draft left over for later resolution. There was no further significant progress during the term of office of Mr Kyprianou.

In February 1988 *George Vassiliou* was elected President of Cyprus with the support of the AKEL (Communist) and DESY (right wing) parties. Vassiliou, a businessman with no previous political background, pledged to resolve the Cyprus problem. In August 1988 the two sides accepted an invitation from the UN Secretary-General to take part in direct negotiations aimed at reaching a settlement by 1 June 1989. Although some progress was made, no agreement was reached by the target date. However, talks continue.

Since 1974, the negotiations aimed at achieving a federal solution of the Cyprus problem have revolved around the same set of interrelated issues. The Greek-Cypriots have consistently argued that Turkish military forces should be withdrawn and that they should recover at least part of the occupied territory. They also hold that refugees should have the right to return to the area under Turkish-Cypriot administration. For the Turkish-Cypriots, the key requirements are political equality with power-sharing at the federal level, a high degree of autonomy in the area under their administration with little or no return of refugees other than in the very long term, and the maintenance of the Turkish guarantee and right of armed intervention.

Chronological Table

The following list of 'periods' or 'eras' or technological stages conforms in the main to the most recent conventional terminology (still in the process of modification) used by archaeologists in describing Cypriot prehistory, etc. BC dates are approximate.

STONE AGE	Neolithic,		
	Khirokitia culture		7000–6000 BC
	Sotira culture		4500–3750
	Chalcolithic	I	3500–2500/2300
BRONZE AGE	Early Cypriot	I	2500/2300–2075
		II	2075–2000
		III	2000–1900
	Middle Cypriot	I	1900–1800
		II	1800–1725
		III	1725–1650
	Late Cypriot	I	1650–1475
		II	1475–1225
		III	1225–1050
IRON AGE	Cypro-Geometric	I	1050–950
		II	950–850
		III	850–750
	Cypro-Archaic	I	750–600
		II	600–475
	Cypro-Classic	I	475–400
		II	400–325
	Hellenistic		325–50
	Graeco-Roman		50 BC–AD 395
	Byzantine		395–1191

RULERS OF CYPRUS SINCE 1184

1184–91	Isaac Ducas Comnenos, Emperor of Cyprus
1191–92	Richard I of England, Lord of Cyprus, and the Knights Templar

The Lusignan Dynasty 1192–1489

Note. The relationship of each king to his predecessor is shown in brackets; likewise the dates of their marriage/s to their respective consorts. At the time they would have been known as Amaury, Hughes, Henri, Jean, Pierre, and Jacques, respectively. From 1194 the Lord of Cyprus was known as King of Cyprus; from 1269 as King of Jerusalem and Cyprus; and from 1368, of Jerusalem, Cyprus, and Armenia.

1192–94	Guy de Lusignan	—Sibylla of Jerusalem (1180)
1194–1205	Aimery (brother)	—Echive d'Ibelin
		—Isabel of Jerusalem (1198)
1205–18	Hugh I (son; born 1195)	—Alice de Champagne (1208; died 1246)
1218–53	Henry I, the Fat (son; born 1217)	—Alice de Montferrat (1229; died 1232/3)
		—Stephania de Lampron (1237; died 1249)
		—Plaisance of Antioch (1250; died 1260)

1253–67	Hugh II (son; born 1252/3)	—Isabel d'Ibelin
1267–84	Hugh III (cousin)	—Isabel d'Ibelin (died 1324)
1284–85	John I (son)	
1285–1324	Henry II (brother; born 1271)	—Constance of Aragón and Sicily (1317)
1324–59	Henry IV (nephew; born 1329)	—Marie d'Ibelin (1307) —Alix d'Ibelin (1318)
1359–69	Peter I (son; born 1354)	—Echive de Montfort (1342) —Eleanor of Aragón (1353; died 1417)
1369–82	Peter II (son)	—Valentina Visconti (1372)
1382–98	James I (uncle)	—Héloïse de Brunswick-Grubenhagen (died 1422)
1398–1432	Janus (son; born c 1374)	—Louise Visconti (1400) —Charlotte de Bourbon (1409–11; died 1422)
1432–58	John II (son; born 1418)	—Medea of Monferrat (1437–40) —Helena Palaeologina (1442; died 1458)
1458–60	Carlotta (daughter; abdicated 1485; died 1487)	—John of Coimbra (1456; died 1457) —Louis of Savoy (1459; died 1482)
1460–73	James II, the Bastard (half-brother, by Marietta de Patras; born 1438/9)	—Caterina Cornaro (1472)
1473–74	James III (son; born 1473)	
1474–89	Caterina Cornaro (born 1454; abdicated 1489; died 1510)	

The Venetian Occupation 1489–1571

The Turkish Occupation as an Ottoman province 1571–1878

Under British administration 1878–1960

(It is a curious coincidence that the duration of the British occupation of the island—82 years—was exactly the same as that of the Venetians.)

a. UNDER THE SUZERAINTY OF THE SULTANS OF TURKEY 1878–1914
Administrators, High Commissioners, or Governors

1878–79	Lt-General Sir Garnet Wolseley
1879–86	Colonel Sir Robert Biddulph
1886–92	Sir Henry Bulwer
1892–98	Sir Walter Sendall
1898–1904	Sir William Haynes-Smith
1904–10	Sir Charles King-Harman
1910–14	Sir Hamilton Goold-Adams

	b. ANNEXED TO THE BRITISH CROWN, 5 November 1914
1915–18	Sir John Clauson
1920–25	Malcolm Stevenson
	c. BRITISH CROWN COLONY, 1925–60
1925–26	Sir Malcolm Stevenson
1926–32	Sir Ronald Storrs
1932–33	Sir Reginald Stubbs
1933–39	Sir Herbert Palmer
1939–41	Sir William Battershill
1941–46	Sir Charles Woolley
1946–49	Reginald Fletcher, Lord Winster
1949–54	Sir Andrew Wright
1954–55	Sir Robert Armitage
1955–57	F.M. Sir John Harding (later Lord Harding of Petherton)
1957–60	Sir Hugh Foot (later Lord Caradon)

Republic, 16 August 1960–

Presidents		*Vice-Presidents*	
1960–77	Abp Makarios III Mouskos	1960–64	Fazil Küchük
1978–88	Spyros Kyprianou	1973–	Rauf Denktash (who assumed the title 'President of the Turkish Republic of Northern Cyprus')
1988–93	George Vassiliou		
1993 –	Glafcos Clerides		

INTRODUCTION TO THE FOOD AND WINE OF CYPRUS

By IRO and DAVID HUNT

At several excellent restaurants in Nicosia, Larnaca, Limassol, and Paphos, and also in the larger hotels, it is possible to enjoy all the standard dishes of the international cuisine. In smaller places you can usually find the British soldier's favourites, with plenty of chips. But presumably those who have travelled as far as the Eastern Mediterranean will want to add to their other experiences by sampling the local dishes, accompanied by the local wines. The following brief appreciation is intended as a guide to some of the less familiar specialities of the island.

The principal influences on Cyprus cookery come from mainland Greece, Asia Minor, and the Levant. The most typical dishes are rich because they are usually prepared with olive oil and contain plenty of vegetables cooked with the meat to improve the flavour. Many are prepared with tomato purée, a method called *yiahni*. There are many varieties of *pilaffs*, made with rice or *bourghouri* (boiled crushed wheat). It is usual to start with *mezedhes* (sing. *meze*) or HORS D'OEUVRES; or you can make a whole meal of them, in which case they will be accompanied as time goes on by samples of whatever is cooking in the kitchen. They include olives, tomatoes, cucumbers, *houmous* (an Arab purée of chick-peas with sesame oil and cayenne), *taramosalata* (paté of smoked cod's roe), *melintzanosalata* (roasted pulp of aubergines flavoured with garlic and lemon), sardines, sausages, *lountza* (smoked pork), fried squid, octopus, *haloumi* (a sheep's milk cheese unique to Cyprus), *moungra* (pickled cauliflower), and *dolmadhakia* (vine leaves stuffed with minced lamb and rice). Another speciality, produced in the mountain villages and sometimes included in mezedhes, is *hiromeri*, leg of pork marinated for 40 days in red wine and sea salt, pressed under millstones to reduce it to one-sixth of its size, and smoked for a whole winter; it is very good with melon. Lastly *sheftalia* is the name for the ubiquitous pork, veal, or mutton sausage.

A SOUP speciality is *trahana*, made with crushed wheat and yoghourt. Another one, *avgolemono*, is made with chicken broth, rice, egg, and lemon juice.

Although Cyprus is an island, FISH is neither plentiful nor cheap. However, *xiphias* (swordfish) is grilled on charcoal; *barbouni* (red mullet) is prepared with wine vinegar, tomato purée, rosemary and garlic; octopus is cooked in wine; and whitebait *(maridha)* can sometimes be found.

MEAT. Lamb is served in a number of ways, especially as *souvlakia* (also known as kebabs), marinated in lemon juice, and cooked on a spit over charcoal, with tomato, onion, and green pepper pieces between the meat cubes. Another method is *kleftiko*, chunks of lamb cooked in a sealed clay oven, scented with bay leaves and origanum. *Tava* is a lamb stew, with plenty of onions.

Pork dishes include *aphelia*, a stew prepared with plenty of red wine and ground coriander seeds; *kolokassi*, which is a kind of sweet potato, stewed with pork, and tomato purée; and *zalatina*, head brawn with Seville orange juice.

The main beef dish is *stifado*, a stew of beef (or hare) cooked very slowly in a casserole with wine vinegar, onions and spices.

Dishes with dried vegetables include *louvia* (black-eyed beans) and dried broad beans cooked together with spinach or turnip leaf and dressed with olive oil and lemon; *moukendra*, a lentil dish made in the form of a pilaff, mixed with rice and fried onion rings. Salads are dressed with olive oil and lemon, and usually incorporate local herbs such as *glystirida* (or *glytisterida*) and *roka* (rocket plant). Fresh vegetables, beans, peas and broad beans are either boiled and dressed with oil and lemon, or are sometimes cooked in what is called the *yiahni* way, with plenty of oil, tomato purée and onions. *Okra* (or ladies' fingers) is also prepared in a similar way.

SWEETS are mainly Middle Eastern in style. *Loukoumi* is what is called in Britain 'Turkish Delight'; *baklava* is rather like a millefeuille pastry with nuts, cinnamon, and syrup; *kadeifi* has a similar filling in a cover resembling 'Shredded Wheat'; *loukoumades* are honey puffs; *galaktopoureko* is a strudel-pastry tart filled with semolina pudding.

Apart from *haloumi*, which is strongly recommended, the CHEESES you are likely to be served in Cyprus will be internationally known wrapped or packaged varieties. You may also find some *graviera*, a version of gruyère, or the rather similar *kefalotiri*, or *feta*, a soft white goat's milk cheese.

Cyprus is famous for its FRUIT: melons, water melons, apples, cherries, peaches, apricots, plums, oranges and tangerines. More exotic are *nespole* or *mousmoula* or *mespila*, which are loquats, like a big rose-hip but tasting more like an apricot; pomegranates, whose juice is often drunk iced in summer; and prickly pears, the fruit of the Opuntia, whose local name is *papoutsosika*. You will also find in the coffee shops, and may be offered if you visit a Cypriot home, fruit preserved in syrup. For 'Turkish coffee' and its varieties, see p 63.

The following list includes most of the more common foods found in Cyprus:

Soups, *soupes*

Avgolemono, chicken broth with rice and a sauce of egg and lemon
Faki, lentil soup
Hortosoupa, vegetable soup
Patcha, made from sheep's brains and eyes
Trahana, made with crushed boiled wheat and yoghourt

Hors d'Oeuvre, *mezedhes*

Bourekia, pies filled with meat, cheese or brains
Haloumi, sheep's milk cheese
Hiromeri, slices of locally-cured ham
Houmous, an Arabic dish of chick-peas and oil
Kalamaria, squids (fried or boiled in their ink)
Karaoli, snails (often used in a pilaff)
Kaskavali, a type of local cheese
Koupepia or *dolmadhes*, vine-leaves stuffed with rice and minced meat (turnip leaves or marrow flowers are sometimes used instead of vine leaves; in Lent the meat is omitted)
Koupes, minced meat enclosed in an oblong case made of *bourghouri*; see below
Loukanika, sausages
Lountza, smoked pork
Melintzanosalata, roasted pulp of aubergines
Oktapodi, octopus

Sheftalia, a type of sausage made of minced meat wrapped in peritonium skin and grilled

Talatouri, a salad of cucumber cubes mixed with strained yoghourt to which oil and mint have been added

Taramosalata, smoked cod's roe beaten up with bread, olive oil and lemon juice

Fish, *psaria*

Bakaliaos, cod
Barbouni, red mullet; if small *(barbounakia)* usually fried
Garidhes, prawns
Lithrinia, grey mullet
Maridha, whitebait
Melanouri, a local black-tailed fish
Mineri, tunny
Orfos, garfish
Pestrophes, trout
Synagrida, sea bass
Xphias, sword-fish

Main Dishes

Aphelia, cubes of pork stewed in red wine with crushed coriander seed

Bourekia tou keima, small pies made with pastry and filled with minced meat.

Bourghouri, boiled crushed wheat with meat (in North Africa known as *couscous*)

Dolmadhes, stuffed vine-leaves

Dolmadhes melintzanes, stuffed aubergines

Keftedes, meatballs, usually lamb and beef (or pork) mixed, often in a flattened oval shape

Kleftiko, lamb roasted in a sealed oven or sealed earthenware pot

Kolokassi, Cyprus sweet potatoes cooked with pork or chicken, chopped onions and tomato purée

Kreatocoloco, marrow stuffed with rice and minced meat

Kritharaki, a type of pasta resembling barley

Makaronia pastitsio, macaroni in the oven; layers of thick boiled macaroni, minced meat and bechamel sauce

Moussaka, layers of fried aubergine and fried sliced potatoes interspersed with minced meat and covered with a bechamel sauce

Parayemista, 'stuffed'; this applies to things such as stuffed aubergines, marrows, etc.

Perdhikes, partridges

Pilafi rizi, rice pilaff

Souvlakia, kebabs, lamb or pork, cooked on a spit and sometimes served in *pitta* bread together with chopped tomatoes and chopped onions

Stifadho, veal, hare or beef cooked with onions

Tavas, lamb cooked with tomatoes and onions in a sealed earthenware pot

Tyropitta, cheese pie

Yiouvetsi, lamb with *kritharaki*

Yiouvarlakia avgolemono, small meat balls made with rice and minced meat, served with a thick egg and lemon sauce

Zalatina, brawn

Vegetables, *horta*

Anginares, artichokes
Bamies, *okra* or ladies' fingers
Bizelia, peas
Coliandros, coriander
Fasolia, beans
Glystiridha, purslane
Kolokithakia, marrows
Koukia, broad beans
Kounoupidhi, cauliflower
Lahana, turnip leaves, boiled and used as salad
Louvia, black-eyed beans
Manitaria, mushrooms
Maroulia, lettuce
Moungra, pickled cauliflower
Moukendra, lentils; cooked with a rice pilaff and onions
Ospria, dried vegetables (beans, lentils, broad beans, chick peas)
boiled and dressed with olive oil and lemon
Pantzaria, beetroot
Patates, potatoes
Prassa, leeks
Portokolokasso, Jerusalem artichoke
Radhikia, wild chicory
Repania, radishes
Rokka, rocket (for salads)
Spanahi, spinach
Spanakopita, layers of mille-feuille pastry filled with spinach, cheese
and chopped onions

Sweets, *glika*

Amygdalota, sweets made with almond paste and sugar
Baklava, layers of mille-feuille pastry filled with ground almonds and
walnuts in a rich syrup flavoured with cinnamon
Bourekia tis anaris, small pies made with pastry and filled with
unsalted cream cheese
Galaktopoureko, thin pastry filled with semolina custard
Glyko, preserved fruit in syrup, offered to guests who call at a private
house
Halvas, sesame cake
Kadeifi, like baklava but in a casing resembling 'Shredded Wheat'
Kolokotes, pastry and sweet marrow
Loukoumadhes, honey puffs
Pittes, pastry opened up thinly like a pancake and fried; a thicker
version is called *Kattimeria*
Shiamishi, a pastry filled with semolina custard and fried
Vasilopitta, the traditional New Year's Eve cake

Fruit, *fruta*

Akhladia, pears
Dhamaskina, plums
Karpouzi, watermelon
Kerasia, cherries
Mandarina, tangerines
Mila, apples
Nespole (also *mespila* and *mousmoule*), loquats

Papoutsosika, prickly pears
Peponi, melon
Portokalia, oranges
Rodhakina, peaches
Rodhia, pomegranates
Sika, figs
Verikokka, apricots

Some Cyprus Specialities

Eliopitta, bread made with oil and containing olives
Flaounes, a special bread with local cheese for Easter
Ressi, crushed wheat porridge, eaten at weddings
Skordialia, bread sauce made with lots of garlic
Soutzoukos, a sweet made of solidified grape-juice

For information about Cyprus cooking recipes see 'Kopiaste', by Amaranth Sita, and 'Kali Orexi', produced by the Cyprus Red Cross Society and sold locally.

The **wines** of Cyprus were praised in antiquity both by the author of the Song of Solomon and by the Greek poet Hesiod in the 8C BC. In Roman times the elder Pliny speaks highly of them, which is evidence that they were exported since Pliny never visited the island. They had a great reputation in medieval times at the courts of the kings of England and of France and elsewhere in Western Europe. 'In all the world are no greater or better drinkers than in Cyprus': so wrote von Suchen in the mid 14C; while in the early 18C John Heyman recorded that 'The wine of Cyprus is also famous in every part of the Levant, as well as Europe', even if there were objections to its tarry taste (which might imply that at least some *retsina* was drunk then). 'A great deal of this wine was sent to Venice and England', he continued, remarking on it being improved by sea travel, and, so he said, 'accordingly an epicure of an Englishman who lived here, used to send his Cyprus wine to England, whence it was sent back again to him at Cyprus'. When the Portuguese settlers of Madeira wanted the best vines with which to plant their new possessions they sent to Cyprus for them; and when at the end of the 19C phylloxera devastated the vineyards, it was from there that they were restocked.

One of the favourite wines of the Middle Ages was malmsey or malvoisie; both names are corruptions of Monemvasia, the port in the Peloponnese from which it was shipped, but it was produced also in Cyprus. The red malvoisie grape is still grown on the southern slopes of the Troödos. You can come closest to appreciating medieval taste in wine by drinking Cyprus's unique *Commandaria*. Its name is derived from the Grand Commandery of the Knights of St. John at Kolossi. It is made by traditional methods, which include fermentation in open jars, from grapes grown within a restricted area, with an addition of ten per cent of white grapes. Its merit lies in the blending process and above all in the aging, for it is only sold after maturing for a long time in cask and in bottle. Really old wines, which are now hard to come by, are brownish and resemble a fine Bual; the usual bottle, whose label may indicate a vintage of as much as 50 years past, is a deep rich red. It is sweet but with a subtle flavour more reminiscent of Madeira than of port.

The other wines of Cyprus conform more closely to the varieties usual in Western Europe. Almost the whole of the island's wine production is in the hands of four main concerns: ETKO, KEO, LOEL, and SODAP, of which the last is a cooperative marketing union. In all cases the grapes are produced by individual growers to the number of 10,000 families; the producers exercise strict quality control. All four have large and modern wineries, to which visits can be arranged. Modern methods of production have brought about great improvement. The four main producers and the government have also encouraged the introduction of grape varieties from Western Europe, especially from France. As a result quality is consistently maintained and is steadily rising.

Cyprus sherry has enjoyed a good reputation in Britain, not necessarily connected with the price advantage derived from Commonwealth preference. The best selling brand is ETKO's *Emva Cream*; the other three main concerns produce cream sherries also, of which SODAP's *Lysander* is worth mentioning. There is an EMVA *Pale Cream* in the modern style, rather like a white port. The best dry sherry is KEO's *Fino*, which is made in the traditional way in an open cask with the development of *flor*; it is fully equal to some Spanish finos. There are also in all four ranges very drinkable dry and medium sherries in the amontillado style.

Table wines continue to improve. Twenty-five years ago the whites were better than the reds, then the latter took the lead and now the whites, with the help of imported varieties of grapes and low-temperature fermentation, have perhaps regained first place. Quality control means that in both categories there are wines which are at least equal to the better wines of Italy and Spain.

Among the wines three well-established brands, all dry enough to be refreshing, and forceful enough to accompany spicy foods, are KEO *Hock*, *Arsinoe*, and *Aphrodite*. More recent productions are *Bella Pais*, light and slightly pétillant, *Fair Lady*, and *Thisbe*, a low-alcohol wine (10 per cent by volume) designed to meet the growing wine-bar market in Britain. LOEL has introduced *Palomino*, a rather drier wine, made from the Spanish grape of the same name, which is the basis of sherry, and proposes shortly to produce a Cyprus Riesling. ETKO's challenger for the whites in a Graves-type wine called *Nefeli*, a good, straightforward wine, dry but not acid, with a good back-taste. It competes well with the more exclusive, and expensive, white wine made by the Khrysorroyiatissa Monastery from the local Xynisteri grape and marketed under the name *Ayios Amvrosios*. There is an unpretentious sparking wine, *Duc de Nicosie*, made by the *méthode champenoise*, which is of good quality with a firm dry taste. There are also sweet and semi-sweet white wines, including some made from the Muscat grape.

All four concerns market a rosé wine; *Coeur de Lion* is considered a good example.

The red wines maintain a sound level. *Domaine d'Ahera*, KEO *Claret*, *Olympus Claret*, and *Afames* are solid, well-made wines with some sublety of taste. *Semeli* is a more recent production; full, fruity and dry, it should preferably be decanted a little time before drinking. An even newer wine is *Carignan Noir*, made from recently introduced grapes of that name. *Otello* is reminiscent of a good Rhône wine and improves greatly with bottle-age. The successful vintage of 1959 can still sometimes be obtained and is worth trying. The red wine of Khrysorryiatissa, made from local grapes grown on the north-facing slopes, is marketed under the name of *Ayios Elias* It is light, almost pink, in colour but has plenty of body. Perhaps the most interesting of the new generation of red wines is *Ino*, produced by ETKO from locally-grown Cabernet-Sauvignon grapes; the vines were planted in the 1970s. It has a long taste, with some tannin, and is a good example of the Cabernet-Sauvignon character, by which is meant equal to the Bulgarian and not far behind the better Australian.

The locally produced beer, made from imported malts, is excellent. Brandy is made in large quantities. The older and more expensive brands are very acceptable for drinking after dinner and the cheaper ones for making the popular local aperitif, brandy sour, where the sharp and perfumed flavour of the Cyprus lemons matches the special quality of the spirit. The Greek aperitif *ouzo* is also produced: this is an aniseed-flavoured spirit reminiscent of Pernod, and equally potent. The other Greek favourite, *retsina*, a white wine flavoured with pine resin, is hardly ever seen, though some is made. An orange-flavoured liqueur, *Filfar*, is drunk after dinner by those who like Grand Marnier.

TOPOGRAPHICAL INTRODUCTION: DEMOGRAPHY

Cyprus—in Greek, ΚΥΠΡΟΣ (Kypros); in Turkish, KIBRIS—the third largest (after Sicily and Sardinia) and most easterly island in the Mediterranean, lies between latitudes 34° 33' and 35° 42' N and longitudes 32° 17' and 34° 35' E. Its total area is 9251km² (3572 sq. miles), slightly larger than the two English counties of Norfolk and Suffolk combined. Its greatest length—from the *Akamas peninsula* on the W to the tip of the *Karpas peninsula*—is 222km (138 miles); and its greatest breadth— from *Cape Kormakiti* in the N to *Cape Gata* (S of Limassol)—is 95km (59 miles). The two British Sovereign Bases together cover an area of 256km² (99 sq. miles).

The S coast of Turkey lies only 70km (44 miles) to the N; Syria lies 103km (64 miles) to the E; and the coast of Egypt is some 340km (211 miles) to the S. The nearest Greek island, Rhodes, the largest of the Dodecanese, lies 386km (240 miles) to the W, with Crete (8256km²) further W and at the same latitude as Cyprus.

Cyprus's main physical features are the long narrow *Kyrenia* or *Pentadaktylos* range, rising to 1024m (3360ft) at *Mt Kyparissovouni* (or *Akromandra*), which runs NE parallel to the N coast to form what is often known as the 'panhandle'; to the S of this range is the undulating alluvial plain of the *Mesaoria*, so-called from its position between the Kyrenia range and the *Troödos* massif to the SW. This latter, taking up much of the main bulk of the island, rises to 1951m (6401ft) at *Mt Chionistra* or *Mt Olympos*. The coastline measures some 782km (486 miles). There are no perennial freshwater lakes or rivers, but the numerous watercourses, dry during summer and autumn, may in winter become torrents. Many reservoirs have been constructed to store as much water as possible at such times, which would otherwise get wastefully discharged into the sea.

The latest estimated **population** (late 1988) was 691,100 (including Turkish troops and 'colonists' from mainland Turkey, largely from Anatolia). The Government-controlled area is said to contain 562,700 Greek Cypriots, of whom c 363,400 live in S Nicosia, and in the towns of Larnaca, Limassol and Paphos, which have absorbed most of the 180,000 refugees. Only 1000 or so elderly Greek Cypriots remain 'enclaved' in the Karpas. The Turkish controlled area had an *electorate* figure of 94,000 in mid 1985. It is still virtually impossible, and will be so until any entente has been reached and another island-wide census undertaken, to obtain any reliable figure of the population, resident or 'in occupation'.

The last official census of the whole island was held in 1960, the first year of Cypriot independence. Out of a total population of 577,615 there were some 442,521 Greek Cypriots (80 per cent) and 104,350 Turkish Cypriots (18 per cent), while among the remaining 30,744 were 3628 Maronites (Lebanese or Syrian Christians), and 2796 Latins (descendants mostly of Italian traders), the rest being described as 'British, Gypsies, Other and Not Stated'. In 1970 the total figure was 633,000 (518,617 Greek Cypriots, and 114,383 Turkish Cypriots).

In 1960 the representatives of the three Christian minorities— Armenians, Maronites, and Latins (the last being Roman Catholics)—threw in their lot with the Greek Orthodox majority, thus distancing themselves from and thereby effectively isolating the Turkish community, the vulnerable minority, which numbered just less than 20 per cent of the total. It was at this time that the late President Makarios, in making the discrimination, referred to the population of the Republic as being 81.14 per cent 'Greek' as against 18.86 per cent Turkish Cypriots, a ratio constantly reiterated since, although—until 1974—a more correct ratio, which had remained comparatively stable for several decades, was 77 per cent Greeks; 18 per cent Turks; and 5 percent Others (largely Armenians and British).

It has been estimated that the population of Cyprus in 50 BC was as high as 450,000, but this dropped dramatically in the 4C AD to c 50,000 largely through war and famine, before climbing to 300,000 and again falling as a result of the Black Death. In 1489, at the end of the Lusignan period and the beginning of the Venetian occupation, the figure was c 106,000. By the third quarter of the 16C it had risen to between 180,000 and 197,000, while after 1571 the Turks began re-settlement—as is their wont—with Anatolian peasants. Numbers in this Turkish province totalled c 200,000, but varied considerably during the next three centuries. Even though the ratio of Ottomans to Christians increased, this was partly because many of the latter ostensibly changed their religion to avoid the *kharaj* or tax (*Linobambakoi*; see Glossary). Sir Harry Luke, however, concluded that 'at no time were the Turks in Cyprus superior in number to the Christians'. In the early 18C the population again decreased to 80–84,000, with 47–60,000 claiming to be Moslem, and 20–37,000 Christians. During the late 18C and early decades of the 19C it continued to fluctuate between 60,000 and 100,000. In 1815 Turner suggests that there were 40,000 Greeks as against 20,000 Turks. Several informed guesses during the 1840s put the proportions as 70–90,000 Greeks as against 25–33,000 Turks.
   In 1879, the first year after being under British administration, the total was estimated to be c 200,000, 25 per cent of whom were Turkish Cypriots. The first reliable census, however, did not take place until 1881, producing a total of 186,200. By 1911 this had risen to 274,100 of whom 56,000 were Turkish (one sub-classification lists five poets, four chauffeurs, and three Fez blockers on the island). By 1921 the population was 310,700; by 1929, 344,000; and 385,000 in 1931. By 1946 it had increased to 450,000 (364,000 Greek Cypriots; 86,000 Turkish Cypriots); in 1956, 524,000 (421,000 Greeks; 92,000 Turks): but while the total population rose, the proportion of Turkish Cypriots to Greek Cypriots constantly dwindled.

Administration. Cyprus has been divided up into six administrative *Districts*, each normally under the supervision of a District Officer responsible to the central government in Nicosia, namely Famagusta, Kyrenia, Larnaca, Limassol, Nicosia, and Paphos (see p 16 of Atlas).
   Since July 1974 the divisive Attila Line has cut across the island in such a way that only *Limassol* (1382km²; 536 sq. miles; comprising the south central part of the island) and the adjoining district of *Paphos* (1396km²; 539 sq. miles; covering that part to the W of the main Troödos massif) remain entirely under government control. *Larnaca*, centred around the town of that name but extending W towards the Troödos mountains, and covering an area of 1126km² (435 sq. miles), is largely in the Greek Cypriot zone (82 per cent). *Famagusta* (1970km²; 761 sq. miles), which includes most of the Mesaoria and the NE and E of the island, is at present largely in Turkish Cypriot occupation, as is the whole of *Kyrenia*, the coastal strip N of Nicosia (639km²; 247 sq. miles). Conterminous with the above five districts is that of *Nicosia*, covering the centre of the island and the N flank of the Troödos range, with an area of 2727km² (1053 sq. miles), of which 37.5 per cent is in Turkish Cypriot hands.

Glossary of Architectural, Topographical and Allied Terms

AGORA, public square or market-place

AMVON, pulpit in a Christian basilica (pl. AMVONES)

AYIA, Saint (female); AYIOS (male); (pl. AYII)

AYIASMA, Holy water

BEMA, chancel or sanctuary in Byzantine churches into which women are not allowed; cf. Stavrovouni

BOTHROS, pit or deposit of votive offerings and sacred objects discarded from a sanctuary

DIACONICON, compartment to the right of the bema used by the deacons: the sacristy

EKKLISIA, a church

EXEDRA, semi-circular recess in a classical or Byzantine building

ICONOSTASI, screen separating the apse or bema from the nave in Orthodox churches, and hung with icons, paintings or mosaics, etc., of sacred personages, and themselves regarded as sacred: women are not normally allowed to pass behind

KAKO-, bad

KALO-, good

KATHOLIKON, the main church of a monastery

KATO-, lower

KHRYSO, golden

LINOBAMBAKOI, literally 'flax-cottons'; the chameleon-like inhabitants of certain villages during the Turkish period, in fact Orthodox Christians compromising with Islam, to avoid paying excessive taxes

MEGARON, hall of a Mycenaean palace

MIHRAB, niche in mosque facing in the direction of Mecca

MIMBAR, pulpit in mosque

NAOS, nave or church

NARTHEX, vestibule or porch at the W end of a Christian basilica

NEA, new

PALEA or PALEO, old

PANAYIA, the Blessed Virgin Mary

PANTOKRATOR, the Almighty, often a half-figure of Christ in the central dome of a church

PANO, upper

PAPAS, a priest

PETRA, stone

POTAMOS, a river or stream

PRODHROMOS, St. John the Baptist (the Forerunner)

PROTHESIS, the compartment to the left of the bema, where the preparation of the eucharist takes place

RINCEAU, a leaf-scroll (usually vine) decoration

STAVROS, the Cross

STIRRUP JAR, a closed pot for the storage of wine or oil, with a spout on the shoulder and a handle (in a form reminiscent of a stirrup) over the closed top

STOA, portico or roofed colonnade

SYNTHRONON, a semi-circle of seats in the main apse, for the clergy

TÉKKÉ, Muslim equivalent to a monastery

TEMENOS, a sacred enclosure

THOLOS, a circular building

BIBLIOGRAPHY AND MAPS

The bibliography of works in English alone on the topography, archaeology, history, and culture of Cyprus is extensive, and the list below does not pretend to be more than a general compilation of titles—largely in English—which may be useful for reference, or of interest in providing background for visitors. Many contain comprehensive bibliographies.

There are of course a large number of recent works in English, Greek, and other languages, many of them tendentious, and bookshops in Cyprus, Athens, and London (in particular, the *Hellenic Bookservice*, 91 Fortess Rd, NW5 1AG; and also *Zeno*, 6 Denmark St; apart from other antiquarian dealers) can frequently offer helpful advice.

The British Council Library in Nicosia should not be overlooked. In Nicosia, the *'MAM'* bookshop (the House of the Cyprus Publications), 13 Aristokypros St (Laiki Yitonia) is recommended. *Kemal Rustem* has been long established near Atatürk Sq, in the north part of the town.

Among the more comprehensive bibliographies are G.H.E. Jeffery and C.D. Cobham, *An Attempt at a Bibliography of Cyprus* (new ed., Nicosia, 1929), and that entitled *Cyprus* (Clio Press, Oxford, 1982), and those contained in Sir George Hill's monumental *History*, still the most scholarly survey, but somewhat too long and detailed for the general reader.

GENERAL DESCRIPTIONS: among the more recent are Ismene Hadjicosta, *Cyprus and its life* (Nicosia, 1943); Barbara Toy, *Rendezvous in Cyprus* (1946); Patrick Balfour (Lord Kinross), *The Orphaned Realm* (1951); Lawrence Durrell, *Bitter Lemons* (1957); Sir Harry Luke, *Cyprus, a Portrait and an Appreciation* (1957; revised ed. 1965); Gordon Home, *Cyprus then and now* (1960); Colin Thubron, *Journey into Cyprus* (1975); Sir David Hunt (ed.), *Footprints in Cyprus* (1982; revised ed. 1990), published by the Trigraph Press, who have also published several reprints of books on the island, as have Zeno.

Among earlier accounts containing descriptions of the island are: Sir Samuel White Baker, *Cyprus as I saw it* (1879); R. Hamilton-Lang, *Cyprus; its present resources, and future prospects* (1878); Lady Annie Brassey, *Sunshine and Storm in the East* (1880); Louis Salvator of Austria, *Levkosia, the capital of Cyprus* (1881; new edition 1983); Mrs Scott Stevenson, *Our Home on Cyprus* (1880); John Thomson, *Through Cyprus with the Camera in the autumn of 1878* (1879; new edition 1985); William Hurrell Mallock, *In an Enchanted Island* (1889); Mrs Lewis, *A Lady's Impressions of Cyprus in 1893* (1894); Sir Henry Rider Haggard, *A Winter Pilgrimage* (1901); David George Hogarth, *The Nearer East* (1902); also Jens Holmboe, *Studies on the Vegetation of Cyprus* (Bergen, 1914).

Claude Delaval Cobham's *Excerpta Cypria: Materials for a History of Cyprus* (1908; reprinted 1969 in both Cyprus and New York) is a unique compilation of descriptive and historical extracts from 80 writers in 12 languages between AD 23 and 1849, and an invaluable source-book; also by the same editor, Giovanni Mariti, *Travels in Cyprus in 1769* (1909; reprinted 1971). The Cobham Collection is now housed in the Royal Commonwealth Society Library, London. *Supplement to Excerpts on Cyprus*, compiled by A.H. Mogabgab, were published in 1941–45.

Early editions of the *Handbook for Cyprus* (first published in 1901, ed. by C.D. Cobham and Sir J.T. Hutchinson; 7th ed. (1913), 8th ed. (1920; ed. by Harry Charles Lukach, later Sir Harry Luke, and Douglas James Jardine), and 9th ed. (1930; ed. by Sir Ronald Storrs and Bryan Justin O'Brien), contain much detailed and curious information.

GENERAL HISTORY: Sir George Hill, *A History of Cyprus* (4 vols, 1940–52; reprinted 1972); Doros Alastos, *Cyprus in History* (1955; reprinted 1976); Costas P. Kyrris, *History of Cyprus* (1985); Stavros Panteli, *A New History of Cyprus* (1984); Stavros G. Lazarides, *Cyprus 1878–1900* (1984; largely reproductions of plates from the *Illustrated London News* and *The Graphic*); Philip Newman, *A Short History of Cyprus* (1940; 2nd ed. 1953); Sir Harry Luke, *Cyprus under the Turks, 1571–1878* (1921; reprinted 1969); John Hackett, *A History of the Orthodox Church of Cyprus* (1901; reprinted 1972); William Hepworth Dixon, *British Cyprus* (1887); C.W.J. Orr, *Cyprus under British Rule* (1918; reprinted 1972); H.D. Purcell, *Cyprus* (1969); C. Spyridakis, *A Brief History of Cyprus* (1964; rev'd ed. 1974); Sir Ronald Storrs, *A Chronicle of Cyprus* (1930); also of interest is *Orientations* (1937; definitive ed., 1949), his autobiography; G.S. Georghallides, *Cyprus and the Governorship of Sir Ronald Storrs* (2 vols: 1985; 1990). Steven Runciman, *A History of the Crusades*, particularly the third volume (3 vols; 1951–54), is also relevant, as is vol. 4 of K.M. Setton, *A History of the Crusades* (1977), containing A.H.S. Megaw on the military architecture of Cyprus.

RECENT HISTORY: François Crouzet, *Le Conflit de Chypre, 1946–1959* (2 vols; 1973); S.G. Xydis, *Cyprus, Conflict and Conciliation* (1974), *Cyprus, Reluctant Republic* (1973); T. Ehrlich, *Cyprus, 1958–67* (1974); Nancy Crawshaw, *The Cyprus Revolt: an account of the struggle for union with Greece* (1978); Robert Stephens, *Cyprus: a Place of Arms* (1966); Charles Foley, *Legacy of Strife* (1964); Michael Harbottle, *The Impartial Soldier* (1970); Sylvia Foot, *Emergency Exit* (1960); P.G. Polyviou, *Cyprus: The Tragedy and the Challenge*; Michael A. Attalides, *Cyprus: Nationalism and international politics* (1979); George S. Georghallides, *The Political and administrative history of Cyprus, 1918–1926* (Nicosia, 1979); N.M. Ertekun, *The Cyprus Dispute* (1981); Pierre Oberling, *The Road to Bellapais* (1982); Christopher Hitchens, *Cyprus* (1984); J.T.A. Koumoulides (ed), *Cyprus in Transition, 1960–1985* (1986); John Reddaway, *Burdened with Cyprus: the British connection* (1986).

ARCHAEOLOGY, EARLY HISTORY, ART AND ARCHITECTURE: Stanley Casson, *Ancient Cyprus* (1937); L.P. di Cesnola, *Cyprus: its Ancient Cities, Tombs, and Temples* (1877); D.G. Hogarth, *Devia Cypria: Archaeological Journey in Cyprus* (1889); Rupert Gunnis, *Historic Cyprus* (1936; 2nd ed. 1947); George Jeffery, *Historic Monuments of Cyprus* (Nicosia 1918; reprinted 1983); H.-G. Buchholz and Vassos Karageorghis, *Prehistoric Greece and Cyprus* (1973); Vassos Karageorghis, *Salamis in Cyprus* (1969), *Kition* (1976), *The Civilization of Prehistoric Cyprus* (1976); *Cypriote Antiquities in the Pierides Collection* (1973, and since revised), *Cyprus* (*Archaeologia Mundi* Series, 1968); N.K.Sandars, *The Sea Peoples* (1978; revised ed. 1985); R.M. Dawkins (ed.), *The Chronical of George Boustronios, 1456– 89* (1964), and *Recital concerning the Sweet Land of Cyprus* entitled 'Chronicle' (a translation of Leontios Makhairas's Chronicle; 1932; reprinted 1980); J.L. Myres, Handbook of the Cesnola Collection of Antiquities from Cyprus (1914; reprinted 1974); Robin Feddon and John Thomson, Crusader Castles (1950; in part); Andreas and Judith Stylianou, The Painted Churches of Cyprus (revised ed. 1985); Fernand Braudel, The Mediterranean (2 vols; 1972–73); A. Papageorghiou, Icons of Cyprus (1969), Masterpieces of Byzantine Art of Cyprus (1965); A.C. Brown and H.W. Catling, Ancient Cyprus (Ashmolean Museum, Oxford, revised ed. 1986); Osbert Lancaster, Sailing to Byzantium (1969); E.J. Peltenburg, Early Society in Cyprus (1989); F.G. Maier, Cyprus from the Earliest Time to the Present Day (1966); H.D. Robertson, The Archaeology of Cyprus; Recent Developments (1975); H.W. Catling, Cyprus in the Neolithic and Bronze Age Periods (in Cambridge Ancient History, 3rd ed., 1968); David Talbot Rice, The Icons of Cyprus (1937); L. de Mas Latrie, Histoire de l'île de Chypre sous le règne de la Maison de Lusignan (Paris, 1852–61); René Grousset, L'Empire du Levant (Paris, 1946); R.B. Francis, The Medieval Churches of Cyprus (1949); Veronica Tatton-Brown, Cyprus B.C.: 7000 years of history (1979: British Museum exhibition catalogue), Ancient Cyprus (1987), and (edited by) Cyprus and the East Mediterranean in the Iron Age (1989); B.F. Cook, Cypriote Art in the British Museum (1979); Desmond Morris, The Art of Ancient Cyprus (1985); F.G. Maier and Vassos Karageorghis, Paphos, history and archaeology (1984); Musée de l'Homme, Paris, Chypre, la vie quotidienne de l'antiquité à nos jours (1985); H.W. Swiny (ed.), Ancient Kourion area (1982); Einar Gjerstad, Ages and Days in Cyprus; W.A. Daszewski and Demetrios Michaelides, Mosaic Floors in Cyprus (1988); Vassos Karageorghis (ed.), Archaeology in Cyprus 1960–1985 (1985), and Cyprus, from the Stone Age to the Romans (1982).

Camille Enlart's Gothic Art and the Renaissance in Cyprus (Paris 1899) was translated by David Hunt and published in London in 1987 by Trigraph Ltd. It contains 429 figures and 65 plates, including 17 drawings by Tessa Henderson. Together with an introduction by Nicola Coldstream and editorial notes by David Hunt, it contains — in spite of its date — a vast amount of information in its 684 pages concerning the architecture of this important period which cannot possibly be detailed in this Guide.

MISCELLANEOUS: H.M. Denham, Southern Turkey, The Levant and Cyprus: a sea-guide to the coasts and islands (1973); Andreas Stylianou, A History of the Cartography of Cyprus (1981); Peter Loizos, The Greek Gift: Politics in a Cypriot Village (1975), and The Heart Grown Bitter (1981); Ed. David and Iro Hunt, Caterina Cornaro, Queen of Cyprus (1989); J.K. Campbell, Honour, Family, and Patronage (1964); David and Mary Bannerman, Handbook of the Birds of Cyprus (1958; reprinted by Kemal Rustem, 1989); J.M.E. Took, Common Birds of Cyprus (1973); P.R. Flint and P.F. Stewart, Birds of Cyprus (an annotated check-list; 1983); Ann Matthews, Lilies of the Field (a book of Cyprus wild flowers, Nicosia, 1968); R.D. Meikle, Flora of Cyprus (R.B.G., Kew, 1977; 1985); Ioannis Ionas, La Maison rurale de Chypre (1988); Jack C. Goodwin, A Toponymy of Cyprus (Nicosia, 2nd ed., 1977; cyclostyled; since expanded); Elektra Megaw, Wild Flowers of Cyprus (40 colour-plates; 1973); Christos Georgiades, Flowers of Cyprus: Plants of Medicine (1985, and 1987), Nature of Cyprus: Environment; Flora; Fauna (1989), Trees and

Shrubs of Cyprus is forthcoming; Sonia Halliday and Laura Lushington, *Flowers of Northern Cyprus*; B.S. Turner, *The story of the Cyprus Government Railway* (1979). Walkers will find G. Daniel's *Landscapes of Cyprus* (Sunflower Books; 1990) of help.

Maps. For general purposes the *Cyprus Administration and Road Map* (Series D.S.L.14 1:250,000; revised 1984), published by the Department of Lands and Surveys, Nicosia, is adequate, but not always up-to-date or reliable as to the quality or sinuosity of minor roads. It is overprinted with a conventional reference grid (8m. by 12m.), which conforms with the sheet lines of the Cadastral Survey, each of the 59 sheets (1:50,000), indicated by Roman figures, being sub-divided into 64 plans at 1:5,000. Some editions also indicate the position of the present *Green Line* between the Greek Cypriot and Turkish occupied zones. At a slightly smaller scale is the *A.A. Leisure Map*. The *Ministry of Defence* map of the island (Series 1501, sheet NI 36-3, edition 4-GSGS, revised in 1979, at 1:250,000) is also useful. The C.T.O. publishes a Visitor's Map at 1:400,000 (1986).

The *Topographical Maps* (four sheets at 1:100,000; Series D.S.L. 18, revised 1984) cover the island in greater detail and are recommended. Travellers requiring further detail will find the 24 sheets at 1:50,000 (*Ministry of Defence* Series K717, edition I-GSGS, published in 1973) extremely useful, particularly for walkers, but neither these nor others produced by the Department of Lands and Surveys may be—understandably—so readily available while part of the country is under military occupation, and their sale is at present 'restricted' (although some sheets—edition 2-GSGS—were reissued, revised, in 1981). The same applies to some town plans.

Among numerous other maps available are a *Forest Map* (D.L.S. 4; 4m. to 1 inch; 1964), and a *Geological Map* (1:250,000; 1963), which may be obtained from the Department of Lands and Surveys, or from approved agents.

Some of these are stocked by, or may be ordered through, Stanfords, 12–14 Long Acre, London WC2. It may be of interest to note that Edward Stanford also published, in 1885, the first trigonometrical survey of the island, undertaken by Captain Horatio Herbert Kitchener, R.E. (1850–1916; Field Marshal in 1909), and drawn to a scale of one inch to one statute mile.

Visitors to the occupied zone will find it helpful to acquire there a roughly printed map indicating Turkish place-names: see p 12.

PRACTICAL INFORMATION

Formalities and Currency

Passports are necessary for all British and American travellers entering Cyprus, and must bear a photograph of the holder. No visa is required for British and American visitors.

At present (1990) the *only legal ports of entry* into the Republic of Cyprus are Larnaca International Airport, Paphos Airport, and the seaports of Larnaca, Limassol, and Paphos. Visitors are not allowed to enter the Republic through the ports of Famagusta, Kyrenia, or Karavostasi, nor through the airports of Tymbou (Ercan) or Lefkoniko, which have been declared prohibited ports of entry. Visitors having legally entered the Republic may however cross into and return the same evening from the occupied sector of the island through the check-point at the Ledra Palace Hotel, Nicosia; passport necessary. Special permission should be requested in advance should the visitor wish to spend more than 24 hours in the occupied zone. *Foreign residents* living in the occupied sector before 1974 may cross into the southern zone and back with little difficulty.

Permits to stay in Cyprus for more than three months may be issued by the Chief Immigration Officer, Nicosia. Visas are not required for visitors in transit for a stay of up to five days and in possession of a through ticket and an entry visa for the country of destination, and with sufficient funds. Those wishing to obtain *employment* in Cyprus must be in the possession of an employment permit issued by the Cyprus Government *before arrival.*

Embassies and Consulates, etc. The Office of the *British High Commissioner* is at Alexander Pallis St, Nicosia (a short drive NW of the centre). The address of the *Cyprus High Commission* in the UK is 93 Park St, London W1; their *Embassy* in the USA is at 2211 R. St NW, Washington 20008 DC.

Custom House. Except for travellers by air, who have to pass customs at Larnaca or Paphos airports, luggage is scrutinised at ports of departure and disembarkation. Provided that dutiable articles are declared, bona-fide travellers will find the Cypriot customs authorities courteous and reasonable. Permits for the importation of pets must be obtained, prior to importation, from the Director of the Department of Veterinary Services, Nicosia. Dogs and cats are subject to a six months period of quarantine. Parrots and budgerigars are prohibited. Sporting guns require a temporary permit from the Ministry of the Interior, but the importation of all other firearms is absolutely forbidden.

The export of any kind of antiquity without permission and a licence from the Department of the Director of Antiquities is totally prohibited.

Currency Regulations. The Cyprus pound is theoretically equivalent to the £1 sterling, although since 1972 Cyprus has ceased to be a member of the Scheduled Territories (Sterling Area), but in practice the present exchange rate is unfavourable to the visitor. The amount in Cyprus banknotes which may be imported or exported is limited to £50, and any Cyprus currency not expended should be exchanged before departure.

Money. The monetary unit since October 1983 has been the *Cyprus pound* (C£), divided into 100 *cents*. The coinage consists of 1 cent, 2 cents, 5 cents, 10 cents, and 20 cents. Notes for 50 cents, C£1, C£5, and C£10 are in circulation.

Cyprus pounds are also current in the occupied zone, although one is likely to receive change in Turkish *liras*, which cannot be used elsewhere on the island.

Approaches to Cyprus and Transport in Cyprus

Travel Agents. General information may be obtained gratis from the *Cyprus Tourism Organisation* (C.T.O.), 213 Regent St, London W1R 8DA, and any accredited member of the Association of British Travel Agents will sell tickets and book accommodation.

The address of the C.T.O. in the USA is 13 East 40th Street, New York 10016. See below for branches in Cyprus itself.

In view of the distance involved, both the cheapest and most practical way of reaching Cyprus from Britain is by air, there hiring a car.

Travellers overland must allow for the *return* journey six days by rail or about ten days by road to Piraeus (see Blue Guides to Greece and to Yugoslavia), thence there is the journey by sea to Limassol. Those preferring a longer sea voyage may embark on a ferry (with limited car-carrying facilities) from a variety of ports, among them Marseille, Genoa, Venice, Trieste, Bari, Ancona, Brindisi and Naples, the majority of which also call at Piraeus.

Direct regular **Air Services** between London and Larnaca (and others from Manchester and Birmingham) are maintained by *Cyprus Airways* working in conjunction with *British Airways*, while the airport of Paphos, serving the W part of the island, has been in operation since December 1983 . Full information regarding flights may be obtained from British Airways, 75 Regent St, London W1, and from Cyprus Airways, Euston Centre, 29/31 Hampstead Rd, London NW1 (a short distance N of Warren St tube station), or any travel agent. There are, in addition, a number of flights to Larnaca from Athens (in conjunction with *Olympic Airways*) and from the majority of European and Middle-Eastern capitals.

The Nicosia office of British Airways is at 52A Makarios Av.; that of Cyprus Airways, 50 Makarios Av., with branches in Limassol, Larnaca, Ayia Napa, and Paphos. That of Olympic Airways is 17 Homer Av., Nicosia. *Cyprus Turkish Airlines*, who at present fly to the occupied north of the island via Turkey, have offices at 28 Cockspur St, London SW1Y 5BN.

Cars may be brought into Cyprus without formality by visitors for any period up to three months. An international driving licence is required, or a national licence valid in the driver's own country for the class of vehicle he wishes to drive (if hiring a car: see below). Also required is a Certificate of Foreign Insurance, available free of charge from the Register of Motor Vehicles, 24 Byron Av., Nicosia, and at the port of entry. Motorists not the owners of their vehicles should possess the owner's permit for its use abroad. Drivers in Cyprus, as in Britain, keep to the *left* of the road. The use of seat-belts is compulsory. The *Cyprus Automobile Association* offices are at 12 Chr. Mylonas St, Nicosia.

Transport in Cyprus. Although the country **buses** (usually market buses) are rarely of much use to the tourist, the **inter-town buses**, and **Service** (shared) **Taxis**, both run by private operators, are the main form of communication other than private car, for the island's railway (commenced in 1905) was discontinued in 1952. Tourist Offices can supply timetables, schedules and prices, etc., and a list of addresses and telephone numbers of such radio-controlled taxi firms, who will collect one from and deliver one to any reasonably central area of the main towns, between which they travel regularly, but they do *not* serve the airports, and travellers must change at central Larnaca to a local taxi to the airport, for example. They are *shared* between 4–7 people—some are 12-seater mini-buses—and are comparatively inexpensive, the cost being about one-eighth to one-tenth of that of a normal private taxi. Travellers using them must expect some delays due to the time taken making detours to collect and deliver. Taxis are distinguished by an illuminated sign, and taximeters are now enforced. For long distances payment is computed by the time taken, while private arrangements should be made in advance of any planned excursion into the country by chauffeur-driven car. Tourist Offices and hotels can usually advise on what the cost is likely to be. Taxis are not allowed to cross into the occupied zone.

During the season a number of **Coach Tours** are organised, details of which may also be obtained from the larger hotels, and Tourist Offices.

Car Hire. Numerous firms provide **self-drive** (or chauffeur driven) **facilities**—some with offices at the airports—which offer greater independence to those travellers wishing to explore the island and visit its archaeological sites, churches and monasteries off the beaten track. They may not cross the 'Green Line'. Hire-cars will also be delivered to ports (or to airports) and hotels by prior arrangement, and in the case of the larger companies the car may be returned to any of their branches. Prices vary, depending on the size of the car; they are slightly lower between 1 November–31 March, and reduced tariffs apply for cars hired for over a week. A list of car-hire firms is available from branches of the C.T.O., but the hirer should have a very precise understanding of the contract entered into, and should inquire about additional insurance, etc.

Roads. The one dual carriageway, most of it of motorway standard (and referred to in this Guide as such) runs S from Nicosia, bearing SW near Kophinou to beyond Limassol. The speed limit is 100km per hour on the motorway, and 60km per hour elsewhere unless otherwise indicated. Regrettably, many Cypriots still drive too fast and too recklessly. It is planned to continue the motorway parallel to the present road between Episkopi and Paphos, and beyond. Two extensions are also projected: from Kophinou to Larnaca, and from Perakhorio (midway between Nicosia and Kophinou) to Larnaca (almost completed), while a by-pass will circle Larnaca from W of the airport to Dhekelia, to serve the Ayia Napa area.

The other few main roads are mostly well-cambered and in good condition, but the hard shoulder is often abrupt and the edges broken. The minor or mountain roads and forest tracks are still largely unsurfaced, and are liable to provide a rough passage after wet weather. Such dirt tracks are only rarely smooth, and although at their best preferable to deteriorated tarmac, they are often dusty and can reduce average speed to a crawl, particularly when climbing through the Troödos mountains. Provided the vehicle is robust and the driver experienced, a faster speed can, paradoxically, give a less uncomfortable drive. Sufficient time should always be given to cover the ground when off the main roads, particularly towards dusk, when traversing narrow winding mountain tracks, often with vertiginous drops into an adjacent valley. **Petrol stations** are normally open from 6.00 to 18.00 (to 16.00 on Saturdays) although some shut on Tuesday or Wednesday afternoons, and others on Sundays and holidays, but it is always advisable to keep the petrol tank topped up when driving off the beaten track. Petrol and diesel oil are sold by the litre.

Motorists should avoid, if possible, driving W during the late afternoon, when the glare of the setting sun can be unpleasant and even dangerous. When driving at dusk or after dark, a sharp look out should be kept for unlit carts, bicycles and straying animals, etc. Road signs are of the international type, while—except in remoter areas— place-names are indicated in English as well as in Greek capitals.

For **Maps**, see p 49.

Distances may still be indicated in miles, but will be changed gradually to kilometres; see p 12.

Bicycles may be hired in the main towns and resorts.

Postal and other Services

Most **Post Offices** are open from 17.30–13.00 (13.30 in winter). Correspondence marked 'poste restante' (to be called for) may be addressed to any post office, and is handed to the addressee on proof of identity (passport preferable). Parcels and registered letters should be called for at central P.O.s on notification of their arrival. Pillar-boxes are painted yellow.

Post offices with *poste restante* services are: Eleftheria Sq., Nicosia; Gladstone St, Limassol; King Paul Sq., Larnaca; and Themithos and St. Paul St, Paphos.

Telephones. The telephone service is maintained by the Cyprus Telecommunication Authority (Cy.T.A.) in conjunction with external services, and has automatic or S.T.D. connections with most other countries. Most operators speak fluent English. The following codes may be useful: Nicosia 02; Limassol 051; Larnaca 041; Paphos 061; Paralimni 031; Polis 063; and Ayia Napa 037. For Fire, Police or First Aid, dial 199 (in the main towns).

Banks are found in the main thoroughfares of the major towns, and are open from 8.30–12.00 daily except Sundays and holidays; and until 11.30 on Saturdays. Exchange facilities are available at Larnaca and Paphos airports during the hours of flight arrivals and departures. Centrally located branches in the main towns also offer exchange facilities for tourists during weekdays from 15.30–17.30.

Press, T.V., and Radio. The 'Cyprus Mail' appears daily in English, as does the 'Cyprus Weekly'. UK and other foreign newspapers are regularly obtainable—at an inflated price—at central kiosks in Nicosia and the larger towns. Radio and television services are mostly in Greek, but they also have programmes in English. 'Cyprus Time Out', or 'Nicosia This Month', among others, are serviceable guides to ephemeral practical information (shopping, entertainment, etc.).

An earth satellite station to facilitate automatic telecommunication and television services, etc. was inaugurated in September 1980 at Kakoradjia, S of Nicosia. In much of the island the British Forces Broadcasting Service radio programme can be picked up. There is a tourist programme, with news in English, on the radio in summer.

Tourist Offices. The head office of the C.T.O., for postal enquiries only, is at 18 Th. Theodotou St, Nicosia (Telex 2165; Fax 366744; P.O. Box 4535). Tourist Information offices are at Larnaca airport (24-hour service) and Democratias Sq., Larnaca; Laiki Yitonia, Nicosia; 15 Spyrou Araouzo St (opposite the Customs House), Limassol, and also E of the town; 3 Gladstone St, Paphos; and at Paphos airport; also at Ayia Napa (opposite the Monastery) and Platres (in summer only).

Hotels and Restaurants

Writing 300 years ago, Van Bruyn observed that one might 'travel where you will in the island without fear, and in as great security as you might at home. The Greeks of the country are naturally polite and good-natured'; and, one might add, hospitable; and the quality of accommodation in the main towns, in the Troödos resorts, and in certain coastal areas—E of Limassol, at Ayia Napa, and along the coast N of Cape Greco—which are being exploited, is now of European standard. Holiday accommodation is likely to be booked up early in the season, so visitors should book well in advance; but see below. There seems to be a tendency in the construction of hotels to concentrate too much on the large luxury type fettered to the exigencies of tour operators, and there is a dearth of medium-sized family-run hotels.

For those touring the southern half of the island it is recommended that they base themselves at one of the main towns (such as Larnaca or Paphos) and radiate into the hinterland from one such centre before moving on to another; one of the Troödos resorts can be a base for the exploration of that massif, although its N flank can be approached with ease from Nicosia, also a base for travellers planning to visit the occupied zone.

Some form of simple accommodation can almost always be found, perhaps with the help of the local police, or by applying to the coffee shop.

The situation has considerably improved since 1890, when Sir Lambert Playfair's 'Handbook to the Mediterranean' suggested—as there were no hotels except at Larnaca—that the traveller should provide himself with 'complete camp equipment, as, though the natives are most hospitable, and fair accommodation can be obtained at the monasteries, yet there are few if any native houses where the traveller could pass an undisturbed night in a native bed'. He goes on to say that an India-rubber bath and a canteen would provide entire independence. ....Henry Rider Haggard, visiting the island in 1901, confirmed that the accommodation was still primitive, for 'Until the tourist comes, it is idle to expect that conveniences for his reception will be provided'.

A list of hotels, giving their classification, facilities and charges, is published regularly by the C.T.O., which together with travel agents in Cyprus, can advise on the renting of villas and hotel apartments, some of which include a daily maid service. Some package holidays can also provide this form of accommmodation in lieu of a hotel.

Travellers are strongly advised to inquire *very specifically as to the exact location* of hotels, should they wish for accommodation in or near a town centre. Many hotels are listed as being *in* Limassol or Larnaca, for example, which are in fact located in (admittedly coastal) suburbs of very slight attraction several kilometres distant.

Monasteries which formerly provided simple (in some cases Spartan) accommodation to travellers, are now reluctant to do so; indeed, that at Ayia Napa specifically refuses to lodge visitors, even when its hostel is not occupied by participants of its occasional ecumenical conferences. Kykko accepts pilgrims.

Limited accommodation—restricted to three consecutive nights—is available at the *Stavros tis Psokas Forest Station* (W of Kykko), but it should be booked well in advance during the summer. Food is available at a simple bar adjacent.

There are *Youth Hostels* at Nicosia, Larnaca, Limassol, Paphos and Troödos. Facilities are also available at Stavros tis Psokas (see above). Members of the I.Y.H.A. should apply to the Cyprus Y.H.A., 18 Solon St, P.O. Box 1328, Nicosia, or direct to the hostel in question.

Camping. The only 'official' camping sites on the island are at Larnaca, the resorts of Troödos, Polis (Paphos District), Governor's Beach (Limassol District), and at Ayia Napa, but private arrangements can be made with the proprietors of certain beach restaurants, should such facilities be available.

Lists of **Restaurants** are also available from Tourist Offices. Many of them are modest or outdoor establishments, but while too many appear to base too high a proportion of their menu on English cuisine—having been so influenced for a century, and also in response to the charter trade—local and more succulent dishes, largely of Greek or Turkish origin, are usually also included and should always be savoured. Better value for money will often be obtained in Cyprus than in some other countries where the ritual and etiquette of eating are taken more seriously, with correspondingly high charges. Some few pretentious restaurants, which can easily be avoided, have been sold the idea that piped music is conducive to a better appetite. It will be noticed that many restaurants are closed on Sundays. Unless they must have the reassuring presence of other tourists, visitors should choose an establishment patronised by locals, where the food will be better (and cheaper) and the atmosphere livelier.

Cafés, bars, and **tavernas** are to be found in or near the main thoroughfares of every town and village. They are open throughout the day and well into the night, and the customer may spend many an entertaining hour watching the passers-by, but be warned that certain modern establishments in the main towns have begun to charge exorbitantly for this pleasure. 'French' coffee *(gallicos)* is available, but a proprietary powder and a jug of hot water is usually supplied in its place.

What is still called 'Turkish' coffee may be ordered in a variety of forms: *skéto* = plain, without sugar; *me oligi* = with a little; *métrio* = medium; *mallon* = rather more sugar; *gliki* = sweet; *varigliki* = heavy. This is served with an accompanying glass of iced water. The visitor will soon be aware of the hospitable and ubiquitous custom, on entering many offices, certain shops, and elsewhere, of being offered cups of coffee, which are conveniently brought in on a round metal tray suspended by wire struts. When entering a Cypriot house one may formally be offered preserves *(glyko)* with coffee and water; this should be taken sparingly, but must never be refused.

GENERAL INFORMATION

Climate and Season. Climatically the best months are March to mid-June and from September to November. Generally speaking it is dry and healthy. Some will find the summer heat excessive, but this is somewhat mitigated by sea breezes. The island enjoys constant sunshine during a high proportion of the year, rain falling rarely other than within the period October–February. The driest town is Nicosia, with an average rainfall reading of 14.72 inches; while Kyrenia is the wettest (21.15 inches). The high-lying resort of Troödos has an annual average of 48.95 inches of rain, most of it falling between late October and early May, but between January and March much of this precipitation is in the form of snow, and woollen clothing is desirable during winter months, particularly in the chilly evenings, when there is often a sudden fall of temperature.

The table below indicates the average air and sea temperatures, the average maximum day temperatures in the hill resorts, and the *percentage* of sunny days in the months concerned. Temperatures are given in degrees Centigrade or Celsius.

Month	Air	Sea	Mountain	Sunshine
Jan.	16.6	16.4	6.3	57
Feb.	16.0	16.9	5.9	63
March	18.4	17.3	10.4	67
April	22.8	18.6	14.3	71
May	27.2	21.0	18.8	79
June	30.5	24.0	24.1	87
July	33.3	26.3	26.3	90
Aug.	33.6	27.7	26.9	88
Sept.	30.8	26.6	23.2	88
Oct.	27.3	25.1	18.4	80
Nov.	22.9	21.9	14.1	71
Dec.	19.2	18.9	9.6	59

July and August are the hottest months, with a maximum temperature of 44.5°C (112°F), while December–February are the coolest, with a minimum of −5.5°C (22°F).

Travellers should also remember that in Cyprus, because of its position, darkness falls both suddenly and comparatively early during the winter months, and an early start should be made if planning a long excursion.

Language. The two official languages, used by their respective communities, are Greek and Turkish, although English is spoken in hotels, restaurants, bars, banks, shops, taxi offices, etc., and generally by the better educated members of the community, and visitors to the island with no knowledge of modern Greek will have little difficulty in making themselves understood, except in the more remote villages, but even there someone with sufficient knowledge of English can usually be found. Certainly to speak even a few words in modern Greek will in itself enlist the native courtesy of the Cypriot to the assistance of the visitor in difficulties, while a knowledge of at least the Greek alphabet is desirable, and is given below. A phrase book or pocket dictionary will also be found useful. A number of topographical prefixes are included in the Glossary. Attention should be paid to the more formal conventions of the Greek Cypriots, although perhaps English influence in the past has to a certain extent eroded this and has made them less formal than their mainland neighbours. When greeted in Greek, it is polite to reply in a like manner.

The Greek alphabet comprises 24 letters:

Α α, Β β, Γ γ, Δ δ, Ε ε, Ζ ζ, Η η, Θ θ, Ι ι, Κ κ, Λ λ, Μ μ, Ν ν, Ξ ξ, Ο ο, Π π, Ρ ϱ, Σ σ ς, Τ τ, Υ υ, Φ φ, Χ χ, Ψ ψ, Ω ω.

Vowels. There are five basic vowel sounds in Greek to which even combinations written as dipthongs conform: α is pronounced very short, ε and αι as e in egg (when accented more open, as in the first e in there); η, ι, υ, ει, οι, υι have the sound of ea in eat; ο, ω as the o in dot; ου as English oo in pool. The combinations αυ and ευ are pronounced av and ev when followed by loud consonants (af and ef before mute consonants.

Consonants are pronounced roughly as their English equivalents with the following exceptions: Β = v; γ is hard and guttural, before a and ο like the English g in hag, before other vowels approaching the y in your; γγ and γκ are usually equivalent to ng; δ = th as in this; θ as th in think; before an i sound λ resembles the lli sound in million; ξ has its full value always, as in ex-king; ϱ is always rolled; σ (ϭ) is always hard, never like z; τ is pronounced half way between t and d; φ = ph or f; χ, akin to the Scottish ch as in loch, a guttural h; ψ = ps as in lips. The English sound b is represented by the Greek double consonant μπ, d by ντ. All Greek words of two syllables or more have one accent which serves to show the stressed syllable. In the termination ον the n sound is disappearing in speech and the ν is often omitted in writing.

The correct reply to καλώς ωρίσατε (kalós orísate: welcome) is καλώς σας βρίκαμε (kalós sas vríkame, glad to see you). To the enquiry τι κάνετε (ti kánete, how do you do?) or πως είστε; (pos íste, how are you?) the reply should be καλά ευχαριστώ, και σείς (kalá efkharistó, ke sis; well thank you, and you?), or έτσι και έτσι, και σείς (étsi ke étsi; so-so, and you?). General greetings are χαίρετε (khérete; greetings), or less formally υιά σας (ya sas, hello). Στο καλό (sto kaló); keep well) is used when bidding farewell to one who leaves, not when one is leaving oneself. Περαστικά (perastiká) is a useful word of comfort in time of sickness or misfortune meaning 'may things improve'.

It is still customary to greet shopkeepers, the company in cafés, etc., with καλημέρα (kaliméra; good day) or καλησπέρα (kalispéra; good evening). Σας παρακαλώ (sas parakaló; please) is used when asking for a favour or for information, but not when ordering something which is to be paid for, when θα ήθελα (tha íthela; I should like) is more appropriate. The Greek for yes is ναι (né) or, more formally, μάλιστα (málista); for no, όχι (ókhi).

Health, etc. The island—long plagued by locusts—also suffered from an evil reputation for malaria, but with pest control and drainage during the last century this had been virtually eradicated by 1949, while the veterinary services have now controlled to a great degree the hydatid disease of echinococcosis, carried principally by stray dogs, which are automatically put down. (Cats, in contrast, continue to thrive.) Dog bites, nevertheless, require immediate treatment. Infective hepatitis (jaundice) can still be a hazard. Mosquitoes can be an irritant, and an insect repellent should be taken. Climate and food alike may cause gastric disorders, but plain unsweetened lemon-juice can be efficacious, and chemists' advice is generally knowledgeable. Dishes involving reheating, and made-up dishes, are best avoided.

Insurance. Although hospitals will naturally provide casualty treatment, the social insurance scheme does not yet include the free treatment of foreign visitors, who should take out temporary insurance in advance against illness and accident while abroad.

Snakes, etc. Cyprus, once known as Ophioussa—the abode of snakes—had also the undeserved reputation of being infested by venomous reptiles, but the viper *(Vipera lebetina)* and the 'Coupli', up to 1m long with a green skin and dark spots, are now comparatively rare. Venomous-looking spiders, locally called tarantulas, are in fact quite harmless.

Equipment. Even in winter the light in Cyprus is strong, and sun-glasses will be needed. It can be dusty, and a clothes brush will not come amiss; nor will a hat, for the sun can burn. A pocket torch will be useful when exploring the darker recesses of Byzantine churches, their murals still too often smoke-blackened, and a pocket compass can on occasions be helpful when off the beaten track.

Photography. There is normally no restriction, but owing to the present Turkish military presence, certain areas near the Green Line, both in Nicosia and elsewhere in the country, will have signs prominently displayed indicating that photography is forbidden: ΑΠΑΓΟΡΕΥΕΤΑΙ (apagorevetai). Photography may not be allowed in some museums and churches, and it is always as well to request permission first. See also p 61.

Public Holidays, Religious Festivals, etc. The main public holidays for the Greek Cypriot community are: 1 January; 6 January (Epiphany); Kathara Deftera (the Orthodox Shrove Day); 25 March (Greek Independence Day); 1 April (EOKA Day); Orthodox Good Friday; Easter Saturday; 1 May; 15 August (Dormition of the Virgin); 1 October (Cyprus Independence Day); 28 October ('Okhi' Day, celebrating Greece's defiant 'no' to the Italians in 1940); Christmas Day; and 26 December (St. Stephen; Boxing Day).

Those applying for the Turkish Cypriot community are 1 January; 23 April (Children's Bairam); 1 May; 19 May (Sports and Youth Bairam); Birthday of the Prophet; Sheker Bairam (Ramadan; 2 days); Qurban Bairam (Feast of Sacrifices; 3 days); 30 August; 29 October (Turkish Independence Day); and 15 November.

There are any number of very local religious festivals, when some curious relics of the imperfect assimilation of pagan superstition with Christian rites may be observed. Details of these, and of more commercialised events, may be obtained from Tourist Offices. Among them are 'The Submersion of the Holy Cross' (6 January), which takes place at some seaside towns; and Kataklysmos (50 days after Easter Sunday). The Limassol Carnival and Wine Festival take place in March and late September, respectively. Festivals are held at Paphos in June and at Kourion (Curium) in July, when drama performances are held in the restored ancient theatres, etc.

Shops are normally (May–September) open from 8.00–13.00 and 16.00–19.00; 14.30–17.30 in winter, except on Wednesday and Saturday, when they close in the afternoon. Many are owner-run, and their hours tend to be more elastic, while the smaller *kiosks*, which are a characteristic feature of Cypriot urban life, are open at all hours. Products of rural industry can usually be found for sale in towns, whether silver or brassware, pottery or Lefkara embroidery and lace (although there is much mass-production of the genuine articles), while the boxes of succulent Turkish Delight or *loukoumi* will attract many. The showroom of the *Cyprus Handicraft Service* of the Ministry of Commerce and Industry (which is doing much to foster the abilities of refugees) is at 186 Athalassa Av., Nicosia.

Sports. Local Tourist Offices can provide the names of firms selling and hiring equipment for water sports (water-skis, aqualungs, etc.), organising cruises and hiring motor boats; likewise the names of hotels offering special facilities.

Angling. For obvious reasons, there is little river fishing, and the island has no native freshwater fish, but during recent years a variety of fish have been introduced into some reservoirs. Offices of the C.T.O. can provide lists of reservoirs, and information on the regulations in force, obtaining a fishing licence, etc.

They can also provide lists of *Tennis-courts, Skiing* facilities on Mount Olympos (January–March), etc.

Visiting Monuments, Museums and **Churches.** Most museums, ancient monuments and sites are administered by the Department of Antiquities, the Cyprus Museum, Nicosia, from whom an up-to-date list of opening times may be obtained. Most of the sites are open daily from 7.30 or 8.00 until dusk, an enlightened policy which it is hoped might be followed by the ecclesiastical authorities with regard to churches: see below. Bona fide students and archaeologists may apply to the Nicosia Museum for a pass allowing them free access to these. In those places most visited by tourists, the way to the ancient site is generally signposted—indeed new, indestructable signs are being put up to replace those vandalised. The site is likely to be enclosed: the guardian is often most helpful.

Rose Macaulay once remarked of Cyprus that 'no island comparable in size carries so many ruined religious buildings'. She continued by observing that the enchantment of ruinous Cyprus was cumulative rather than individual. Ruins one will still see in plenty, but not all are in such a state of dereliction, although it has been said that this is preferable to some recent restorations. In some of the island's monasteries it appears that the aesthetic quality of the monastic church and its contents is in inverse proportion to the wealth of the community. Indeed, it has been remarked that far more buildings and their contents in the Greek-Cypriot-Government-held half of the island have been irreparably injured and disfigured by the taste of the Orthodox Church than those which have suffered the depredations of ignorant Turkish troops and international art thieves in the occupied north; see below.

Many village churches are kept locked, but normally there is no great difficulty in finding the priest *(papas)* or guardian, and the local coffee-shop should be resorted to when seeking for a volunteer to find them. Even in the most out-of-the-way places there is usually someone available who can understand and speak English. In some cases the custodian will be found at some distance from the church in question: that of Stavros tou Ayiasmati, for example, lives at Platanistasa, with some 5km of winding dirt track between them, and much time and energy will be saved making enquiries in advance.

It will be noted that the Greek Orthodox churches are laid out on a set plan, and, unlike churches in Western Europe, have no range of chapels. Women are still forbidden to pass beyond the *iconostasis* into the *bema* or sanctuary (except in specific cases), nor should men use the Holy Doors, but may enter the side openings of the screen. Some priests will expect or specifically request a donation for the upkeep of the building, even if it is obvious that nothing will ever be done to improve the filthy condition in which many of them are found.

Few priests and monks, whose hirsute appearance often proclaims their ascetic character, would pretend to have any interest in the aesthetic appeal of the church in their care, and until they are placed under the supervision of a more responsible body, and the guttering candles and oil-lamps removed, any number of Byzantine murals will continue to be destroyed; others continue to be progressively obliterated by the osculations of the Faithful. Thousands of early icons—often half hidden behind lace curtains—have disappeared, to be replaced very often by affected modern examples in the most vile taste, while the extravagance and metallic lustre of some recently hung chandeliers has to be seen to be believed. Such misplaced charity at this time in the island's history has been the subject of much criticism. It is of interest that priests—but not monks—of the Greek Orthodox Church may be married before they are ordained, but are then unlikely to rise in the hierarchy.

Many *Mosques* in 'unoccupied' Cyprus may be closed, but visitors entering that of Hala Sultan Tékké, near Larnaca, for example, which is a national monument, are reminded to remove their shoes beforehand.

No one would deny that significant material damage has been done and that theft and looting has taken place since July 1974 in the Turkish-occupied part of the island. Greek Cypriots have repeatedly and vociferously denounced the 'plundering of a 9000-year-old civilisation', even organising an exhibition devoted to the subject in Athens in 1985. All are sympathetic: no one can condone the destruction of any part of a country's heritage, be it pagan, Christian, or Moslem.

Much of the destruction took place immediately after the Turkish troops landed. Certain churches were later entered, sometimes forcibly, and murals and mosaics were detached, some intact, while others were destroyed in the attempt. In most cases this was done by thieves using sophisticated professional techniques for their removal, export and eventual sale. The most serious examples known were the lifting of the mosaics in the church of *Kanakaria* (Lythrangomi); and of the murals in *Panayia Pergaminiotissa* (Akanthou), already much decayed; of *Antiphonitis*, the lower parts of which had been previously defaced; and of *Ayios Ephimianos* (Lysi). And there are several others.

The churches of *Panayia Absinthiotissa* (damaged in the fighting) and *Ayios Khrysostomos*, both near Koutsovendis, are still in military hands (at the time of writing), the latter being used for storage. Both are out of bounds, as is the site of *Lambousa*, and no reliable reports of their conditions are available. Some graveyards have also been vandalised; some icons—the best having usually been taken earlier—have been stolen, and others—some already in poor condition—have been removed by the Turkish Cypriot authorities for safe keeping. Certain private and public collections of antiquities were looted (notably in Famagusta), and the contents of other collections, ostensibly protected, at Morphou, Kyrenia, and elsewhere, have appeared in the international art market for stolen goods. The necropolis at *Vounos* (near Bellapais) was systematically dug over and its tombs pillaged.

It should be emphasised that there is no trace of any deliberate policy of desecration of churches, either on religious or ethnic grounds, by Turkish Cypriots, despite allegations of such. In 1975 their authorities locked up several hundred Greek Orthodox churches to prevent damage, although some were put to use as mosques (such as the early 20C one at Akanthou). Many of them were in an unedifying state already. Bona fide inquirers may apply to the local *muhtar* for the keys of many.

It appears that Christian cemeteries have been allowed to be desecrated by the occupying power; among them have been the British cemeteries at Kyrenia and Famagusta.

Several archaeological sites recently excavated have been back-filled to protect them from the elements and from pilferers; others await such provisional attention. No other archaeological activity is at present in progress, and professional foreign archaeologists, even if previously in charge of excavations in the north, are unable to visit their sites to check conditions, or on the whereabouts of the artefacts, or to implement better protection for them. Such constraints would appear to be counter-productive, but this is not the place to discuss the ethics of the effective boycott which has been instituted, whereby archaeologists working in the north could be banned from ever working again in any Greek-speaking country. Exposed sites are inevitably deteriorating, owing to the limited means of those in the north endeavouring to maintain them. Meanwhile, the Turkish Cypriot authorities are restoring a number of buildings, both Moslem and Christian, among them the *Büyük Khan* and the dilapidated church of *Ayios Loukas* in N Nicosia. They are also strenuously attempting to stop all forms of trafficking in stolen antiquities, part of an international racket and a serious problem which also dogs the Government-controlled south.

Northern Cyprus. Travellers are advised *not* to approach too closely the buffer zone of varying width known as the Green or Attila Line, lying between the Government-controlled part of the island and that at present occupied by Turkish forces, and which is patrolled by UNFICYP troops.

Photography is *not* allowed in its vicinity, and signs are displayed to this effect in Greek (see p 58), and also in English in sectors of the British Sovereign Base areas. In the Turkish-occupied part the following orders should be obeyed, which are printed on red hordings.

DIKKAT Attention
YAVAŞ SÜRÜNÜZ Drive slowly
DURMAK YASAKTIR No stopping
ASKERI BÖLGE: GIRILMEZ Military area: no entry
FOTOĞRAF ÇEKMEK YASAKTIR No photography

The Turkish military can be fairly abrupt when requesting the unsuspecting and innocent traveller to turn back on both main and minor roads, or in the vicinity of camps.

It is sensible to carry some form of identification at all times, preferably a passport, which should not be retained by a hotel, although requested when booking in.

Check in advance if a hotel will accept credit cards, and what they may charge you should you wish to use them.

Sterling currency is frequently accepted.

Turkish Cypriot food. The following list of dishes may be found useful:

Soup, *Çorba*

Domates Çorbasi, tomato soup
Et Suyu, Consommé
Sebse Çorbasi, vegetable soup
Tavuk Suyu, chicken soup
Yayla Çorbasi, mutton soup with yogurt

Hors d'oeuvres, *Mezes*

Arnavut Ciğeri, spiced liver
Börek, pastry filled with soft white cheese and herbs. Sometimes deep-fried
Cacik, yogurt flavoured with grated cucumber, garlic and olive oil
Fava, broad bean paste
Pilaki, white beans and onion with vinegar
Sardalya, sardines
Tarama, a paste of red caviar, yogurt, garlic and olive oil

Salad, *Salata*

Rus Salatasi, mixed Russian salad with carrots, peas in mayonnaise
Çoban Salatasi, mixed chopped salad of tomatoes, cucumbers, peppers, etc.
Karişik Salata, mixed salad
Patlican Salatasi, cooked aubergines with yogurt
Yeşil Salata, green salad

Fish, *Balik*

Alabalik, trout
Barbun, red mullet
Kefal, grey mullet
Lüger, bluefish
Palamut, tunny

Meat, *Et*

Bonfile, fillet steak
Döner Kebab, slices of lamb roasted on a vertical spit
Kofte, croquettes of lamb in gravy
Pirzola, lamb chops
Sebzeli Rosbif, roast beef served with vegetables
Şis Kebab, charcoal-grilled chunks of lamb and tomatoes
Şeftali, minced meat and herbs in a sausage-type skin, grilled
Şis Köfte, grilled croquettes of lamb

Vegetables, *Sebze*

Bezelye, peas
Biber, sharp green peppers
Havuç, carrots
Kabak, marrow or pumpkin
Lahana, cabbage
Taze Fasulye, French beans

Dessert, *Tatli*

Baklava, layers of filo pastry filled with nuts and covered with syrup
Dondurma, ice cream

Fruit, *Mevya*

Erik, plums
Incir, figs
Kiraz, cherries
Kavun, yellow melon
Karpuz, water melon
Şeftali, peaches
Üzüm, grapes

Drinks

Ayran, yogurt diluted with water and chilled
Çay, tea, served black in a small glass with cubes of sugar.
Kahve, Turkish coffee. Sugar is added during preparation so you should tell the waiter whether you want it *sade*, without sugar; *az şkerli*, with a little sugar; *orta*, moderately sweet; *çok şekerli*, very sweet.
Maden Suyu, mineral water.
Raki, an aniseed-flavoured spirit of considerable potency resembling the Greek Ouzo.

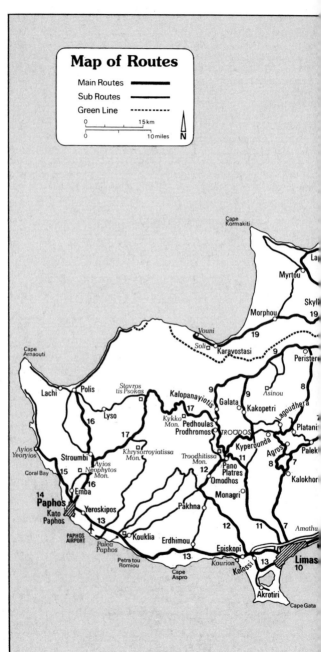

Map of Routes

Main Routes	
Sub Routes	
Green Line	-----

0   15 km
0   10 miles

N

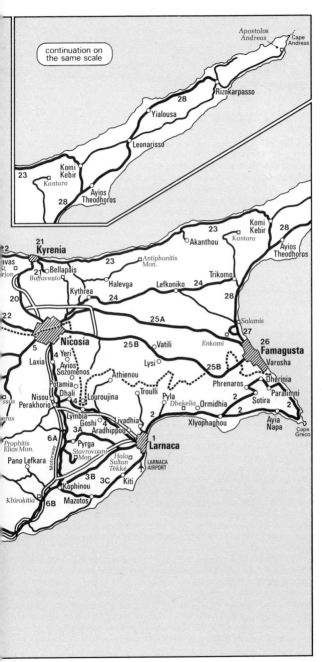

continuation on the same scale

Apostolos Andreas
Cape Andreas

Rizokarpasso

28

Yialousa

Leonarisso

23
Komi Kebir
Kantara

28
Ayios Theodhoros

23
Komi Kebir
28

Kantara

Akanthou
Ayios Theodhoros

21
Kyrenia

2
avas
St.
rjon
21
Bellapais
Buffavento

23
Antiphonitis Mon.

Trikomo

Halevga

Lefkoniko
24

28

Kythrea
24

20

25A

Salamis

22

Nicosia

25B
Vatili

Enkomi

27

26
Famagusta

5
Laxia

4
Yeri
Ayios Sozomenos

Lysi

25B

Varosha

Athienou

Phrenaros

Dherinia
Paralimni

Potamia
Dhali

Louroujina

Troulli

Pyla
Dhekelia
Ormidhia

2
Sotira

2

ssus
eras

Nisou
Perakhorio

4

Lymbia
Goshi
4
Livadhia

Xlyophaghou

2

Ayia Napa

Cape Greco

Prophitis
Elias Mon.

6A

3A
Aradhippou

1
Larnaca

Pano Lefkara

Pyrga
Stavrovouni
Mon.

Hala
Sultan
Tekke

LARNACA AIRPORT

3B
Kophinou

3C
Kiti

Khirokitia

6B
Mazotos

PART I

1 Larnaca

A. Southern Sector

Until the 1960s a comparatively small and sleepy old port with a long history, **LARNACA** (19,800 inhab. in 1960; approx. 53,600 in 1988, including the suburbs of Aradhippou, Dromolaxia, and Livadhia) has grown in importance since the opening of its international airport, some 5km S, now the Republic's main airport, and it is the town many visitors first enter. It is of special interest for the Pierides Collection of Antiquities and for the adjacent site of Kition, and is a good centre from which to explore the SE of the island.

Larnaca airport was in fact the first landing-field in Cyprus (from 1939), and was used by the RAF. It was entirely reconstructed in 1975 to replace the International Airport at Nicosia, by then in No Man's Land and occupied by UNFICYP; it was extended later to handle commercial jets.

Tourist Offices at Democratias Square, and at the airport—the latter providing a 24-hour service.

Originally known as *Kition* (or *Kitium*), it was settled in the Early Cypriot period, later growing in importance. From perhaps the 9C BC it was dominated by the Phoenicians and continued to prosper; its harbour, which may have been enclosed, was used for the export of copper from the mines of Tamassos, c 40km to the NW, while the town itself may have stood a short distance back from the sea. Its sympathies were with the Persians during the Graeco-Persian War, and in 450 BC it was besieged by the Greek fleet under Kimon, who died here. During the Roman period it was of comparatively little importance, and in the 7C it was occasionally raided by the Arabs.

Under the Lusignans its name changed to *Salina* or *Salines*, on account of the neighbouring salt lake. During the siege of Famagusta by the Genoese (1373–74) many foreign traders moved to Larnaca or *La Scala* (the landing stage, as its roadstead had become known) the name Larnaca (Greek: 'a hollow place', rather than from 'larnax', a coffin) not being generally in use until c 1600. During the Turkish occupation it grew in importance as a port, and was long the main place of residence of a small English colony and (from 1683) of foreign consuls in Cyprus. Some of these occupied themselves searching for ancient remains in the vicinity; an English Consulate is first heard of in 1626.

J.-B. Tavernier, writing c 1650, refers to the population of the island as being 'all clad after the Italian manner, both men and women'. At carnival time masquerades were in vogue, but the practice was forbidden in 1681 because some young gentlemen were visiting the bazaars in female attire. John Heyman (Professor of Oriental Languages at Leyden), who visited Larnaca during the first decade of the 18C, remarked that the consuls did not 'affect anything of that state and ceremony in their visits and conversation, as at Smyrna; for I once saw the English consul very readily offer his hand to the wife of the first dragoman of the French consul, and led her upstairs; a civility to which a Smyrna consul would by no means have condescended'; continuing: 'The English consul's house here is the best in the whole island, though the outside of it is only of clay, but nothing can be more neat, or elegantly ornamented than the inside. It has also the largest hall I saw in any part of the Levant; but, what is of much more importance, the English consul is highly respected all over the island, as jointly with his company he advances money to the inhabitants, for getting in their several harvests, in which otherwise they would be at a great loss'. It is believed that the original building (which was dismantled some years ago) was erected by the less reputable consul and merchant Mr Treadway, who—the story goes—as he was much in debt, invited all his creditors to a meal, at the commencement of which he begged to be excused, and forthwith boarded a friend's ship (on which he had stowed all his valuables under cover of darkness the previous night), set sail, never to be seen again; there is some doubt whether the dinner ever reached the table.

Chamber music was cultivated among the English colony in particular, and old letters contain requests for scores by Purcell, among others, to be sent out to Cyprus.

In 1778 some 40 Maronites lived here, but, with no priest of their own, they were attended by Franciscans. In 1800 Lieutenant-Colonel William Martin Leake (1777–1860; the topographer of Greece) visited the town briefly, off which lay a small squadron under Sir Sydney Smith, who had just signed a treaty for the evacuation of Egypt by the French. Leake remarked that the stone foundations of ancient walls and other remains of antiquity were being 'removed for building materials almost as soon as they were discovered'. In 1815, according to William Turner, Larnaca contained about 1000 houses, and in the Marina or port area there were about 700 more. Turner also complained of being kept awake at nights by the croaking of frogs in the marshes, and of its muddy streets.

In 1841 it was slightly larger than Nicosia, and out of a population of 13,000 some 9500 were Greek Cypriots. It has been estimated that in 1816 there were some 1000 Europeans at Larnaca, 200 of whom were 'in transit'. By 1847 this number had dropped to 400, still a considerable figure in comparison with less than a dozen each at Nicosia and Limassol. As an entrepôt for business in the Near East the town—thus more 'European' than Nicosia—thrived, and a branch of the Ottoman Bank was established here in 1864. In the following year Gen. Luigi Palma di Cesnola was appointed American consul at Larnaca, holding the post of Russian consul simultaneously. Hence he undertook his depredations 'with the countenance and indulgence of the authorities and public officers', to quote his own exculpatory words; and, apparently, with financial backing from John Ruskin to the tune of £1000. The authorities were still Turkish.

HMS *Minataur*, flagship of the Channel Squadron, commanded by Vice-Admiral Lord John Hay, sailing from Suda Bay, Crete, dropped anchor in the roadstead of Larnaca on 4 July 1878. Captain Harry Rawson landed during the following two days to be briefed by Charles Watkins, the British consul. On the 10th Rawson, together with Walter Baring, second secretary at the British Embassy at Constantinople, and Sami Pasha, representative of the Porte, who had meanwhile disembarked, made their way to Nicosia to initiate negotiations for the transfer of power. Rawson returned to collect 50 marines and 50 bluejackets, who on the morning of the 12th, together with Hay, entered Nicosia by the Famagusta Gate. Within hours the sultan's firman had been presented to the Turkish governor, Bessim Pasha, who thereupon handed over the administration to Hay, as agreed. The Union Jack was hoisted, and the curious crowd applauded enthusiastically. On the 23rd Sir Garnett Wolseley landed at Larnaca with some 1500 troops, including a detatchment of the Indian Army contingent from Malta, 400 strong, who for the next six months made Larnaca their H.Q. Wolseley himself entered Nicosia on the 30 July.

It was here in January 1879 that John Thomson (whose description of the island, and photographs, have recently been reprinted), landed to tour Cyprus.

Two of the 'Invincibles' who turned Queen's evidence after the assassination of Lord Frederick Cavendish in Phoenix Park, Dublin (in 1882) were eventually sent for their own safety to Cyprus, but both died shortly after, and were buried in the Roman Catholic cemetery here.

The population in 1881 was 7833 (5058 Greek Cypriots, and 1965 Turkish Cypriots). Although a new pier was constructed in 1882, from the 1940s the port was gradually superseded in importance by those at Famagusta and Limassol; but since 1976 work has been in progress to extend its facilities. The area was crowded with Greek Cypriot refugees in 1974–75, mostly from Famagusta, while in the spring of 1976 thousands of Christians from the Lebanon sought temporary refuge here.

Larnaca was the birthplace of Zeno the Stoic (335–263 BC, who left for Athens in 313), and in c 50 BC of Apollonius, the Alexandrian physician and commentator on Hippocrates. Robert Hamilton Lang (1836–1913) was British Consul in Cyprus in 1871–72. Claude Delaval Cobham, editor of 'Excerpta Cypria' (see Bibliography), to whom all with an interest in the island's past are indebted, was Commissioner of Larnaca from 1879–1907, where he resided in the old English Consulate (see above).

The centrally sited *Tourist Office* is in Democratias Square, and is adjacent to the Post Office, banks, etc.

A few steps to the SW, at 4 Zenon Kitios Street, in a white verandahed building of 1856 standing in its own garden, is the Swedish Consulate, accommodating part of the important **Pierides Collection of Cypriot Antiquities*, largely gathered together by Demetrios Pierides (1811–95), and since further enriched by members of the family. It is expected that most of the collection will be moved to the five renovated *Warehouses* (from 1882) standing a short distance E of the Tourist Ofice. This should take place in 1991. Medieval objects, and the collection of Roman glass, will remain here.

From the ENTRANCE HALL, with its chests and carved woodwork, we enter **R1**. Neolithic II–Middle Cypriot pottery; picrolite idols from Erimi and Souskiou; anthropomorphic pitchers, including one showing two deer.—Pyxides of Red Polished ware from Margi and Kochati; on wall shelves, trays and plates of Cypro-Geometric III and Cypro-Archaic I periods.—Bichrome ware, and further examples of Red Polished ware.—White Painted I ware from Philia (Middle Cypriot).— Female idols of the Goddess Astarte type; Late Cypriot II rhyton in the shape of a dog's head, and other ware of the same period; stirrup jars, bowls, etc., some of alabaster (1400–1050 BC).—Bird-shaped askoi; pottery of Cypro-Geometric II period.—In the centre: ritual bowls of Red Polished II ware (2000–1850 BC) from Margi, and another superb example displaying pairs of birds; and recently discovered at Souskiou, a remarkable terracotta *Male figure on a stool,* of the Chalcolithic period, 36cm high.

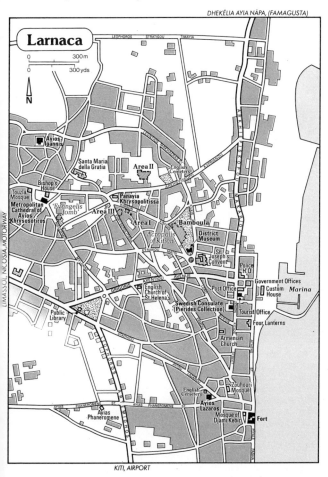

R2. Bichrome IV ware (700–600 BC) and of the 'Free field' style, decorated with birds and fishes; (right) of the Cypro-Archaic period, including anthropomorphic pitchers, etc. On the right-hand wall: terracotta funerary statue (seated) from Marion (400–325 BC), and another (reclining). Adjacent is a terracotta idol of a goddess with arms raised (800–700 BC), and model chariots, mounted warriors, and other figurines, and female statuettes of the Cypro-Archaic I period. On the other side of the room are more small statuettes, and heads of various periods, including a number holding 'discs' and other votive offerings.

Mounted warrior, Pierides Collection

R3. Pitchers from Marion with mould-made female figures holding miniature jugs on their shoulders, of various periods.—Attic Black Glazed ware (imported; 525–400 BC), and alabaster vases (Hellenistic).—Attic Black-figured, and Red-figured pottery (6–4C BC).—Terracotta figurines, lamps, and lagynoi (flasks).—Note the head in a separate case, and the 'mask' on the wall.

R4. Medieval glazed pottery of brown and green scraffito ware (early 14–15C), including cup; also 13C scraffito ware.—A fine collection of ancient glass (200 BC–AD 300), including glass birds and fishes. Note the female head between the cases.—Here also is a collection of stone heads; moulded heads; glass, and shell jewellery.

In the adjoining HALL is an inscription from Kition from the grave of a certain Kilikas. On the right-hand wall are three shields of lions rampant, and opposite, a sculpted flamingo, and part of a lion. On the walls of the stair-well is a collection of early maps of Cyprus. Note also in the hall a brass-studded leather trunk (English; late 17C?), once belonging to Rupert Gunnis (see Bibliography), and the firearms on the wall. The stair-well itself contains furniture and a rare collection of Cypriot embroidery and costumes.—We may make our exit through a room on the left, containing carved and painted woodwork, and a Bride's Chair; and the adjacent *Library*, displaying family portraits, etc.

The Larnaca Club, opposite the main entrance, with a high doorway to admit laden camels, was once a *khan*.

Hence we turn E towards the *Customs House, Marina*, and old harbour. The modern harbour lies some distance to the N.—We bear S along the palm-lined PROMENADE (Athens St), flanked by hotels and restaurants, and overlooking the beach—not one of the best bathing beaches, which are several kilometers to the N; see Rte 2.

Continuing S, we approach ***Larnaca Fort**, a Turkish building of 1625, used as a prison and barracks during the early period of British rule, and now containing a small collection of objects from Kition and from the Hala Sultan Tékké (see Rte 5C). Note the huge conch, lined with stone anchors, constructed in the thickness of the sea-wall, and the two cannon-ports. Steps ascend to a wall-walk.

Nearby is the renovated *Mosque of Djami Kebir* (late 16C), with some tombstones adjacent, in what was until recently the Turkish Cypriot quarter of the town.—Another mosque (of *Zouhouri*)—derelict, and with only the base of its minaret—lies a short distance to the NW. Some early 19C shops in its vicinity have been restored.

A short distance to the W stands the principal architectural monument of Larnaca, partially hidden by ugly entrance gates and dependencies, the church of ***Ayios Lazaros**.

According to the legend, Lazarus, after his resurrection at Bethany, was expelled by the Jews and sailed to Kition, where he definitively died and was buried. In 890 his tomb was miraculously discovered, but his remains were then sent to Constantinople, whence they were subsequently removed by the French, and may have eventually settled at Marseille. It is said that the original church was built in the 9C, but in 1570 it was taken over by the Turks who sold it back to the Orthodox Church in 1589, after which, until 1758, it was shared by the Orthodox and the Latin Church. The building was reconstructed in the 17C, and later embellished by a large campanile, one of the few the Turks permitted before 1857.

The English Cemetery, Ayios Lazaros, Larnaca, photographed by John Thomson, 1878

To the S of the ornate four-square tower is an open porch, from which steps descend into the interior of the church, with its three aisles, the central nave being covered by three domes (boarded in), and the roof supported by four twin piers, in which several re-used Byzantine capitals have been incorporated. In the thickness of one, a stair ascends to a rococo pulpit, elaborately gilt. Note the icon of the Virgin and Child on the N pier at the crossing, and another colourful icon of St. George and the Dragon (1717); also a silver filigree icon of 1659 depicting the Raising of Lazarus, and another of the same subject on which is seen a man holding his nose. The saint's empty marble sarcophagus is reached by steps descending from the bema near the S apse. The 18C iconostasis was damaged by fire in 1970. The modern candelabras, and icons ranged round its walls, detract considerably from the church's otherwise impressive interior.

Immediately behind the NW corner of the church is a tiny *English Cemetery* containing a number of graves dating from c 1685–1850, mostly of members of the Levant Company (incorporated 1581) and of consuls and their families. The roof is an unfortunate addition.

Among them are: Captain Peter Dare, Commander of the ship 'Scipio', died 1685; Ion Ken, 'of London, Merchant' (1672–93) and William Ken, Merchant of Cyprus, died 1707, both nephews of the famous Bishop of Bath and Wells; Mary, the wife of Samuel Palmer (died 1720) and her infant daughter; George Barton (died 1739; consul prior to 1730, and from 1738), Michael de Vezin (consul 1785–92), and James Lilburn (consul 1840–43), not overlooking Lorenzo Warriner Pease, 'Native of the United States of America' and missionary (died 1839), and William Balls, 'late seaman on board HBMS Volage' (died 1849), engraved with the words: 'this tomb is erected as a token of respect by his shipmates'.

Some minutes' walk to the W, approached by Ayias Phaneromene St, stands *Ayias Phaneromene* (1907), built adjacent to two rock chambers, the inner one covered by a huge stone, and apparently a tomb dating from c 80 BC.

An ALTERNATIVE return to the town centre from Ayios Lazaros is made by following the narrow Zenon Kitios St (near the Zouhouri mosque), passing near the *Armenian Church*, to regain the Swedish Consulate.

B. Northern Sector and Kition

Turn left a few paces N of the Tourist Office and follow Grigoris Afxentiou Av. (which later passes the *English Church* of St. Helena, in the Byzantine style, 1907) before taking the next main turning to the right (Kimon St).—To the right stands the *Convent of St. Joseph* (1848) and, opposite, the **Larnaca District Museum**.

A circular mosaic pavement, tombs, capitals, and stone anchors are seen in the garden.—To the left of the entrance is a room displaying SCULPTURE, mostly of limestone, including several female votive torsos from Arsos, among them one retaining colour, and also a head wearing a crown; a bearded head from Pergamos, and another, wreathed and bearded, from Larnaca (c 500 BC); inscribed funerary stelea, etc. In a wall-case is a collection of terracotta figurines (female) of various periods, including a mother and child (Larnaca; Late Cypriot II); many wear head-dresses, and some show traces of paint; and also a number of limestone statuettes and heads.

The room to the right contains the CERAMIC COLLECTION, mostly from Kition (from the Early Cypriot III period) and Livadhia (Middle Cypriot); Mycenaean craters and vases (14C BC), and from Kornos (Cypro-Classic). Among objects displayed are recent finds from Khirokitia, Kalavasos 'Tenta' (including an Early Bronze Age bowl), Pyla, Athienou, and Maroni: also alabaster vases from Kition, and an ivory figure of the Egyptian god Bes.—In a wall-case are stone, clay, glass, faience, ivory, and bronze ornaments, jewellery, paste amulets (7–6C BC), and seals of the 8–7C, together with cylinder-seals (Late Cypriot), a limestone seal (Middle Cypriot); picrolite scarabs (Cypriot type), and faience scarabs of Egyptian type.—Another case displays glass of the Roman period, alabaster bowls (6–3C BC), and clay lamps of various periods.—Silver staters of the Cypriot Kingdoms, and coins from the mint at Kition (and elsewhere) found in the district; examples of 'Base Ring' ware (Late Cypriot); bronze tools, weapons, metalwork, mirrors, etc. (2000–4C BC); also Neolithic I stone vases from Khirokitia and Neolithic II pottery from the same site; a case of flint and bone implements, another of stone tools, and conical and engraved stones and stone idols, likewise from Khirokitia.

The far room displays objects of various periods found on specific sites, among them those of Bamboula (Pamboula); the necropolis of Kition; the necropolis of Ayios Georghios (including scarabs, a clay chariot, and equestrian figures); Tremetousha and Alethriko; Dhekalia, Pyla, and Ormidha; Kalavassos, Lefkara, and Meneou; Ayios Theodoros, Kornos, Atheniou, Kophinou, and Klavdhia. A central case contains hoards of coins from Larnaca and Kition; another displays jewellery. At the far end of the room are tombs from Ayios Prodromos, the lids of two with carved heads.

Kimon St climbs gently NW, passing (right) the so-called **Acropolis** of Kition, probably dating from the 13C BC, on part of the BAMBOULA HILL, indiscriminately levelled by the British Army in 1879 to fill in an adjacent marsh, the site of Phoenician ship-yards and harbour, now being excavated. It was not until 1930 that what remained of the hill was recognised as being the ancient site of the acropolis, and probably of an open-air temple.

Another view may be obtained from near the tennis-courts in Kilkis St, which later leads near (left) the *English* or *Protestant Cemetery* (containing also the victims of an air crash in 1967), and by continuing ahead along Leontios Makhaeras St, we reach (left at the third turning, almost hidden by a rash of new houses) the entrance to the main site of ancient **Kition**.

This, known as *Area II* of the excavations, is the most extensive so far uncovered. From the Guardian's lodge, immediately NW of the site, a raised wooden gangway has been erected to allow the visitor a more comprehensive view of the excavations, which are continuing.

This complex area lies at the N end of the ancient city and abuts its N wall, constructed of mud bricks with limestone bastions; while the earliest architectural remains date back to the late Cypriot II period (13C BC). The original form of one building (known as *Temple 2*) is to be seen to the SW of Temple 1 (the main temple): both lie N of the ancient street, and right and left respectively of the wooden cat-walk as we turn N. In about 1200 BC the area was rebuilt, possibly by Achaean refugees using pottery of the Mycenaean IIIC period, and the earlier wall was replaced by a more substantial *Wall*, the lower part of which was of Cyclopean blocks, many removed during the Phoenician period. *Temple 1* was then built, measuring 35m by 22m, and approached by a monumental entrance to the NW of *Temenos B,* adjacent to a cistern. Its S, W and E walls were constructed of rectangular blocks of ashlar stone with a rubble fill, while on the outer façade of the S wall are crude graffiti of ships. To the E of the temenos lie two smaller temples (*4* and *5*; excavated in 1974/5, the former abutting the city wall), between which the 'streets' lead E towards an as yet unexcavated area. Some of the foundations of Temple 4 are re-used anchor stones.

Kition appears to have been partially destroyed by an earthquake in c 1075 BC and, although rebuilt, was later abandoned. It was re-inhabited in the 9C BC by Phoenicians from Tyre, and remained a Phoenician city until 312 BC. (It may be of interest to quote Sir Ronald Storrs' earlier observation, when he wrote that none of the recorded Phoenician remains had 'survived the determination of the Greek majority that Cyprus shall possess proofs of none but Hellenic origin'.) Temple 1 was rebuilt as a temple to Astarte, but it was destroyed by fire in about 800 BC. It was again rebuilt, and remodelled in 650 BC, when its four rows of wooden posts were replaced by two rows of six masonry pillars. Little remains—with the exception of several cisterns—of the Hellenistic period, nor is there any clear evidence of Roman structures in the area.

The lesser sites and monuments in the NW sector of the town may be visited by returning to the corner by the English Cemetery and walking W along Kyprianos Av., shortly passing (left) the church of *Panayia Khrysopolitissa,* dating from 1815, with a badly restored top-heavy tower and execrable iconostasis.

Continuing due W along Dianelos St, we pass (left) an *Orphanage* and *Technical Institute,* and bear left to the Metropolitan Cathedral of **Ayios Khrysosotiros** (adjacent to the residence of the Orthodox Bishop of Kition), largely rebuilt in 1853. Note the gargoyles, the ornate bishop's throne (1779), pulpit (high on the N wall), tortoise-shell and ivory icon-stand (1730), and carved iconostatis.

Behind the *Bishop's Palace* stands the *Touzla Mosque,* while not far SE of the cathedral was the site of the former British Consulate (see History).

Just to the left, a few paces down Nikodemos Mylonas St, is an ancient vaulted *Tomb,* known as the 'Evangelis tomb'; another, 'Cobham's tomb', lies to the W off Dhedhalou St. A third (Tomb 9), discovered in 1972, also part of the 'Tourabi' cemetery, lies a few minutes' walk to the S, in Mykonon St, near the Greek Secondary School.

Lanes lead N from the Bishopric to **Ayios Ioannis** (17C, but extensively repaired in 1850), containing an iconostasis of c 1700 with repainted icons, and a Venetian black and white marble doorway built into a room by the narthex. Note also the adjacent open-air pulpit and painted wooden balcony.

Hence, turning SE, we may regain Panayia Khrysopolitissa, first passing (left) the large domed church of *Santa Maria della Gratia* (or *Terra Santa;* restored 1843), with its gargoyles.

By turning down Kimon St, we pass (right) **Area I** of the Kition excavations, of little interest to the casual visitor.

In 1962–63 it nevertheless produced a wealth of objects, including Mycenaean IIIB pottery, alabaster vessels, faience ornaments and scarabs from Egypt, carved ivories, gold jewellery, and a superb enamelled rhyton decorated with hunting scenes (mid 13C BC), discovered in chamber tombs in the courtyards of its houses (dating from the Late Cypriot II period) as at Enkomi, and Ugarit in Syria. A complex of copper workshops was later uncovered.

Tombs of the same and slightly later eras, and what appears to be a bathing complex of the Hellenistic period, have been found at **Area III**, in Khrysopolitissa St.

Continuing down Kimon St, we shortly pass (left) the Acropolis (see above) to regain the District Museum.

The only other monuments in Larnaca (apart from the *Aqueduct*; see Rte 5A), and of slight interest, are the monasteries of *Ayios Yeoryious tou Kontou* (the Near; rebuilt c 1840), off the Nicosia road; and further from the centre, that of *St. George the Distant*, with a small domed church (?12C).

2   Larnaca to Ayia Napa

42km (26 miles).

Two short sub-routes are first described.

FROM LARNACA TO TROULLI (14km). Driving NE along the coast road, we turn left after 3km through **Livadhia**, in 1198 the property of the Abp of Tyre, and known for its basket-weaving. *Ayia Paraskevi* is an early 19C building on an ancient site, preserving fragments of an earlier edifice, and containing a number of 18C icons.—We continue N to **Kellia**, a re-settled village of little interest except for the relics of an old Turkish cemetery to the left as we enter, and *Ayios Antonios*, on a low hill surrounded by a stone wall. It is a cruciform building, provisionally restored, preserving a number of medieval fragments. Built into the wall of the W narthex is the coat of arms of the Gourri family. The whitewash has been removed to uncover early 11–13C wall-paintings; the icon of the Virgin (1695), in an early 17C iconostasis, has been overpainted.

Cars are usually stopped at this point, but to the E, 4km beyond, is the monastery of *Ayios Yeoryios Mavrovounos*, probably a medieval nunnery, with a barrel-vaulted church, largely rebuilt in 1711, with a number of marble columns from its Byzantine predecessor lying in the vicinity. The iconostasis and altar have been savagely 'restored'; the conventual buildings now shelter cattle.—**Troulli**, dating from c 1600 or earlier, lies near copper and iron pyrite mines and *terra umbra* quarries. *Ayios Mamas* (16C) is a barrel-vaulted building with an open arcade on the S side. Its 16C iconostasis is of interest, but its icons have been disastrously 'restored'; that of St. Mamas (1708) is reputed to have the power, nevertheless, of curing sore throats!—The road beyond Troulli shortly reaches the Attila Line; before the Turkish occupation it continued N to meet the road from Athienou to Famagusta at *Arsos* (see Rte 25B).

FROM LARNACA TO PYLA (12km). Following the coast road, after 5km we pass a turning to **Voroklini** (1150 inhab.), among its olive trees, a small market-gardening and basket-weaving centre, which has grown rapidly in the last decade, but which is of slight interest apart from the fact that the French poet Arthur Rimbaud supervised a local quarry here in 1878; cf. Troödos.

2km beyond this turning we bear left for **Pyla**, the only jointly controlled village in the island, and of ancient origin. A 5–4C BC tomb was excavated here in 1934. In c 1350 the place belonged to De Brie, Prince of Galilee, and later to the Gibelet family. Near the village centre rises a partially restored medieval tower, once entered by a drawbridge. Nearby stands *Arkhangelos Michael*, medieval in origin, in which are preserved fragments of a painting of the archangel; the iconostasis contains some late 15C woodwork.—*Panayia Aspromoutti*, some distance to the SW, contains a fine 16C carved wooden cross set in a silver base dated 1758.—The road climbs steeply beyond Pyla to a junction where we turn right, and after passing a landing-strip to the left, gains the Dhekalia crossroads (see below) some 4km from the village.—*Pergamos*, in the occupied zone, lies NE of Pyla: between them is a lobe of the Eastern Base Area, which acts as a buffer between the Turkish and Greek Cypriot forces in this corner of the island.

The main road, along which several hotels have been built recently, skirts LARNACA BAY to reach crossroads at 11km.

From here the former main road to Famagusta climbed inland to **Xylotymbou** (2000 inhab.), one of several villages swollen by re-housed Greek Cypriot refugees, beyond which is *Ayia Marina* (15C, with much-damaged murals), and the restored chapel of *Ayios Vasilios* (c 1470); nearby are remains of a Hellenistic necropolis with some rock-cut tombs.—After 4km the road by-passes *Athna*, in the occupied zone, previously a Greek Cypriot village, but now deserted.

We bear right, skirting the **Dhekelia Cantonment**, containing the H.Q. of the DHEKELIA BRITISH SOVEREIGN BASE AREA, largely constructed 1954–55, with its extensive cantonments, military hospital, and cemetery, etc., here looking curiously neat and exotic.

Ayios Nikolaos, in the NE lobe of the Base Area, near Famagusta, came into the news in 1985. It was GCHQ's listening-post at which the seven British signals servicemen were monitoring prior to being charged with 'spying'. Their trial lasted 119 days and cost the British taxpayer some £4.5 million. It ended with their acquittal, putting the Intelligence establishment itself in the dock!

Passing the *Dhekelia Power Station*, we shortly reach another road junction, and bear right for *Xylophaghou*; see below.

The left-hand fork leads shortly to **Ormidhia** (3250 inhab.), a village dating from the Byzantine era. In the 18C it served as a summer resort for many of the European merchants and foreign consuls of Larnaca, and, according to Captain Kinneir who sought shelter here during a storm in 1818, had already seen better days, for he was shown into a 'ruinous building, filled with broken chairs and tables, worm-eaten couches, and shattered looking-glasses...'. *Ayios Konstantinos Alamos*, replacing an earlier structure, is of little interest except that it preserves the 12C saint's bones, said to have been found in a seaside cave nearby (see below). Cesnola did much digging for antiquities at Ormidhia, which in 1878 caused him to be brought to court and those in his possession confiscated.

FROM ORMIDHIA TO AVGOROU (10km), for Phrenaros. The road climbs NE to the fertile red-earth plateau on which lie the 'Kokkinochorio' villages, passing (right) *Ayios Yeoryios Angonas*, a domed building of the 14C or earlier, with remains of murals in its apse. The principal church of **Avgorou** (3100 inhab.) is of less interest than the unpretentious chapel of *Ayios Yeoryios*, while the dome of *Ayios Yeoryios Terrachotis* (of the carob trees), some distance out of the village, is prominent, although little has survived a disastrous internal restoration and re-painting of frescoes.—Not far E of the road junction 2km N is the 16C monastery of *Ayios Kendeas*, aesthetically unpleasing, but well-sited.—*Phrenaros* (see below) lies 6km E of Avgorou, and is reached by traversing a well-irrigated potato-growing district.

The main road continues E to **Xylophaghou** (4000 inhab.), a market-gardening centre. Its unimposing church of *Ayios Yeoryios* is a 15–16C building, with murals damaged by fire.—Some 3km S are remains of a *Venetian watch-tower* on *Cape Pyla*, marking the E end of Larnaca Bay; below the cape is the *Cave of Forty Martyrs* (or *Spilia Macaria*) which contains petrified bones, not of martyrs, but of the once indigenous pigmy hippopotami *(Phanourios minutus).*

FROM XYLOPHAGHOU TO CAPE GRECO VIA SOTIRA (28km); the inclusion of Phrenaros and Dherinia will add c 7km to the excursion. Driving NE, at 5km we enter **Liopetri** (2850 inhab.), long a haunt of

Linobambaki (see Glossary). Domed *Panayia*, with a verandah and belfry, is a medieval building, later lengthened, but of slight interest. Nearby is *Ayios Andronikos* (15C; possibly earlier), with remnants of murals in its apse, and with an octagonal dome.—On approaching (5km) Sotira, we pass near (left) the restored domed cruciform church of *Panayia Khordajotissa* (16C). NW of it is the domed narthex of *Ayios Theodhorous*; to the NE, within an enclosure of boulders, is *Ayios Yeoryios* (12C; its dome reconstructed recently), probably once serving 'old' Phrenaros; see below. In **Sotira** itself (3000 inhab.) is the church of *Metamorphosis* with a pleasing belfry; and a few paces to the NE, partially ruined *Ayios Mamas* (?12C, but later much rebuilt), containing late 16C frescoes. Hence we may skirt the S bank of its lake to (3km) Paralimni; see below.

3km to the NW lies **Phrenaros** (2700 inhab.), probably replacing an older abandoned town further S. Just S of the ugly modern church shelters *Arkhangelos Michael*, a two-domed building with its belfry, which survived restoration in 1883, but its murals and icons (with the exception of two dating from c 1550) were ruined.—1km E is the small, well-preserved and unrestored church of *Ayios Andronikos*, just beyond which stands *Ayia Marina*, a barrel-vaulted 15C edifice containing wall-paintings of two periods.

4km NE of Phrenaros lies **Dherinia** (3350 inhab.), on entering which we pass *Ayia Marina* (15C). The church of *Panayia* preserves 17C icons; while just NE of the village centre is *Ayios Yeoryios*, a small domed medieval building. Another *Ayia Marina*, a mid-Byzantine edifice, lies just over 2km E, but it is at present inaccessible. A close view of *Famagusta*—and of the skyscrapers of *Varosha*, its S suburb—may be gained from the N slope of the village, with the Karpas peninsula in the distance, extending to the NE.—Paralimni lies 2km SE.

PARALIMNI, now a small town of 5900 inhab., was damaged by an earthquake in 1941. It has an ancient but unenviable reputation for its massacre of *beccafico* or *ambeloboulia* (Sylvia atricapilla), or Black Cap, a small migratory fig-eating bird, which is snared, pickled, and largely exported as a delicacy which should be crunched up whole, as described by Durrell in 'Beccafico: a Tragic History' (reprinted in 'Spirit of Place', 1969). The twin-vaulted church of *Panayia* is decorated with 18C porcelain plates.—*Ayia Napa* lies 6km S; see below.

We now bear E, passing several windmills, shortly circling to the SE to skirt the flank of the peninsula extending towards Cape Greco. Regrettably this stretch of coast, almost deserted until the 1980s, is being developed, and a rash of hotels and apartments has sprung up. We pass the new resorts of *Pernera* and *Protaras*, on Fig Tree Bay; on a rocky outcrop between the two stands the chapel of *Prophitis Elias*. **Cape Greco**, the SE tip of Cyprus, with its lighthouse, radio-relay antennae (of Radio Monte Carlo), and radar devices, lies beyond. The cape itself is marked 'out of bounds', but trespassers are not usually prosecuted. It was off this point that a large and heavily laden Genoese ship was sunk in the 15C, and still lies undiscovered. *Ayia Napa* lies 6km W, approached by an improved road.

A new road has been constructed from Xylophagou to Ayia Napa (see below), off which a minor road, rough but passable, turns right to the little estuary of *Potamos tou Liopetriou*, E of Cape Pyla—with the restored medieval chapel of *Ayios Yeoryios*—and skirts the shore to the well-sited small church of *Ayia Thekla*, surviving from an earlier monastery, and later, restored *Ayia Varvara* (15C). We continue E past *Nissi Beach*, with its hotels, to enter the outskirts of **Ayia Napa** (1359 local inhab.), an old fishing village spoiled by commercialisation.

When Pietro della Valle visited it in 1625, he found it 'almost destroyed, partly by the usual tyranny of the Turks, partly through the great pestilence which had wasted the island a few years before, killing most of the inhabitants'.

The main attraction of the place, which lies on a gentle slope inland from the shore, is the **Monastery of Ayia Napa*, enclosed by a high wall (possibly to defend it against the incursions of pirates, who apparently landed nearby to obtain fresh water). It was so-named by 1366, and a monastery may have existed before that date. It was completed by the Venetians just prior to the Turkish occupation of 1570, and is comparatively well-preserved; it had continued to exist as a monastery until 1790. In the centre of the partially cloistered courtyard, entered from the N through a gate with finely carved windows, is a charming marble *Fountain* (1530), with floral swags, and covered by a large dome resting on four pillars. Water was conveyed hence by a much-repaired Roman aqueduct ending in another fountain, and gushes from a carved boar's head (probably Roman). The *Church*, with an unusual entrance portal, is partially underground—being cut into the rock—and is entered by a descending flight of steps. The belfry is built on a rock base. Adjoining a Latin chapel are steps leading down to two 600-year-old sycamore trees (*Ficus sycomorus*) standing by a reservoir, whence we get a seaward view.

The monastery of Ayia Napa; detail

To the W of the church is a hostel, which provides accommodation to participants at the *Ayia Napa Conference Center* (an ecumenical organisation), but—as the author has been requested to point out—

tourists 'expecting to have lodging provided for them' will be turned away, for 'accommodation is not available here for unannounced visitors': there is no room at this inn, part of property belonging to the Archbishopric of the Orthodox Church of Cyprus.

3   Larnaca to Kophinou, for Limassol

There are three alternate routes: A, the most northerly and more interesting, taking in *Pyrga* and the excursion to *Stavrovouni* monastery; B, the direct road; and C, nearer the coast and taking in the *Hala Sultan Tékké* and the church at *Kiti*, which should not be overlooked.

Perhaps the most comprehensive route is to follow C as far as Kiti, and then return to *Meneou*, there turning left through *Dhromolaxia*. After another 3km of rough road we reach the junction on the direct road, where Rte A bears off to the NW, which we then follow.

A. Via Pyrga and the Monastery of Stavrovouni

48km (30 miles) including the ascent to Stavrovouni.

We follow the main Nicosia road, near the outskirts of Larnaca turning left onto the Limassol road, later passing (left) the *Aqueduct of Larnaca*, of three sections (altogether 75 arches), erected in 1746 by Bekir Pasha, abandoned in 1939, but partially restored recently. The main camps of British troops to occupy the island in 1878 were established between the aqueduct and the coast.—On reaching crossroads we turn right onto an improved road, bearing NW towards low limestone hills, and pass the ruins of *Ayios Mamas* before traversing *Kalokhorio* (1400 inhab.), where *Ayios Vasilios* (1732) contains an iconostasis of 1852.—The road winds through more attractive country, with a view SW towards Stravrovouni on its commanding peak, through *Ayia Anna*, and later bears left; the right-hand fork continues W through *Mosphiloti* (named after the white hawthorn tree to which the Cypriots graft pear shoots): see Rte 6.

We shortly reach **Pyrga**, a pleasant little village praised by Mariti for the neatness of its olive-groves and the size of its trees; there are also a number of carob trees in the neighbourhood. To the left as we enter is *Ayia Marina* (15C), in which fragments of murals survive, while the *Mosque* (c 1830) has been built on earlier foundations. Just beyond the village centre a path to the left leads to the *Royal Chapel of **Ayia Ekaterina**.

Restored in 1977, it was built as a Latin church in 1421, and was probably founded by King Janus, a wall-painting of whom (with his wife Charlotte de Bourbon) is preserved, which was completed prior to his death in 1432. It remains one of the most interesting structures surviving from that period, with a plain vaulted interior and three doorways, two now blocked. On the lintel above the S door is a Catherine-wheel, while in the interior are colourful murals of the Last Supper, Crucifixion, and the Raising of Lazarus (somewhat over-restored), with their titles in French below. On the ribs of the vaulting are paintings with the royal badges of the House of Lusignan.

We approach the Nicosia–Limassol motorway, but before reaching it turn left along the old road.—*Kornos* (see Rte 6) is not far beyond this junction.

The monastery of Stavrovouni

We shortly fork left for the slow ascent to the *MONASTERY OF STAVROVOUNI* ('the mountain of the Cross'), spectacularly perched on an isolated rocky peak to the SE (689m, or 2260ft). The road climbs gently past an army camp and the dependant monastery of *Ayia Varvara* (late 18C), of no interest, before we commence the steep winding ascent to the summit, which commands extensive *Views over the whole of the SE of the island.

The road has been much improved. Formerly it was a narrow loose stone and earth track, hardly recommended after rain. Nevertheless it should be treated with caution, care being taken when passing other cars descending or ascending.

In Classical times the mountain was called Olympos, and was crowned with a temple dedicated to Aphrodite, which was the goal of pilgrimage long before the Empress St. Helena, mother of Constatine the Great, is said to have brought the relic of the True Cross from Jerusalem and founded the monastery c 327.

Among many earlier travellers it was first mentioned by Abbot Daniel of Russia, who visited Cyprus in 1106. The first monastery was largely destroyed by the Arabs in 1426 after the Battle of Khirokitia, fought not far away. What remained was burned by the Turks in 1570, and it was not until the 17C that it was repopulated by Orthodox monks, who in 1821 were massacred by the troops of Küchük Mehmed, the despotic Governor of Cyprus, who—it is said—had an eye on the site for his Summer Palace.

The monastery was virtually rebuilt during the 19C on surviving foundations. It had been visited earlier, in 1745, by Alexander Drummond (H.M.Consul at Aleppo) who considered the church was built in a 'mean manner' and the painting 'so monstrous, that it would even disgrace a paltry alehouse in our country'. In 1787 Dr John Sibthorp (1758-96), the botanist and author of 'Flora

Graeca', tried to break into the deserted monastery, which was eventually opened to him, and he passed the night on a straw mattress below the altar!
N.B. At present, women are not admitted to the monastery itself, but strong representations will continue to be made to change this discriminatory rule.

From the entrance—providing a panoramic view of the E foothills of the Troödos massif to the W—we ascend stairs to a landing, and pass through a small patio to the main church, itself of little interest except for a wooden cross dating from 1476 (perhaps representing that of the Good Thief, which St. Helena is said to have also brought with her for good measure). This was encased in silver in 1702, and stands to the right-hand side of the iconostasis. A supposed fragment of the 'True Cross', protected by a gold frame (17C work) and set into the larger cross, is all that remains of the relic, splinters of which had been widely distributed throughout Europe over the centuries for the veneration of the devout.—The corridor to the left leads past uninviting guest cells (in which men may be accommodated overnight) to a platform behind the apse commanding very extensive *Views*, and plunging views down the mountainside. On the wall of this N corridor the inscribed prayer of an 11C monk is pointed out.

The remaining monks are occupied with the production of honey and cheese, and it is said that they were the first in Cyprus to cultivate the sultana grape. Some employ their time painting icons, which are of slender merit. Only a proportion of the community reside here at any one time, taking it in turns to stay on the summit, where they are attended by sleek and hungry cats, originally imported to control the local viper population (cf. St. Nicholas of the Cats).

Having regained the main road, we turn left, and traverse attractive wooded country, later descending to (9km) **Kophinou**, 3km short of which, and W of the road, stands the monastery of *Panayia Galakto-trophousa*, founded in 1947 and completed in 1963 by dissident monks preferring to follow the old calendar; access is not easy.—Kophinou, now inhabited by 1250 Greek Cypriots, is an ancient village, and formerly a Turkish Cypriot enclave, gratuitously attacked by Grivas in November 1967.

S of the direct Larnaca road (see below), and to the E, is the domed church of *Panaia* (14–16C), largely ruined, and its surviving frescoes smoke-blackened. On the hillside above are the ruins of *Ayios Heraklios*, retaining the saint's tomb chamber, once painted.

For the motorway continuing SW, via *Khirokitia*, to (40km) **Limassol**, see Rte 6.

B. Direct

26km (16 miles).

The motorway, running approximately parallel to the main road, is expected to be completed in 1991; meanwhile, follow the road described at the beginning of Rte 3A, and 3km beyond the turning for *Kolakhorio*, cross the bed of the Tremithos, and shortly by-pass (right) *Klavdhia*, deriving its name from the Roman 'Claudia', where a Late Bronze Age site was excavated in 1899 by an expedition from the British Museum, where the finds now are. Its mosque was once a

Byzantine church, and the village was the birthplace of Haji Bakis, tyrannical Pasha of Cyprus in 1775–83.

A rough track leads NW from Klavdhia towards Pyrga, passing the relics of the former Cistercian abbey of Beaulieu, now known as the church of **Stázousa**. The nave (?14C) retains a good ribbed vault, while a Gothic doorway survives of a ruined dependency.

Another 4km brings us to (left) *Alethriko*, S of which, at *Kivisil*, is a small domed church in the Byzantine style, but ruinous.

The main road, not completed until l888–92, by-passes the hamlets of *Anglisidhes* and *Menoyia* to the left, and with good views to the N towards *Stavrovouni*, before reaching *Kophinou*; see above.

For the motorway continuing hence SW via *Khirokitia* to (40km) **Limassol**, see Rte 6.

C. Via Kiti

27km (16½ miles).

The *Airport* at Larnaca (see below) is best approached by first gaining the main road immediately W of central Larnaca, and there turning left. We shortly skirt the SE bank of the **Salt Lake**, with an area of c 6km^2, on the far bank of which rises the dome and minaret of the *Hala Sultan Tékké* (see below) amid its exotic oasis of cypress and palm trees.

The LAKE, which is 3m below sea level, has been a source of commercial salt from antiquity, and its collection, which commences in August when the water has evaporated, is largely in the hands of workers from Aradhippou. It is a government monopoly, and has been for centuries, although apparently an Englishman named Pervis was farming the revenue of the Salines in 1603. In the 16C the salt was exported as far as Venice. According to tradition, the district was once covered by vineyards, until St. Lazarus, passing that way, asked a local woman for some grapes she was carrying. She mockingly refused him, saying that more salt than wine was likely to be got from that soil, at which the saint vindictively reacted by forthwith turning the area into a saline lake.

Together with the *Akrotiri Lake* (see Rte 13), it is famous as a stop and winter habitat for migrating birds, especially flamingos (*Phoenicopterus ruber antiquorum*), a thousand or so of which may be seen here at any time between October and March, making a colourful display.

A turning to the left leads to the *International Airport*, a landing-field since 1939, but in 1975 entirely reconstructed; in late 1976 its runway was extended to accommodate jet aircraft. It acts as the substitute airport to that at Nicosia (its new terminus only inaugurated in 1968, but closed on account of the Turkish occupation in 1974 and since occupied by UNFICYP), from which the entire air traffic of the Republic has now been diverted, to the benefit of Larnaca and Paphos.

A right-hand turning immediately beyond the bridge across the Salt Lake leads directly to the *Hala Sultan Tékké, otherwise known as the *Tékké of Umm Harãm*, as it preserves the remains of the maternal aunt of the Prophet Mohammed. While accompanying her husband to Cyprus on one of the periodic Arab raids on the island, she fell from her mule here and, according to the chronicle, 'broke her pellucid neck and yielded up her victorious soul, and in that fragrant spot was at once buried'.

Beautifully sited within gardens and surrounded by trees, the octagonal *Mosque* with its minaret (restored) was built in 1816 by the then Turkish Governor of Cyprus, Seyyit Mohammed Emin. Note the fountain and water-tank for ablutions. Shoes should be left at the entrance. The octagonal columns of the interior are painted green; to the right is the Women's Gallery. The *mihrab* faces Mecca, while below the *mimbar* or pulpit are votive offerings. Hence we enter the inner domed sanctuary of 1760 through a medieval doorway above an antique marble step. The uprights of the trilithon covering the tomb itself are partly of timber construction, the origin of which has given rise to various legends, and are screened by green curtains and other trappings. In the cloister is seen the tomb of King Hussein of the Hedjaz's second and Turkish wife, who died in Cyprus in 1929. A white marble slab outside the entrance bears an inscription referring to the Venetian Lieutenant-Governor of Cyprus from 1489–91, Baldassare Triviziani.

The shrine, ranking third in importance after those at Mecca and Medina, is still frequented by Muslims at the festivals of Sheker Bairam and Qurban Bairam in particular, and it used to be the custom for Turkish vessels as they passed—for the mosque and minaret are clearly visible from the sea—to dip their flags in homage and fire a salute.

Excavations W of the Tékké have brought to light a Bronze Age town, probably fortified, but destroyed in c 1175 BC, although temporarily re-occupied in the 4C BC. Finds include Mycenaean IIIA and B and Late Minoan IIIB pottery, ivory objects and bronze weapons, tools and utensils, and a lotus-shaped faience sceptre head decorated with the cartouche of Pharaoh Horemheb (18th Dyn.); the cartouche of Seti I (end of 14C BC) had been discovered previously at the Tékké. In 1978 a hoard of 24 objects of gold (beads, earrings and pendants), bronze, agate, carnelian, picrolite, and faience, was also found, probably Late Cypriot II, together with an alabaster bowl imported from Egypt, and several rhyta of fine quality. In 1979 a tomb in the town area was found to contain a magnificent bronze trident, weapons, and jewellery.

2km due W of the turning to the Tékké lies the village of **Dhromolaxia** (3800 inhab.) with a Bronze Age site first excavated in 1898. Its name has given rise to much speculation, *Vromolaxia* being used as late as 1865, meaning 'stinking gulch'. It has been presumed that the Phoenicians may have here produced a purple dye from the mollusc of the genus Murex, which has an offensive smell, but nevertheless was much in demand for dyeing the robes of royalty and the priestly hierarchy. In 1425 the village was burnt by the Arabs. Marble Corinthian capitals lie in the churchyard, and another supports the font of the late 18C church, in the women's gallery of which is a damaged icon of the Baptist (1794).

2km *Meneou*, with an 18C aqueduct, had an old church used as a quarry for the construction of the Tékké, 2km beyond which we enter **KITI** (2100 inhab.), probably settled from Kition (Larnaca) in the 4C AD.

Peter I built a castle-palace here in 1376 known as *Le Quid*, and Charles de Lusignan, a later owner, was deprived of it by James II, the usurper, for remaining loyal to Queen Carlotta. In 1425 Kiti was sacked by the Arabs, while under the Venetians it belonged to the Podocatoro family, the last member to posses it being killed at the siege of Nicosia in 1570. A Venetian bridge is still to be seen in the village, which is today a centre of market-gardening.

A few paces N of the village centre stands *Panayia Angeloktistos ('built by angels'; otherwise known simply as *Kiti Church*). Architecturally impressive in itself, it is famous for the outstanding mosaics it contains. The key is available from the house facing its S side. Several covered stones have also been incorporated into the surrounding wall.

The church was constructed c 1000 on 5C foundations, rebuilt in the 12C and restored in the 16C. The central nave and transepts are of unusual height, and the crossing is crowned by a lantern dome. A Latin chapel (13C) now serves as the narthex, in which, built into the wall above the main porch, are three coats of arms; and a gravestone of 1302 is preserved, that of Lady Simone, wife of Sir Regnier de Gibelet and daughter of Sir William Guers. The icons and iconostasis have been much repainted and are of little interest except for the large Archangel Michael (mid 17C) to the right of the entrance.

Panayia Angeloktistos, Kiti

But the glory of the church is the ***Byzantine Mosaic** in the central apse, and a request should be made that it be lit up (even if the plastic lamps are a distraction). The Virgin stands on a footstool, supporting the Child on her left arm, and is flanked by archangels Gabriel and Michael (the latter damaged), with peacock-feather wings. Note also the elaborate border of the conch. There is some controversy about the date, which may be any time between the 5C and the 9C, but more probably the 6C, it being argued that the central apse was part of the earlier basilica largely destroyed in the 7C in Arab raids. The balance of the composition and colouring of the mosaic equals in quality much of contemporary (?) work at Ravenna. The only other mosaics of this kind in Cyprus *were* in the church of Kanakaria, near Lythrangomi, in the Karpas (see Rte 28).

To the S lies the village of **Perivolia** (1150 inhab.), and beyond, to the SE, CAPE KITI, with a lighthouse of 1864, to the N of which stands well-sited *Venetian watch-tower* (restored). A Phoenician temple of the 9C BC was discovered here at the ancient site of *Dades* in 1969, while the underwater exploration of the area has brought to light a Byzantine shipwreck S of the cape, and three Bronze Age stone anchors, etc.—Some 2km NW of Kiti lies *Tersephanou*, near which is the source of the wells once feeding the Aqueduct of Larnaca.

The main road traverses citrus orchards and the largely abandoned village of *Sophtadhes*, and runs parallel to the sea for some distance before veering inland to (9km) **Mazotos**, which during the Middle Ages was the capital of one of the four Venetian provinces which had a Cypriot as Commissioner.

To the S are remains of a Roman settlement on the Roman Road circling the island, known as *Laconicos* or *Alamina*. According to Gunnis, it was off the coast here (or at unidentified *Ceramaea*) that in the 740s the entire fleet of Calif Yezid III was destroyed by Constantine Kopronymos, with the exception of three *dromods* which were allowed to escape and carry news of the disaster back to Egypt.—The old road, now little more than a track, bears off to the left just S of Mazotos and continues close to and parallel with the coast as far as *Zyyi* (see p 110), some 16km SW.

From Mazotos we continue 4km due W to the 'modern' village of *Alaminos* (see above), owned by Philippe d'Ibelin in c 1300, and in 1464 given by James II to Giovanni Loredano. We pass a small 15C *Tower* on approaching the village. In the dome of *Ayios Mamas*, to the S, its interior once painted but largely whitewashed over, survive a bust of the Pantokrator and a frieze of angels.

We gain the old Larnaca–Limassol road to the NW at *Kophinou* (see Rte 5A).

4   Larnaca to Nicosia via Dhali

42km (26 miles).

The previous main road between Larnaca and the capital, via *Pyroi*, having been cut by the Turkish occupation of 1974, recourse was made to improve the road via Dhali, which followed to a large extent the old camel route. Until the projected motorway is completed (?1991),which will facilitate communications considerably, this is the main artery between Larnaca airport and Nicosia.

An alternative route is that via *Mosphiloti*, which is described in part in Rte 3A.

Driving NW from Larnaca, we by-pass (right) **Aradhippou** (4900 inhab.), of slight interest. Greek Cypriot refugees have been rehoused in the neighbourhood since 1974.

Known as *Radipe* under the Lusignans, Aradhippou was in 1352–54 the residence of Hugh IV, but was burned by the Arabs in 1425. In the 17C the camel route from Nicosia to Larnaca passed through the place. In 1905 there were still some 348 camel-drivers in Cyprus (five of them women), but by 1965 only 90 camels remained, ten per cent of the camel population two decades previously, most of them having been sold abroad. They were first referred to in Cyprus in c 1340.

Under the Turkish occupation Aradhippou's inhabitants were formally allowed to keep pigs, a rare favour, and it is said that the place is still pervaded by a porcine aroma, the law requiring most animals to be kept outside villages not always being observed. Many inhabitants traditionally worked in the

Larnaca Salt Lake during the season, while also adjacent are mines of *terra umbra* and gypsum (for plaster of Paris).

After by-passing (left) *Goshi* we bear left away from the old main road and the present road to *Athienou*, 9km NE beyond a spur of hills.

Athienou (3550 inhab.), site of a settlement connected with metal-working active from c 1600 until c 700 BC, and partially excavated in 1971–72 by an Israeli expedition, was also once of importance as being the main centre for the muleteers of the island, the honesty and efficiency of whom did much to safeguard and promote its commerce before the advent of the automobile. It is also an important centre for the production of sheep- and goat-milk cheese (a factory was established here in 1915), and honey. It was also reputed for its embroidery, known as 'Copto' or 'cut work'. At present it is closely confined by the Attila Line, which runs not far N of the town.

The principal church of *Panayia*, dating from 1711, contains a Baroque iconostasis, while above the E window of the apse is a stone lintel (inserted upside down) on which three medieval coats of arms are carved. Also of architectural interest is the old building known as *Zanetti's House*.

The ancient and extensive site of **Golgi** (or *Gorgus*), immediately NE of the town, was settled by Greeks from Gorgus, near Corinth. It was partially ransacked by Cesnola in 1860, and the temple site stripped of its statues, some of heroic dimensions, which are now in the Metropolitan Museum, New York. A number of scattered fragments still lie here, and much excavation has still to be done.

The road next by-passes the dilapidated village of **Lymbia** (1700 inhab.). It is overlooked to the N by outposts of the Turkish Army near *Louroujina*, once a Linobambaki district (see Glossary), where in the early 1930s a temple of the 6C BC was discovered.

In the village stands abandoned *Ayios Epiphanios*, a domed Late Byzantine building, its painted interior whitewashed in 1864.—3km further NE, nearer the old main road, is ruined *Ayia Ekaterina*, its paintings still visible.

Passing (right) the Byzantine church of *Ayios Yeoryios*, partially constructed with stone from Idalion (see below) and containing paintings, we enter the outskirts of **Dhali** (3900 inhab.).

Immediately S of the town a lane leads left to the ancient site of **Idalion**, on the slope of and below two limestone hills, discovered in 1850 and not yet fully excavated.

Idalion dates from the Bronze Age, and survived until at least 400 BC. Traces of its walls can still be seen. It was said to have had as many as 14 temples, among them the sanctuaries of Aphrodite; of Aphrodite Kourotrophos, found ransacked in 1883; and of Athena (between the two hills). It was near here that Adonis is said to have been killed by a wild boar. Among a number of important discoveries here was a statue of Sargon, King of Assyria, of c 700 BC (sent by Hamilton Lang, the British consul, to the Berlin Museum).

Recent excavations have uncovered substantial sections of a massive wall of ashlar limestone blocks (early 5C BC), which stand 6.5m high, built on the foundations of earlier fortifications. Remains of a large public building are also being excavated by an American archaeological expedition. At present, permission to view must be sought from the neighbouring military post. *Photography is prohibited.*

Dhali was on the camel route, but by the mid 19C had dwindled to a sad village; nevertheless in 1866–69 Cesnola spent his summers here, while, as he himself boasted, opening up some 'ten thousand tombs' in the area. The village itself is dominated by a modern church; to the NE stands Late Byzantine *Ayios Dhimitrianos*, strengthened in 1964, domed, and with partially restored murals. *Ayios Mamas* (early 16C) is now a cemetery chapel; while to the NW, adjacent to the 'old road', stands rock-cut *Ayios Theodhoros*.

Potamia, 3km NE of Dhali, is close to the Attila Line, which here projects S to include *Louroujina* (see above, and Rte 25B), and certain sites mentioned may be out-of-bounds.

Potamia was known during the later Lusignan period for the Castle of Peter II, built here c 1380, and the refuge of the Royal family from plague-stricken Nicosia in 1402, but this structure was razed by the Arabs. Although partially rebuilt, it was dismantled by the Venetians, and little remains. Cesnola reported that an iron chest full of gold and silver objects had been found in its garden by the Turkish occupants in the mid 19C.

Just N of the village are the foundations of *Ayia Ekaterina*, while to the NE of Potamia are the recent ruins of Late Byzantine *Ayia Marina*. Further NE are those of *Panayia Pallouriotissa*, of the same period, preserving remnants of a 17C fresco and two icons of that era.—Between Potamia and the hamlet of *Ayios Sozomenos* (2km N) is the Bronze Age site of *Elinos*, where a head of Apollo (500 BC) was found in 1933 (now in the Cyprus Museum, Nicosia). The empty tomb of St. Sozomenos, after whom the place was named, lies in a rock-cut cave in which are preserved wall-paintings; the village church of *Ayios Mamas* (early 16C, on earlier foundations), now derelict, preserves two Renaissance tombs and a good W doorway.

From Dhali we bear due W across an area called VASILIKA (the King's Land) to join the motorway at *Perakhorio* (see Rte 6).

The old road shortly by-passes (left) *Nisou*, a village given by James II to Nicholas Morapiton of the Lusignan family in 1460; the church of *Ayia Paraskevi* (18C) contains 15–16C relics.

Some distance to the N and to the right of the road is the rock-cut chapel of *Ayios Eftykios*, built over the marble sarcophagus of St. Epaphras, probably the Bishop of Tamassos who attended the Council of Chalcedon in 451 and not the 1C Bishop of Paphos sent to Cyprus by St. Paul; a Byzantine cross has been carved on the lid.

After 8km we traverse *Laxia*, in a setting of orchards, with several small factories in the neighbourhood, and uninteresting in itself. A Middle Cypriot site was excavated here in 1885, and near by is a curious deposit of fossil sea-shells.

Yeri (ancient *Phoenikiais*), a somewhat squalid village 4km to the E, retains a 16C church rebuilt in 1814, preserving fragments of frescoes and an icon of 1542.

We shortly approach a range of low hills from which Nicosia was bombarded by the Turks in 1570.

Some 3km to the E lies the outer suburb of **Athalassa**, the gift of Peter I to his mistress Echive de Scandelion. In 1898–99 it was a refugee camp for some thousand Doukhobors after their expulsion from Russia, and before making their way to Canada (cf. Kouklia). Because of its use as a quarry for building the Phaneromeni Church in Nicosia in 1870, little remains of its castle, *La Cava* (on the road to Yeri), with its rock-cut cistern, originally built for James I and later accommodating one of the two convents of Clares in Cyprus.

On descending towards *Nicosia* (see below), we pass (right) the *Agricultural Research Institute*, the masts of the *Cyprus Broadcasting Corporation*, and the *Police Headquarters*, to meet the S end of Abp Makarios III Av.

5   Nicosia

A. General

NICOSIA (*Leucosia* or *Lefkosia* in Greek; *Lefkosha* in Turkish), is the capital of the Republic of Cyprus, with a population of c 166,900 in the Government-controlled area in 1988. In the census of 1960 the whole city contained 95,515 (73,381 Greek Cypriots; 22,134 Turkish Cypriots), since when the city boundaries have been extended in several directions. It lies at 163m (536ft) above sea level in the centre of the Mesaorian plain, with extensive views towards the Kyrenia range to the N, and S to the more distant Troödos massif; and it was here that the highest temperature on the island was recorded, in 1956; 44.4°C or 112°F.

Nicosia contains few outstanding buildings, but its many trees and flowering shrubs, and the comparatively low density of its traffic—except at rush hours—make it a pleasant place to visit. The *Cyprus Museum* is of paramount importance for an understanding of the early history of the island. A good collection of icons may be seen in the *Byzantine Museum*. The medieval *Walls* of the old city are also of considerable interest.

Attractive relics of more leisurely days are the few remaining brown-stone bungalows, with their colourful verandahs, now frequently adapted to commercial use, and too often overshadowed by modern blocks in a prosaic international style. The municipality has recently restored part of the old city (cf. *Laiki Yitonia*) and the *Famagusta Gate*.

Hotel accommodation, particularly near the centre, is not always easy to find at short notice, or when international conferences are in progress, and should be booked well in advance.

The fast-growing city is at present divided by the so-called 'Green Line' (see Pl. pp 96–7), and in its suburbs this is extended by the Red Line, forming part of the Attila Line, separating the Greek Cypriots from the Turkish Cypriots and the military forces of their mainland neighbours.

Nicosia is the residence of the President of the Republic of Cyprus, as it was of the earlier British Governors, and present High Commissioners.

The old *Walled Enceinte* lies immediately NE of the modern centre: see Rte 5D (Pl. pp 100–1) and Rte 18.

It is generally believed that the present city lies adjacent to the ancient settlement of *Ledra* or *Lefcontheon*, named after Lefkos, son of Ptolemy Soter (c 300 BC). There are slight ruins extant of the Roman period as well, but it was not of much importance at that time. It grew to be the seat of an Orthodox see, and later of one of four dioceses of the Latin Church, enforced by Pope Alexander IV's *Bulla Cypria* of 1260. (It is still the residence of the Archbishop of the Orthodox Church.) A Byzantine castle, its exact site undetermined, in which some hundred Templars took refuge during a popular rising on Easter Sunday 1192, was replaced soon after by a more substantial fort, the first Lusignan palace. This was in turn replaced in c 1376–82 by a more extensive walled château, monastery, and citadel, which probably stood between the present Tripoli Bastion and the old Gate of St. Dominic, to the E of the present Paphos Gate.

It was at the former palace that Von Oldenburg saw his first ostrich, in 1211; while a later visitor, Louis IX of France, resided there for some months in 1248–49 as guest of Henry I before setting sail for Damietta; and here his son Louis, the Dauphin, died. Martoni, in 1394, complained that 'there are no innkeepers who keep beds to lodge strangers in' in Nicosia.

From about 1372 Peter II was engaged in surrounding the old town with ramparts, which extended further E and S of the present concentric ring of bastioned walls. These latter, over 3km in circumference (see Rte 5C, and plan on pp 100–1), were not constructed until very shortly before the siege of 1570. All buildings, both churches and palaces, *without* this circumvallation, were razed, including the royal monastery 'to which were attached two cloisters full of oranges and paved with fine marbles...'. The walls were dry-moated, although possibly fed occasionally by the seasonal river Pedieos, which in 1330 had inundated the city. Other floods occurred in 1547 and in the mid 19C, before the stream was diverted to its present course. Nicosia was also visited by plague in 1402 and 1505, and shaken by several earthquakes, those of 1491, 1547, 1735, and 1756 being the most severe. In 1426 it was sacked by Mamelukes after their victory at Khirokitia, and some thousands of captives were transported to Egypt.

Part of the Lusignan palace, Nicosia, now demolished. The Flamboyant Gothic window is preserved in Jeffery's Museum. Compare with photograph on p 175

In 1540 its population was estimated as being 16,000, but this had grown considerably by the time the city, defended by Cypriot and Venetian troops during the six-week siege in the hot summer of 1570 (25 July–9 September), fell to the invading Turks, who then subjected it to an unbridled orgy of rapine, slaughter, pillage, and destruction, before marching on Famagusta. Some say 20,000 were butchered, including the incompetent Venetian governor, Nicolo Dandolo.

It was reported by Van Kootwyck (in 1598–99) to be 'full of ruins, squalid and defenceless, for the walls are breached or decayed, and could not withstand a regular attack or siege', while his contemporary Girolamo Dandini observed that the church bells had been turned into ordnance by the Turks: church towers had been reduced to mere stumps; while Cornelis van Bruyn, who visited the place in 1683, found remaining 'many fine buildings, palaces almost, but little inhabited, and worse cared for'.

In 1814, Captain Kinneir, another traveller, on entering the city by the Famagusta Gate, was horrified by the state of its unpaved narrow alleys, in which his horse 'was nearly buried in mud and filth'. This ordure was occasionally dumped into the old moats, which were then filled with earth and rubbish, and, partially cultivated, yielded 'a considerable quantity of corn'. At this time the larger houses had pleasant gardens, abounding 'in fig, olive, mulberry, orange, lemons and pomegranate trees', according to William Turner.

Nicosia was the scene of rioting in 1764, when the despotic and avaricious Turkish governor Chil Osman was killed, while in 1821 Abp Kyprianos, three other bishops, and some 200 leading Christians were massacred by another fanatical governor, Küchük Mehmed, in anticipation of a Greek rising and as an excuse to confiscate their property.

The native Cypriots resembled the Irish in the 16C and onwards in that they regarded their Church as a bulwark against cultural domination, and gave more allegiance to their priests in political matters once the native secular leaders had been killed, driven out, or forced to compromise with the invader. That the Church over-reached itself in more recent years in endeavouring to combine both ecclesiastical and political power in one man is now generally admitted, its uncompromising policies having to a great extent precipitated the present divided state.

The Famagusta Gate abutted by the former aqueduct (since removed), photographed by John Thomson. Compare with photograph on p 98

Nicosia suffered from a serious epidemic of cholera in 1835, and from fire in 1857. On 12 July 1878 the British flag was hoisted in Nicosia by Admiral Lord John Hay, and ten days later Sir Garnet Wolseley formally took up his post as High Commissioner. He entered Nicosia on 30 July. The original Government House, erected SW of the town centre, was burnt in October 1931 during riots incited by the Bishops of Kition and Kyrenia (Nicodemus Mylonas and Makarios Myriantheus, respectively). The municipality of Nicosia was formed in 1882. The population of the city in the previous year (including the suburbs) approached 15,000, half Greek and half Turkish, growing to 53,000 in 1946 and 74,000 in 1955.

From the late 1950s it was a centre of anti-British, and later, intercommunal, disturbances. In 1964 the Greek and Turkish sectors of the city were separated by the so-called 'Green Line', after the 'incident' of the previous 21 December and subsequent 'troubles'. In July 1974 Turkish mainland forces entered the NW outskirts of Nicosia, after which the N half of the capital was effectively isolated from the S, the only crossing point between the Republic and the Turkish occupied zone being beside the Ledra Palace Hotel, immediately W of the old walled enceinte.

B. Southern Nicosia

The Nicosia *Tourist Information* bureau is at the E end of *Laiki Yitonia*, just N of the D'Avila bastion; see p 102 and plan on p 100.

The main buildings of interest in the S sector of the city lie to the SW of the walled enceinte, the majority of which are N of Evagoras 1st Av., leading SW from Eleftheria Sq. and shortly crossing Abp Makarios III Av., the main thoroughfare (in which many banks and some of the better shops are located) leading SE.

From a short distance W of this intersection we follow Diagoras St to the NW to reach Homer Av., where we bear left, passing (right) the *United States Information Service and Library*. Adjacent, also on the right, are the buildings of the *Cyprus Museum*, with its main entrance in Museum St; see Rte 5C, below.

A few steps N of the Museum, at 3 Museum St, is the building (1972) of the **British Council**, containing a good library of English books and records, and the venue for film shows and exhibitions, etc. Its predecessor, containing the finest British library in the Middle East, was burnt down (by schoolboys using petrol) on 17 September 1955. They have a branch at 23 Mehmet Akif Av. (Shakespeare Av., in the building of the High Commission's Residence until the Turkish occupation).

Further N is the building of the *Cyprus Telecommunications Authority*, facing the *Roccas Bastion*; see p 99.

From the roundabout here, Marcos Dracos Av. bears N past the *Armenian Cemetery* towards the *Ledra Palace Hotel*, now used by UNFICYP forces, beside which is the Republic's checkpoint, and some distance further N, that of the Turkish occupied zone: see Rte 18.

Opposite the Museum are the shady *Municipal Gardens* flanked to the N by the classically designed *Municipal Theatre* (1967).

Continuing NW along Homer Av., we pass (right) the unpretentious building (1955) of the *House of Representatives*, beyond which (right) is what some would consider an inappropriately placed *Bust of*

Mahatma Gandhi (1869–1948), that inspirer of the policy of Civil Disobedience, donated by the Indian Government on the centenary of his birth. To the left is the *General Hospital*.

A few paces further brings us to a roundabout, a short distance N of which are the *Law Courts*, much of the business of which takes place in the actual courtyards.

By turning left here we cross a bridge spanning the course of the PEDIEOS RIVER, the longest on the island (74km), but dry much of the year.

Iroon St bears NW towards the offices of the *British High Commission*, the *Central Prison*, and the present 'Green Line' (just beyond which stood the *Nicosia Club*).

Museum St is continued to the S by Byron Av., on the left of which, at the junction of Grigoris Afxendiou St, stands **St. Paul's** (C. of E.), a very English 'village church' of 1893–94, enlarged in the 1950s, and its interior renovated in 1975. It is the 'cathedral' of the diocese of 'Cyprus and the Gulf'.

Some distance S in the latter street is (left) a somewhat derelict *Stadium*, just beyond which (right) is the brown-stone block of the *Ministry of the Interior*. From the crossroads here one may return towards the centre by Evagoras 1st St.

The main E–W thoroughfare—George Grivas Dhigenis Av.—is shortly crossed by Demeter Severis Av., which, ascending a gentle slope, passes (right) the buildings of the *Public Information Office*, and beyond, the entrance to the **Presidential Palace**, twice the object of arson.

Sited among gardens near the bank of the Pedieos, and the traditional place of Richard I, Coeur de Lion's encampment, the original *Government House* was a prefabricated bungalow destined for Ceylon, but re-routed at Port Said for Cyprus and erected in 1878. Sir Harry Luke (who, as private secretary to the High Commissioner in 1911–12, resided there) remarked that 'it was no aesthetic, architectural or domestic loss when it was burnt down by a Greek Cypriot mob during the riots of 1931'. Sir Ronald Storrs' personal library and irreplaceable collection of works of art were nevertheless destroyed.

The building was replaced by a stone structure incorporating Byzantine, Gothic and Turkish elements, designed by Maurice Webb, but this in turn was burnt out during the coup d'état of 15 July 1974, its shell only surviving. Since 1960 it had been used as government offices by President Makarios. Plans for its reconstruction were under way by 1976, and work has now been completed.

Almost opposite this entrance is that to the extensive grounds and playing-fields of the well-sited *'English School'*, as it has been known since its establishment in 1900 by the Rev. Canon F.D. Newham, on the lines of an English Grammar School. It has much expanded during intervening decades.

Hence Kyriakos Matsis Av., forking right, bears downhill to approach the town centre.

C. The Cyprus Museum

The *CYPRUS MUSEUM, headquarters of the Department of Antiquities, was first established in 1883 (when Claude Delaval Cobham was on its council, and Captain Horatio Herbert Kitchener was curator; cf.), and maintained by private subscription until refounded in 1908 as a memorial to Queen Victoria. It was transferred the following year to part of the present brown-stone building, designed in the Classical style with a marble portico, which was enlarged between 1913 and 1918, and further extended in 1959–61. In 1942 the important *Louki Pierides Library* was donated to the museum, while in 1950–51 the central courtyard was roofed to provide space for reserve collections. Many of the more valuable treasures were removed temporarily to Athens for safe-keeping after the Turkish invasion of 1974.

There is a long-term project to build an entirely new museum worthy of the collections, but it is unlikely that this will be accomplished for several years. Photography is allowed on request. Postcards, etc. may be bought at the bookstall by the main Entrance Hall. The reader is referred to the Introduction to the Monuments of Cyprus and to the Chronological Table; see pp 15 and 33.

It should be emphasised that the displays in the museum are not static, and that the objects described below may not always be found in the same place, or may be on exhibit elsewhere, and replaced by other items.

From the entrance we turn right into **R1**. Artefacts of the Neolithic IA period from Petra tou Limniti, Mari, and Cape St. Andreas, including stone, flint, and bone objects; of the Neolithic IB period from Troulli and Dhenia; and from Khirokitia (Neolithic IA and II). A reconstruction on a reduced scale of the settlement at Khirokitia is also displayed.—A ritual deposite from Kissonerga–Mosphilia, including cult objects of c 3000 BC, excavated in 1987; a wall-painting of a human figure with upraised arms, from Kalavassos–Tenta; artefacts of the Neolithic IB and II periods from Philia and Sotira, including stone (andesite) bowls, phalli, and pottery; Neolithic II and Chalcolithic I flints and ornaments from Kalavassos; obsidian and picrolite ornaments; Chalcolithic I artefacts from Erimi, and shell and picrolite necklaces from Souskiou; also Chalcolithic II artefacts from Ambelikou. Note the stylised picrolite idols with outstretched arms (Chalcolithic I), the jug of Red-on-White ware from Erimi of the same period, and the limestone idol from Lemba (c 2500 BC).

R2 Glazed ware with combed design from Vounous, and clay figurines, and clay models of a sacred enclosure and of plowing scenes from the same site (Early Cypriot III). Also an Early Bronze Age alabaster bowl.

R3 Mycenaean crater from Kourion, decorated with female figures in 'windows'; another from Pyla (c 1400 BC) decorated with chariots, and others displaying birds, bulls, and octopes; other important Mycenaean ceramics of the Late Cypriot II period, and decorated ware of the Middle and Late Cypriot period, including Syrio-Palestinian and Egyptian imported pottery; work of the Cypro-Geometric and Cypro-Archaic periods, including some jugs with curious female figures (one winged), mould-made, leaning on the shoulder near the spout, and themselves holding miniature jugs. Cypro-Classical, Hellenistic, and Roman pottery; and imported ware, some Corinthian but mostly Attic. Also a faience Rhyton from Kition (13C BC) and stone mortar and 'conical' pestle.

R4 Terracotta votive figurines excavated in 1929 near Ayia Irini (N of Morphou) of the 7–6C BC. Of some 2000 figurines found around the altar of the temenos only two were female. Others included minotaurs (which might indicate the cult of the bull as a god of fertility), some charioteers, and some hermaphrodite figures. Most of them appear to wear a soft conical cap or helmet; some suggest perhaps a bronze helmet.

R5 A collection of clay and limestone statuary and votive statuettes, among them two female torsos each carrying a votive bull, and

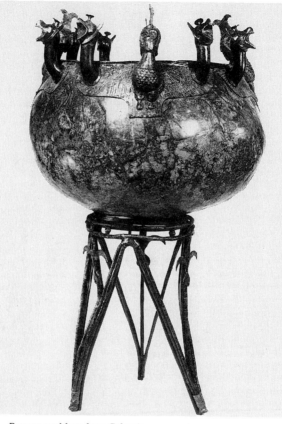

Bronze cauldron from Salamis

wearing necklaces; a bearded head from Troulli (c 450 BC); a female head wearing a diadem decorated with sphinxes and palmettes from Arsos (450–400 BC); a stele of Bacchus, with an erotic scene on the reverse (3C BC); and a marble head of Arsinoë II, from Soli (3C BC).

R6 Limestone female statue in ritual dress and bronze head of a youth, both from Soli (Roman period); Bronze statue of Septimius Severus (AD 193–211) discovered accidentally near Kythrea in 1928, together with its fragments, and reconstructed in 1940.

R7 Bronze objects from Enkomi, including a wheeled stand decorated with bulls and gryphons; helmets, weapons, spearheads, mirrors, tripods, scales and weights, lampstands, and lamps, etc. Among the statuettes is one of a 'Horned God' standing on an ingot and holding a spear and shield, from Enkomi (12C BC); bronze objects recently excavated from an 11 BC tomb at Paleapaphos; a collection of coins, including part of a hoard of 2484 silver Ptolemaic tetradrachms found below a mosaic floor at the House of Dionysos, Paphos; Cylinder and other seals and impressions; and an unusual Late Bronze Age relief pithoi, peculiar to Cyprus. Note also the limestone capital from Vouni of the Hathor type (5C BC). The far end of the room is described below.

Turning to the right we pass (below, to the right) **R9**, with examples of cippi and funerary stelae, one surmounted by a sphinx, from Idalion (4C BC); and terracotta and marble sarcophagi, one showing a woman with an infant and child.

Steps ascend to **R11**. Here displayed is an ivory chair and bed, and an iron chair and footstool from Salamis (8–7C BC), also clay heads; likewise from Salamis is a bronze cauldron on an iron tripod (8C BC), and bronze accessories from chariots and harnesses.—The *Library* is adjacent. **R12** is devoted to the metallurgy of Cyprus, with models and artefacts relating to copper-mining and production processes.

From **R11** we descend to pass (left) a subterranean passage (**R8**) in which reconstructions of rock tombs, together with the artefacts found in them, have been displayed.—To the right, in **R10**, are more funerary stelae, and votive inscriptions, one in Cypro-Syllabic script.

Hence we return to **R7**, where on the wall is a mosaic of a dog and partridge from Mansoura (3-4C BC) and of *Leda and the Swan*, from Palea Paphos (cf.), with a collection of alabaster statuettes and vases, and terracotta lamps of the Hellenistic period, together with bone and ivory objects, and glass: amulets, scarabs, beads, phalli, etc. Also a rich collection of jewellery including much of gold, from the Neolithic to the Early Byzantine periods, and plates from Lambousa (cf.)

R13 Marble statues, including that of Asclepios, God of Medicine, and of Isis, both from Salamis (2C AD).

R14 Terracotta figurines, statuettes (some from Marion of the 4C BC) from the Early Bronze Age to Roman times; and masks, together with several moulds. Note the 'square' or plank figurine of a mother and child (Early Bronze Age); also votive figures, dancers, and goddesses with uplifted arms, etc. Hence we regain the Entrance Hall, and make our exit.

D. The Walled City: Southern Sector

The walls in their entirety are for convenience described here, although their northern half, from and including the Roccas Bastion to the Flatro Bastion, are at present under Turkish military occupation. For the main monuments of Northern Nicosia, see Rte 18.

The **Walls* encircling old Nicosia, over 3km in circumference, were constructed during the third quarter of the 16C (see Nicosia History). In 1565 the Seignory of Venice dispatched Ascanio Savorgnano, an engineer, to report on the condition of the straggling medieval circumvallation, which stood c 350m beyond the present circuit, except to the NW. Two years later Francesco Barbaro laid out the present fortifications, based on Savorgnano's project. They remain substantially the same as when built, although in some sections the stone casing has crumbled (or has been used elsewhere), and at various times since they have been breached and the moat filled in to provide additional entrances to the enceinte. The walls were strengthened by 11 bastions, and were originally pierced by three fortified gates, now known as the Famagusta Gate, the Kyreniá Gate, and the Paphos Gate.

The bastions and present entrances are described in a clockwise order commencing at the **Caraffa Bastion** (sometimes spelt Garaffa) facing due E, and immediately S of an open space known as the *King George II Square*.

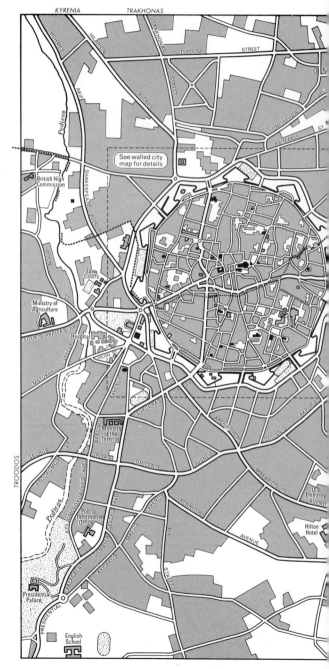

Nicosia (General)

*The restored Famagusta Gate, from the West (interior entrance).
Compare with photograph on p 90*

The S angle of the bastion is flanked by the ***Famagusta Gate**, in
fact a tunnel surmounted by a curious central dome, but now closed to
traffic, which was the principal entrance to the walled city, and the
main monument of the Venetian era surviving in Nicosia. It was built
in 1567 by Giulio Savorgnano (brother of Ascanio) who copied
Michele Sanmicheli's Porta del Lazzareto at Candia (Crete), constructed two years earlier. The interior façade of the portal, with its heavy
wooden gates, probably contemporary with the building, is decorated
by the six coats of arms mentioned by Mariti in 1791, previously
masked by an aqueduct which had been thrown up there. It was
briefly named 'Channel Squadron Gate' in 1878 after the entrance to
Nicosia there on 12 July of 50 British blue-jackets and 100 Marines. It is
now the venue of exhibitions, lectures, concerts, etc.

Nearby, on the ramparts, is a brittle statue entitled 'The Poet', made of pieces of
broken glass (1983; by Costas Varotsos).

Next come the **Podocataro, Costanza**, and **D'Avila Bastions**, the walls
between them now pierced by entrances carried across the moat. On
the **Costanza Bastion** stand the unpretentious remains of the *Mosque
of the Standard-bearer*, said to be where the first Turkish standard
was planted at the siege of 1570. The tomb of the bearer, Bayraktar,
who was instantly killed, lies in a chapel on the N side.
  On the **D'Avila Bastion**, its stonework repaired, stand the *Municipal Library, Central Post Office*, and the *Town Hall* (a structure of
1930 renovated in 1952). Beyond the latter and before reaching the
Tripoli Bastion are two openings, known respectively as ELEFTHERIA
SQUARE and DIONYSIOS SOLOMOS SQUARE, although the former is
little more than a wide street connecting Evagoras Av. with Ledra St,
and the latter an open-air bus terminus. In the moat between the
Tripoli and Roccas Bastions lie the tennis courts of the Field Club,
beyond which was the tunnel of the **Paphos Gate**. It was originally

known as the *Porta Domenico*, named after the former monastery of St. Dominic which stood in the vicinity, and which, together with the Lusignan palace, was razed by the Venetians in 1567. The gate, which was occasionally entered by floodwater from the Pedieos—the bed of which originally ran along Hermes St—was closed in 1878, and the adjacent opening pierced. The city fire-engines were parked near by.

Above the **Roccas Bastion** at present flutters the Turkish flag, for it overlooks the 'Green Line' separating the two communities.

A few paces to the E is the *Holy Cross* church (R.C.), a large building of 1900–02, largely paid for by a bequest of Queen Maria Cristina of Spain. It replaced an earlier Franciscan church (1642), the superiors of which had long been Spaniards (as confirmed in 1746). It contains a bas-relief dated 1524 of St. Mamas and his lion (cf. Morphou) taken from a predecessor destroyed in the siege of 1570. Access to the church, which is of slight interest, is allowed although it is on the N side of the line.

In adjacent Favieros St is a medieval doorway with zig-zag moulding.

A secret tunnel, burrowed by Turkish Cypriots under the previous barricades here, was exposed by heavy rains in 1965, and forthwith sealed by UNFICYP.

Between the *Mula* and *Quirini Bastions* is another minor entrance, and beyond the latter, in which the *Vice-President's Palace* stands (at present designated the 'Palace of the President of the Turkish Republic of Northern Cyprus' (or Kibris)), is the isolated **Kyrenia Gate**, originally the *Porta del Proveditore*, repaired by the Turks in 1821, and again (by the British) in 1931, since when traffic has flowed past either side of the gate, the main entrance to Turkish occupied Nicosia: see Rte 18.

Beyond lies the **Barbaro Bastion**, facing due N, the **Loredano Bastion**, and lastly the **Flatro Bastion**, between each of which is pierced an entrance, but the older *Kaimakli Gate* here has not been used for centuries. The Flatro Bastion here divides the two sectors of walled Nicosia.

The southern half of the enceinte is best explored on foot. It is here that many of the old churches of any interest are to be found, and those visiting Nicosia for a brief period can take advantage of the fact that they are open usually between 6.00–8.00, and from 6.30–10.00 on Sundays, when a good number may be inspected, even if cursorily, during those hours without disturbing any services in progress.

It is unfortunate that the old walled city has been allowed to decay to the extent in which we now see it, but there have been extenuating circumstances during recent decades. Too many attractive old Turkish-style houses with their latticed kiosks have been allowed to disintegrate, or have been deliberately dismantled, although this is less so in the N half of the town (see Rte 18), where more old houses, more mosques with their minarets, more stalls, bazaars, and street kiosks, and in general a busier street life, are apparent. Yet, although too many open spaces serve merely for the accommodation of old cars and refuse, the character of some areas can have changed little, with their numerous shops and workshops. Tailors, cobblers, carpenters, merchants, and retailers of all sorts still ply their trades in spite of the close proximity of the divisive 'Green Line'.

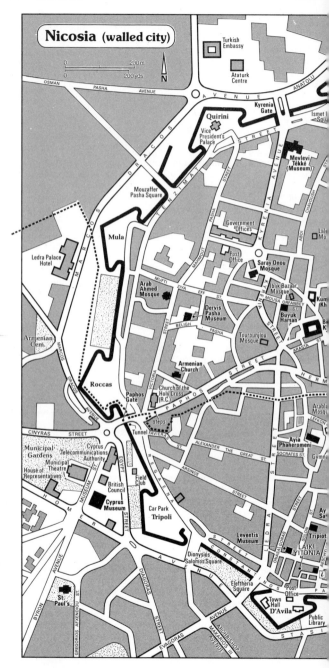

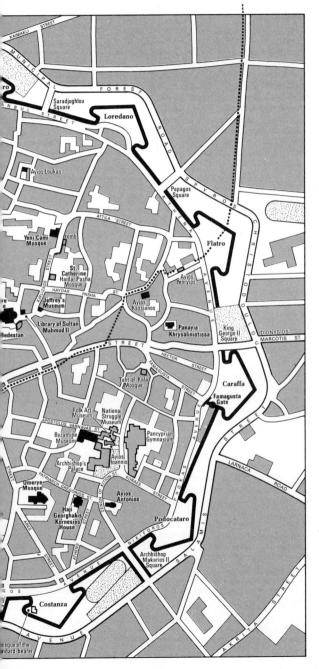

Although the approximate position of the 'Green Line' is indicated on the Plan (pp 100–1), it will be noticed that the barricades of the respective guards are usually some little distance S and N of the line, and normal life peters out in their vicinities.

The walled town is conveniently entered from unpretentious **Eleftheria** (or Freedom) **Square**, formerly Metaxas Sq, a minor centre of animation, overlooked to the E by the *Town Hall* on the *D'Avila Bastion*. From the N end of the square, Regaena St, with its somewhat sordid bars, leads W, and **Ledra St**, once the main, if narrow, thoroughfare, and still lined with shops, leads N.

But before ascending the latter, one should turn E for a short distance along Constantinos Paleologos Av., turning left into the short P. Eliadis St to enter a pedestrian precinct. This area is known as *Laiki Yitonia* (pronounced like-y ye-tone-ia), recently radically but tastefully restored and refurbished, a well-conceived project of preservation of which the municipality is justifiably proud. Hippokrates St, further N, has received similar treatment. At No. 17, a building of c1885, is the **Leventis Municipal Museum**, inaugurated in 1989, and devoted to the history of Nicosia.

The southern part of the area comprises two lanes, those of Praxippos, and parallel to the N, Aristokypros, in which are a good bookshop and, further E, the **Tourist Office**. Several small restaurants, galleries, handicraft shops, craftsmen, a bank, etc., are installed here, and it is a pleasant place to return to after a tiring walk around the old town.

Visitors short of time may prefer—rather than following the itinerary described below—to turn E along Hippokrates St, later bearing left, to take a shorter route which passes the *Ömerye Mosque*, the *House of Haji Kornesios*, and *Ayios Antonios*, there turning left past the Archbishop's Palace to *Ayios Ioannis*, the *Byzantine Museum*, and the *Folk Art Museum*. The *Famagusta Gate* may be approached by working one's way NE; thence returning to Laiki Yitonia by following the avenues SW past the Podocataro and Costanza bastions; see p 98.

Towards the far end of Ledra St one should turn right into Socrates St, at the end of which we bear left to approach the main church of this quarter, **Ayia Phaneromeni**. Erected in 1872 with stones taken from the ruins of the castle of La Cava (at Athalassa; cf.), it incorporates fragments from its monastic predecessor, among them its gargoyles. It is here that the bishops executed by the Turks in 1821 lie buried (see History). The building, with its tower, is in itself of little interest. It contains a 17C iconostasis and a carved Byzantine cross surrounded by 18C gilt filigree work.

Crossing behind the church, and leaving the façade of a *Gymnasium* on our right, we pass the diminutive **Arablar Mosque** (closed), in Lusignan times the church of *Stavro tou Missiricou*. Continuing E along Lefkon St we shortly reach Trikoupis St, which we follow for some distance to approach an open space, and turn left.

To the S is the partly restored **Ömerye Mosque**, with its small minaret, so converted by Mustapha Pasha, the victorious Turkish general, in 1571, who for some reason identified the 14C Augustinian church of St. Mary's as that at which the prophet Omar rested when visiting Nicosia. There may well have been a hospice attached to the monastery. The W door and a chapel retaining the tracery of its rose-window on the W side survive from the original edifice, much damaged in the siege, when its vaulting was destroyed by Turkish artillery.

It had previously been famous as the shrine of St. John de Monfort (died 1248/9), who accompanied Louis IX thus far on the Fourth Crusade. Many of the interesting incised tombstones of the Lusignan period, which had been barbarically re-used to re-floor the mosque, were removed to the Bedestan (see Rte 18) under the supervision of Rupert Gunnis in 1935. Among them were those of the Neville and D'Aubigny families.

Relics of a late Venetian building may be seen near the E end of the mosque.

Continuing E along Patriarch Gregorios St we shortly pass (right) the façade, with its typical overhanging 'kiosk', of the *House of the dragoman Haji Georghakis Kornesios** (Great Dragoman of Cyprus from 1779–1809), one of the earliest and finest 18C examples of traditional domestic architecture to survive in the capital. It has been tastefully restored, and since 1987 the upper floors have housed an *Ethnographic Museum*. Note the carved escutcheon over the Gothic door displaying the Venetian Lion and pomegranates. The *divans* in some of the reception rooms will be noticed together with de Vezin's painted grandfather clock, among several objects of interest.

At the end of the street we are faced by **Ayios Antonios**, architecturally unimpressive except for its intricately carved belfry, restored in 1743. It is said to contain a tombstone of a woman in 16C(?) costume, probably transferred here from an earlier church on or near this site; more visible are the carved iconostasis, throne and pulpit.

Bearing N at this point along Zenon of Kition St we cannot avoid seeing the bulk of a three-storey edifice in a grandiose pseudo-Venetian style commenced in 1956 and composed of superimposed loggias. This is the **Archbishop's Palace**.

Of great pretention and of slight architectural merit, even if displaying some fine workmanship, it has been the object of much well-deserved criticism, not only for being entirely out of keeping with its surroundings, but also as a gratuitous extravagance at a time of considerable economic troubles. Note the peacock plaques. Hence Makarios escaped on 15 July 1974, when it was attacked and set alight by the 'National Guard' in the attempted coup d'état by the Greek military junta five days prior to the Turkish invasion. A gigantic statue of the late Ethnarch dominates the site, the recent erection of which has caused universal criticism.

It is understood that the present Archbishop, Chrysostomos I, intended to build another palace, and was only dissuaded from doing so by public outcry.

The NW part of the palace complex consists of a large building accommodating part of the *Abp Makarios III Cultural Foundation*; other halls have been erected, one of which may display a second collection of icons in addition to those which may be seen on the GROUND FLOOR, and known as the *Byzantine Museum**.

Some 144 icons, the earliest of which dates from the 9C, are to be seen, 92 of which have been collected from churches in Nicosia alone. Although displayed very much out of context, they are at least safer here than they would be if they were left in the churches.

Among the more interesting are: 4, Descent into Limbo (13C); 7, St. Nicholas (late 13C); 8, the Virgin Kamariotissa, with donors (late 15C); 17, a Virgin (12th and 16Cs); 22, St. Marina (13C); 29, St. Mamas, mounted on his lion (c 1500); 36, St. John the Baptist (14C); 46, Christ, with angels and donors (1356); 50, The Baptist, olive-coloured (16–17C); 65, the Virgin Athanasiotissa (damaged) and Deposition; 66, Christ (c 1190); 70, Crucifixion, with the Virgin on the reverse (late 14C); 72, St. Marina (second half 15C); 80, Entry into Jerusalem (1546); 81, Descent into Limbo (1563); 87, Christ, with donors (1549); 88, the Virgin Hodegetria, with angels and donors (1529); 94, the Virgin Orans (with uplifted arms; early 16C); 96, Nativity (16C); 100, the Last Judgement (16C); 106, St. Barbara (16–17C); 107, the Virgin Hodegetria (1557); 118, the Burning Bush

(18C); 126, Virgin and Child between St. George and St. Nicholas (16C); 132, the Baptism (16–17C); 137, St. George (17C); 140, St. Demetrius (late 16C); and 141, Ascension, Pentecost, and the Virgin Orans between angels, a wall-painting of the 14C.

On the FIRST FLOOR is the late Ethnarch's personal collection of 120 European paintings. Many of the attributions would appear doubtful, or the exhibits are very poor examples of the work of the artists whose names appear on the labels.

Two paintings which are notable are a St. Bartholomew (Spanish School), and an *anonymous* 18C Portrait of the Duc de Penthièvre.

Of more interest is the collection of prints and engravings, etc., on the SECOND FLOOR, devoted to Greece, and particularly to the Greek War of Independence. Notable are A girl of Chios, by the Genevan artist *J.-E. Liotard* (1702–89), and several works by *Pierre Bonirote* (1811–91); a number of watercolours and drawings are of quality and several of the maps are also of interest.

The *Library* concentrates on MSS and books in all languages concerned with all aspects of Cyprus; the Foundation will also house a *Research Centre* in the field of Cypriot studies, and publish books, etc.

Immediately to the N of the Palace is the diminutive buttressed church of **Ayios Ioannis*, its predecessor being that of the same monastery and known as the Abbey of St. John the Evangelist of Bibi, where a finger of St. John the Baptist was once preserved until allegedly stolen by light-fingered Marmalukes in 1426 after the Battle of Khirokitia. At the same time the Benedictines left the island and the property passed into Orthodox hands. It was repaired in the mid 17C, and its walls and vault entirely covered with paintings, the majority of them dating from 1730, and since then very smoke-blackened. They include a graphic representation of the Day of Judgement above the S door; opposite is the Creation; and, on the right of the bishop's throne, four scenes describing the discovery of the relics of St. Barnabas. Note also the marble slab on the floor depicting the double-headed eagle, and the sculptures over the W entrance.

Immediately N of the church, installed on the ground floor of the 14–15C monastic dependencies which from 1730 were known as the Archbishopric, and from 1961 as the *'Old Archbishopric'*, is a **Folk Art Museum*. The buildings were restored in 1962–64. At the head of the exterior staircase is an early Byzantine marble panel carved with three palm trees at the foot of which lies a sheep.

The collection was inaugurated in 1937. From 1948, under the enthusiastic directorship of Adamantios Diamantis, the range of its collections was considerably extended.

From the entrance porch, with examples of wooden water-wheels, threshing trays, etc., we pass into **R2**, added to the earlier edifice in the 17C, containing looms (one in use) and dowry chests, one painted. Embroidery and materials woven on the premises may be bought here.—We pass through the original Romanesque entrance and inner Gothic arch, by which are examples of carved woodwork; note traces of murals, and also the wax votive-offerings.—**R4** (right) is devoted to colourful women's costumes from the Paphos District and from the Karpas, including hand-woven cotton *'saghies'*; also men's waistcoats (*ghilekko* and *zimbouni*), some gold-embroidered, and *'vraka'* or baggy trousers, normally worn with black leather boots. Hence we enter **R5**, with a display of wooden moulds for plasterwork, and carved shelves, etc., off which **RR6–7** contain exhibits from Nicosia District, Lefkara ware, and embroidery from the Karpas.—**R8** (note ceiling of split bamboo over the beams), with more embroidery, particularly in reds and yellows.–**R9** Samples of hand-woven materials; silk and cotton sheets and napkins, etc.; a carved and painted Bride's Chair, and carved gourds.—**R10** is devoted to domestic utensils and agricultural implements: sickles, sheep-bells, camel-bells, basketwork fish-traps, etc.; note the slatted wooden seats.— **RR11** and **11A**. Plates and kitchen utensils, etc.–**R12** contains a further collection of 'saghies' (from Paphos), and a selection of musical instruments: flutes, tambourines, and a *bezouki* or *laouto*.

Opposite the Archbishopric are the buildings of the **Pancyprian Gymnasium** (1893; rebuilt after a fire in 1922 on the site of an earlier Greek school founded in 1812 by Abp Kyprianos), at which Lawrence Durrell taught briefly, and which in the late 1950s was to become a hot-bed of youthful demonstrators under their passionately enosist headmaster, Dr Spyridakis.

In adjacent Koraes St is a medieval doorway.

Just N of the museum, on the far side of an arch leading to Apostolos Varnavas St, is the so-called *National Struggle Museum*, devoted to a collection of photographs, booby-traps, arms, and other lethal paraphernalia used in the anti-British activities of the EOKA movement during the troubled years of 1955–59.

By continuing N, and turning right and then left, we shortly pass the *Taht-el-Kala Mosque*, with its minaret. Some restoration is being undertaken in this area. After crossing the next intersection, by bearing right, approach **Panayia Khrysaliniotissa**, much of it rebuilt in 1735– 40. The older part is of various dates from 1450 onwards, when the narthex was added, and until comparatively recently it was surrounded by a monastic enclosure. The exterior arcade and doorway of the elongated S transept is built of 15C materials. The icon of the Virgin (said to have been found in a field of golden flax on this site, and which may have given the church its name) disappeared long ago.

Twenty-eight icons from this church, presumably including several found in 1934 in its dependencies, which were collected together by David Talbot Rice and Rupert Gunnis, and cleaned, now embellish the Byzantine Museum; see above.

A few paces to the NW stands *Ayios Kassianos*, erected in 1854 perhaps on the site of a Latin church destroyed in 1570, into the narthex of which a small 15C bas-relief of the Virgin and Child has been embedded.

Slightly further to the NE is *Ayios Yeoryios*, at present inaccessible, a small 17C barrel-vaulted building, over the W door of which was placed a panel from a 15C sarcophagus, on which are three coats of arms, the central one being that of the Syrian family of Gourri.

Returning to the above-mentioned intersection, we may turn E along Hector St towards the *Caraffa Bastion*, and there bear right along the interior of the circumvallation, to approach (left) the *****Famagusta Gate**; see p 98 for its history.

Hence the circuit may be continued past the *Podocatoro* and *Costanza Bastions*, shortly beyond which turn right into Dioyenis St, shortly continued by Aeschylus St (see *Laiki Yitonia*), on the right-hand side of which stands **Ayios Savvas** (1851), of little interest in itself, containing furniture and (repainted) icons from an earlier building, including a fine silver-gilt chalice of 1501, and a curious early 16C panel of a man wearing a long fur coat and a Persian head-dress.

Returning on our tracks a few paces, we may turn W to gain the glazed porch of **St. Michael Trypiotis**, with an inscription over the door dated 1690. The church is probably of Byzantine origin, however, for many fragments of an earlier style are apparent. Note the lintels over its three doorways: the N door is Renaissance in design; the W entrance is 14C French; and the S door of a much earlier period; while over the E gable is a shield with six fleur-de-lis. The interior is quaint, with a wide iconostasis, but of little intrinsic interest.

By following Solon St to the S we shortly regain Eleftheria Sq., adjacent to the *D'Avila Bastion*. The suburb of **Kaimakli**, to the NE of the walled enceinte, retains several characteristic streets flanked by brown-stone houses. It was once inhabited by the stone-masons of the capital.

6 Nicosia to Limassol

A. Via the Motorway and Khirokitia

73km (45 miles), plus approach roads.

Since September 1984 the two cities have been joined by a dual carriageway of motorway standard, which eases communications considerably. It has several exits and is also the most convenient road to take when driving from the capital to Larnaca (see Rte 4, in reverse, for the second half), with which it should be connected by motorway by late 1990.

The road first by-passes (left) *Laxia*, and then *Nisou* and *Perakhorio*, for which see Rtes 4, and 6A. For sub-routes off the main road, see Rte 6A. The motorway runs parallel to the main road, crossing it several times after *Khirokitia*.

The road next by-passes (right) *Alambra*, and *Kornos*, while to the SE the monastery of **Stavrovouni** is seen on its height; see Rte 3A. We later bear SE past the *Kophinou* exit, crossing the valley of the PENDASKHINOS, and passing (right) *Skarinou*, to approach the Khirokitia exit.

On the W side of a bridge in the valley between the village and the old main road and only a short distance from the latter (from which, of course, it may also be approached) is the Guardian's lodge of the *Neolithic Settlement of **KHIROKITIA**, reached by ascending steps rising steeply up the hill-slope above. This important site, discovered in 1934, dates from the 7–6 millennia BC. It is the second earliest known site on the island; only that of *Kastros* (at the far end of the Karpas peninsula, first excavated in 1971) pre-dating it. The excavations, apart from those of recent decades, have been described in detail by Porphyrios Dikaios in 'Khirokitia' (1953).

It is divided into four main areas, although recent excavations have continued beyond these. We first reach *Area I* by walking along what has been referred to as the 'main street', but which is in fact a defensive wall, traversing the whole length of the site. It is best to veer off this to the left and follow a path to the side of the excavations. Cramped together on either side of the 'street' are the bases of numerous stone 'beehive' type houses, usually circular, although some may be oval or roughly square. It is possible that they may have had flat roofs. As many as five superimposed building levels of houses have been excavated, for after an earlier building had collapsed or been abandoned, it would be levelled off and rebuilt, and with the gradual rising of the ground level new courses of masonry were necessary. It is only the excavation of the accumulation of millennia on either side of the defensive wall which gave it the appearance of a street. The superstructure of these huts would have been mud or sun-dried mud bricks. Graves were dug into the floor, bodies of the deceased were placed in a crouched position, and the floor was then remade; as many as 26 adult and infant burials in eight superimposed floors have been found in one house. Many more *tholoi* have been uncovered in the last decade or so.

Part of the Neolithic settlement at Khirokitia

Note the large 'house' containing two piers in Area I, beyond which we pass *Areas II–IV*, the latter lying on the N slope of the conical hill, from which we may, on the descent, get a more comprehensive view of the site, before regaining the road.

Artefacts discovered include a variety of stone utensils, often manufactured from andesite collected in the nearby river bed; combed ware pottery; numerous querns; flint blades and arrowheads; polished stone axes, adzes, and chisels; primitive idols of stone or clay; and necklaces of carnelian beads and dentalium shells, etc. Many of these finds may be seen in the Cyprus Museum, Nicosia.

For the village of *Khirokitia*, 1km distant, see Rte 6B.

The motorway later passes close to the village of *Mari* (left), and provides a view of the recently excavated site of *Kalavassos Tenta*, on a knoll to the N; see Rte 6B—We circle towards the coast near *Cape Dolos* and then veer inland, approaching the shore again near the *Moni Power Station*, running parallel to it but on the N side of a ridge on which stands the site of **Amathus**; see Rte 6B.

The motorway, after passing (right) a turning to (4km) *Armenokhori* (formerly one of the island's many Armenian villages, and near which Neolithic tools were found in 1962) now approaches Limassol, and has been continued as a by-pass to regain the main road near Erimi; see Rte 13. For *Limassol*; see Rte 10.

B. Via Perakhorio and Kophinou

82km (51 miles).

For the road to (17km) the Perakhorio crossroads, see the latter part of Rte 4, in reverse.

Perakhorio (1650 inhab.) lies just to the W of the road junction. The new main road from Nicosia to Larnaca here bears off to the SE via *Dhali*; see Rte 4. Of more interest than the principal church of Perakhorio, *Ayia Marina* (1853), and slightly further W on a hill (key from the nearest house) is that of *Ayii Apostoli (late 12C), containing remains of contemporary murals, among them a fine frieze of winged angels. In the drumless dome is a damaged Pantokrator, and in the semi-dome the Virgin supported by SS. Peter and Paul, below which are the Fathers of the Church. The murals on the S wall are of later date.

FROM PERAKHORIO TO PROPHITIS ELIAS MONASTERY (16km). Driving SW, we shortly traverse *Ayia Varvara* (1050 inhab.), 2km N of which is the ancient site of *Kochati*, preserving a huge medieval cistern and, further NW, *Margi*, both largely Maronite inhabited.—Continuing SW we pass (left) a modern chapel and an abandoned copper-mine, and (right) *Panayia Khrysogalatousa* (18C), with a painted iconostasis of 1715 and an icon of the same date. We approach the repopulated hamlet of *Mathiati*, in 1878–81 a British Army camp. Three ancient shrines have been found in the vicinity, in one of which was discovered a head of Dionysos (now in the Cyprus Museum, Nicosia).—Some 3km to the SE (S of the road to Sha and Mosphiloti), and surrounded by olives, is the ruined Byzantine church of *Ayios Aftikos*, retaining slight fragments of painting in its dome.

The road NW from Mathiati leads to (5km) *Kataliondas*, and to *Analiondas*; see p 114.

We soon enter (4km SW) **Lythrodhonda** (1850 inhab.). Many of its 'chameleon' inhabitants were Linobambakoi (see Glossary).—A rough mountain track leads S from Lythrodhonda to (c 10km) *Pano Lefkara* (see below).—The ruins of a Byzantine church were discovered here in 1833, while *Ayios Therapon* (early 18C but much rebuilt) contains relics from the monastery of **Prophitis Elias**, some 6km uphill to the SW. The monastery is of post-Byzantine construction. Only one monk was left there by 1735. The buildings were restored in 1899, and again more recently, and are now used by the Forestry Department. Date palms prosper here, even at an altitude of 608m.

From Perakhorio we drive S along the main Limassol road, shortly by-passing (right) *Alambra*, an area SW of which has been undergoing excavation since 1974, when a settlement of the Middle Bronze Age period was uncovered. We reach, 4km beyond, a road junction at *Mosphiloti*, just SE of which is the monastery of *Ayia Thekla*, dating from 1471, but said to have been built on the site of a 4C church erected by St. Helena. The present church contains numerous wax ex-voto figures and a silver iconostasis.

Pyrga (see Rte 5A) lies 2km E of the next road junction, while a short distance to the W is **Kornos** (1150 inhab.), famous for its coarse clay pottery decorated with anthropomorphic designs; the larger storage jars are built up by hand, not thrown on a wheel. The production of tobacco has been introduced recently.—3km further W lies *Delikipo*, with a tiny church dedicated to the Metamorphosis (Transfiguration), dated 1723, but using fragments from an older building; it contains some 18C icons and a 16C alms plate.

The road S of this junction to *Kophinou*, and including the ascent to the monastery of **Stavrovouni**, prominent to the SE, is described in Rte 3.

From Kophinou, the main road veers SW.

The next left-hand turning leads 2km S to **Ayios Theodhoros**, the scene of serious intercommunal disturbances between 1964 and 1974, retaining some old alleys; its much-restored church dates from 1847.

A worthwhile DETOUR is that to *Pano Lefkara*, some 9km to the NW from the next road junction. The road climbs steeply up a spur of the Troödos foothills to a height of 585m at **Pano Lefkara**, which, together with its twin village of **Kato Lefkara**, have a combined population of 1300.

The Bishop of Limassol was banished here in 1222, and a bishop's crown and other relics were found under the floor of the church of *Arkhangelos Michael* in 1865. The villages were sacked by the Venetians in 1570, and many of their inhabitants massacred for taking up the Turkish cause, for which the survivors were later exempted from the poll-tax. It once had an unenviable reputation for mixing mallow-water with its olive oil, but its main claim to fame is its lace and embroidery. This became known in the late 16C, but it is unlikely that it was the present geometrical design of *lefkaritiki* lace that is said to have been purchased for Milan Cathedral by Leonardo da Vinci, for there is no evidence that he visited the island in 1481.

The lace is of extremely high quality and therefore expensive, but not inordinately so. Its manufacture and marketing is in the hands of four main makers, each employing some 150 workers. The base material is now Irish linen. Beware of cheaper imports which may be passed off as Lefkara ware in some less scrupulous shops. The *loukoumia* (Turkish Delight), much of it exported, should also be sampled, and its preparation watched, if possible. Its figs also have a local reputation, as did the medicinal plant collected in the neighbourhood in the 18C called *cistus ladanifera*, a stimulant not to be confused with laudanum.

The village contains a number of well-constructed stone houses, one of which—*The House of Patsalos*—has since 1988 contained a *Museum of Folk Art*, largely devoted to the traditional embroidery, lace, and silverwork of the area. The principal church of *Stavros* preserves an iconostasis and icons and a cross of the 18C; the Byzantine chapel of *St. Mamas* has been much mutilated. *Ayios Timotheos*, prominent in Kato Lefkara, is a well-preserved medieval domed church, while that dedicated to the Archangel Michael is a small Byzantine building with a modern narthex.

A reasonable road, which later deteriorates, climbs NW to *Vavatsinia* (see below).

An ALTERNATIVE to returning directly to the main road is that bearing SW off the approach road just S of the village via *Kato Dhrys* (possible birthplace in 1134 of St. Neophytos) and the *Monastery of Ayios Minas* (15C; rebuilt c 1740; and recently occupied by nuns), its church in the centre of its cloister, to (7km) *Vavla*, a hamlet lying at 455m and surrounded by olive-groves, almond trees, and carobs.

From here another road leads W through the Troödos foothills via *Layia* to (7km) **Ora**, 4km due W of which lies *Melini*, with a church of 1721, which may also be approached from the coast near Amathus.—6km NW of Ora lies *Odhou* (845m), an attractive and well-sited village among mulberries, medlar and walnut trees; its church (*Ayia Marina*; 1777) contains an older iconostasis and woodcarving of an earlier style.—Due N of Ora stands *Ayii Vavatsinias* (690m), reputed for its needlework, and with the peak of MOUNT KIONIA (1423m) as a background; the attractive high-lying hamlet of *Vavatsinia* (850m) is a further 6km NE, also approached from Pano Lefkara.

From Vavla our sub-route climbs SE down another shoulder of the Troödos foothills to (8km left), the village of **Khirokitia**.

Isaac Comnemos was defeated near here by Richard I, Coeur de Lion, in 1191. In c 1300 it was fortified by the Templars, and it was here that the decisive battle took place between King Janus and the Arabs (July 1426), in which the king was captured and taken to Egypt, while the Prince of Galilee (his brother) and the flower of his army were slaughtered.

The medieval church of *Panayia tou Kambou* (insensitively restored in 1920) contains painted fragments of 1509.

The main road can be regained a short distance beyond, just below the *Neolithic Settlement of Khirokitia*; see Rte 6A.

Some 3km to the SW of Khirokitia is **Tokhni**, where it is said that St. Helena, on first landing in Cyprus on her return from Jerusalem in 325, constructed a bridge, with a church in the centre, built to shelter a fragment of the True Cross (cf. *Stavrovouni Monastery*). Part of this building was incorporated into an adjacent 14C church, later destroyed by fire. A 19C bridge and church have been erected on the site of the original edifice.

A legend relates that the Cross was stolen in 1318 and hidden in a hollow carob tree for 22 years until discovered by a shepherd-boy. The cross was said to perform miraculous cures until, declared a fraud, it was taken to Nicosia to undergo a trial by fire. Remaining unconsumed after an hour in the flames, it was taken out with a pair of tongs and, on seeing the relic survive unharmed, Alix d'Ibelin (Queen of Hugh IV), who had for three years remained speechless after entering the sanctuary at Makheras (see Rte 7), cried out her belief that here indeed was wood upon which Christ had been crucified: and so a double miracle was accomplished!

Many of its Turkish Cypriot villagers were massacred on 15 August 1974 by an EOKA-B contingent.

The main road may be regained S of *Tokhni*.

From the Khirokitia junction the main road continues SW, off which a by-road shortly leads left to the villages of *Psematismenos* (with an unremarkable 16C church rebuilt in 1886), and *Maroni*, both ancient Cypriot sites, the latter with Bronze Age and Archaic remains recently excavated, notably at *Vournes*, dating from the 13C BC.

At 4km beyond Maroni, a lane leads left to *Zyyi* (pron. zee-gy), a diminutive port and terminus of the cable from Alexandria laid in 1880, and until 1879 on the main Larnaca–Limassol coast road (see Rte 3C); it is said that St. Helena (see above) may have disembarked here or at adjacent *Vasilikos*. The latter has ore-processing and loading facilities, and is connected by a narrow-gauge railway to Kalavassos.

Kalavassos itself lies 3km NW of the old road, with iron pyrites and gypsum mines further up the valley. Late Cypriot tombs were discovered at *Ayios Dhimitrios*, and there are a number of Neolithic and Bronze Age sites in the area; that at *Tenta* (c 2km S, near the motorway), is the object of recent excavations, now beneath a protective roof. Two Mycenean tombs, one intact and containing jewellery, have been found, together with circular houses, and wall-painting of 6000 BC. A 6–7C basilica has been excavated at the site of *Kopetra* (or *Sirmata*).

Crossing the narrow-gauge railway, the main road by-passes (left) *Mari*, scene of considerable intercommunal fighting between 1964 and 1974. On a slope to the S is the recently discovered Neolithic site of *Mesovouni*. The road soon approaches the sea and *Governor's Beach* before veering inland again.

The next main left-hand turning leads to the monastery of *Ayios Yeoryios Alamanou*, founded in the late 12C; the present building is quite modern.

The road again veers towards the sea, passing a large cement works and *Moni Power Station*, adjacent to which luxury hotels have recently been erected.

Shortly beyond this point a right-hand turning climbs due N to (16km) *Ephtagonia* (beyond which lies *Melini*; see above) through a partially re-afforested district, but few of the villages in the area are of any great interest except **Arakapas** (4km due W of Ephtagonia) and *Sykopetra* (740m), 4km N of Arakapas. On the outskirts of the former, near the larger church with its Baroque tower, and incorporating stones from the earlier building, stands **Panayia Iamatiki, probably of Latin origin, but largely rebuilt in 1717 and restored in 1976. The original arch at the W end and arches and pillars of the main aisle give some indication of its former magnificence; its surviving paintings (including St. Mamas and his lion) and the triangular floor-tiles, deserve attention.–Only two walls remain of the old church of *Stavros*, 1km to the W, seen from the road climbing to *Dhieron*, from which one can regain the coast near Limassol, descending via *Akrounda* and *Yermasoyia*; see below.

4km NE of the main road at this point is the village of *Pyrgos*, of Byzantine origin, and legend relates that a tunnel extended hence to *Amathus* (see below) big enough for the Queen's solid gold carriage to be driven through it.

We pass, just beyond the *Limonia Bay* hotel (right), the slight remains of a basilica, and a number of built and rock-cut tombs on the hillside, including restored *Tomb 3* of the E necropolis, on approaching the important site of **AMATHUS.

To the right of the road lies the 'Lower City', which was at one time practically engulfed by the sea. Remains of walls jut out into the water where the Phoenicians had a harbour c 800 BC. Built and rock-cut tombs lie adjacent to the main road slightly further W.—The present village of *Ayios Tykhonas* (inland, beyond the motorway) is largely built from the ruins.

A settlement prior to 1000 BC, Amathus remained attached to the Persians in the revolt of 499/98 BC, and was besieged by Onesilos; while under the Romans it was the capital of one of the four Districts of the island. Although the town declined considerably during the Byzantine period, it was here on the sandy 'scala' that in 1191 Richard I of England first landed in Cyprus, to marry Berengaria of Navarre at neighbouring Limassol (cf.).

Amathus was used as a quarry by the Franks, and its stone conveyed by sea to Larnaca, while its ruins were combed for treasure. In 1866 the French carried off to the Louvre a stone vase with bull-headed handles (the same as that noticed by 'Ali Bey', who visited the site some 60 years earlier); the Colossos of Amathus was unearthed here in 1873; the contents of tombs and sculptured panels from them, excavated by Cesnola, may be seen in the Metropolitan Museum, New York.

Amathus is said to be the birthplace (in 609) of St. John the Almoner, the famous patriach of Alexandria.

The site has been the object of further excavation since 1975, when houses of the Hellenistic period, apparently still inhabited in the 1C AD, were discovered. Work on the 'Lower City' brought to light a large paved area rich in architectural remains, including Doric capitals, spirally fluted drums of columns, parts of entablatures with triglyphs and plain metopes, etc., what may be the remains of an atrium surrounded by colonnades or stoas, and a bath complex.

On the adjacent hill slope (approached by a track climbing from the road just before reaching the *Amathus Beach* hotel) several defensive walls have been uncovered, and also remains of a palace, but the exact character of the site has not yet been determined. Work was resumed in 1978 on the Acropolis opposite the central gate, on its W edge, and on terraces to the N. The summit of the Acropolis must have been an important temple site dedicated to Aphrodite and Herakles, which has been partially restored. A torso of a female statue (Aphrodite?), wearing a necklace, has been uncovered recently in this area. Nearby was an early Christian basilica.

The road shortly enters the uninviting outer suburbs of Limassol, which extend behind the shore for some distance, passing near several luxury hotels, and crossing the bed of the YERMOSOYIA. Travellers wishing to by-pass the town will join the motorway by turning right here. For the road continuing W for Kolossi and Paphos, see Rte 13.

The river was dammed in 1968 some distance upstream beyond the village of **Yermosoyia** (2950 inhab.), fortified by the Templars c 1300 and later passing to the Hospitallers.

We later veer left to approach the E end of the Promenade, passing (right) Public Gardens, to reach the older centre of **Limassol**; see Rte 10.

7   Nicosia to Limassol via Tamassos and Palekhori

76km (47 miles); 11km more to include the detour to Tamassos; for that to the monastery of *Makheras*, see below.

Much of this road has been improved, but it is still slow through the mountains. It is preferable to take the by-pass driving SW from Nicosia, and thus avoid several suburban villages more interesting for their history than for their remains. The by-pass is best approached from the centre by following Hilon St immediately SW of the Cyprus Museum, later bearing half-left (or alternatively from the W end of George Grivas Dhigenis Av.).

We leave to the left the suburb of *Engomi* (a village dating from c 1567) and then **Strovolos**, both on the W bank of the PEDIEOS.

Near the old village centre of the latter, on the site of *Panayia Khryseleousa*, Henry II of Cyprus died at his residence in 1324; it was also the birthplace of Abp Kyprianos (1756–1821), who was hanged by Küchük Mehmed in Nicosia. The dome and apse of the original church (1357) were retained when it was rebuilt in 1810–17. On the S side is a small chapel of which the capital of one exterior column is in the form of an archpiscopal crown. It may commemorate the martyred archbishop, who was abbot here in 1802 when it formed part of a monastery, little of which remains.

4km. A short distance to the left of the road, among farm buildings, on lower ground towards the river, is the church of the monastery of *Arkhangelos, originally dating from the late Byzantine period but ambitiously rebuilt in 1636, and in 1713 purchased by Kykko Monastery. It contains in the narthex the tomb of its founder, Abp Nikephoros, an iconostasis of 1650, and a large fresco of the archangel

(1785). The whole deserves restoration, being one of the more interesting but least known monuments in the immediate vicinity of the capital.

To the NW lies derelict *Nicosia International Airport*, at present patrolled by UNFICYP.

We shortly reach a road junction. The right-hand turning by-passes the airport, and after skirting *Ayii Trimithias*, regains the main road from Nicosia to *Troödos*: see Rtes 8 and 9.

The main road shortly passes close to the curiously sited chapel of *Panayia Khrysospiliotissa* (left), consisting of a natural cave enlarged to an area of 9m by 7m, which, as a refuge, probably dates from the Early Christian era, but little remains of its painted interior; its Virgin had particular powers of producing rain in times of drought.

Another 3km brings us to *Anayia* (left; by-passed), where our route bears off to the SW.

The recommended DETOUR TO TAMASSOS, 5.5km distant, should be made from here, by turning left through the old villages of *Anayia* and *Argates*, leaving on the far side of the river PEDIEOS the ancient village of **Psomolophou**, once the goatskin-tanning centre of the island; it now concentrates on growing apricots. *Panayia Theotokos* (1847), preserving parts of an earlier structure, contains a large icon frame made up of fragments of a 16C iconostasis.—We cross the river (bed) to *Episcopio*, said to be the village furthest away (34km) from the sea in Cyprus. It was here among the olive groves that the bishops of Tamassos had their residence, and thus the name. For the road hence to *Makheras*, see below.—To the S, approached by re-crossing the river, is the village of *Politiko*, on a hill-slope, immediately to the NE of which is the ancient site of **TAMASSOS**, or *Tamassus*.

It was long famous for its apparently inexhaustible supply of copper, discovered c 2500 BC, and may well be the 'Temese' mentioned in the 'Odyssey'; while Ovid also refers to 'the Cyprian lands, though rich, in richness yield to that surnam'd the Tamasenian field'. It was a Phoenician colony in c 800 BC. The mines were given by Alexander the Great to King Pnytagoras of Salamis after the Siege of Tyre, while in the 1C BC Herod the Great took a lease on them, at which time a number of Jews emigrated to Cyprus. The mines were largely abandoned by AD 100, soon after which there was a widespread revolt of Jews against their Roman master, which, of course, precipitated reprisals.

Tamassos was the birthplace of St. Heracleidios (see below) and St. Mnason. The former was the first bishop of Cyprus, having been so ordained by St. Barnabas for guiding him and St. Paul across the island. He was succeeded by Mnason, who performed a number of miracles, the most impressive being the destruction of the temple of Asklepios at Tamassos. The town was the earliest centre of Christianity in Cyprus, and amongst its first bishops Abbot Nilos (of Makheras monastery; see below) eventually became archbishop (c 1200).

A life-size bronze statue of Apollo was found not far from the village in 1836, but nothing remains of his temple or of the statue, which was hacked to bits by the peasant who exposed it, and sold off gradually as old copper! Numerous other relics have been found in the area, which was not excavated scientifically until 1889–90. In 1894 the two 6C BC tombs were discovered, while since 1975 German expeditions have been active, in 1976 uncovering the sanctuary of and the altar dedicated to Aphrodite Astarte (5–4C BC).

It has been established that the earliest temple on this site dates from the Cypro-Archaic II period, although earlier structures lie beneath. It was destroyed and then rebuilt in the 4C BC, and continued to be used well into the Hellenistic period, although severely damaged in an earthquake. Among the artefacts found have been a sculptured head of a dog, and a small head of Aphrodite (in Lysippian style); some Attic ware (mid 6C BC); a decorated faience vase from Egypt; sherds of Red-Figure Athenian pottery; and incense-burners (*thymiateria*), one of which shows the god Ammon seated on a ram.

From the Guardian's lodge we may descend below protective roofs into the two separate ***Tombs**, possibly those of some 'kings' of Tamassos. One will oberve a hole in the roof of the inner chamber of the larger tomb, through which looters once entered; they left, however, a silver dish on which a figure of a horse was embossed (now in the Cyprus Museum, Nicosia). Note the carved volutes on carved half-columns on either side of the entrances of both outer and inner chambers, and that the stone is cut in a way to imitate wooden panels, etc.; even bolts are represented on the false doors of stone in the larger of the tombs.

A short distance SW of the village is the ***Monastery of Ayios Heracleidios** (see History, above), founded in Byzantine times, the original church of which stood slightly to the S of the present edifice, which was built in 1759 by Bishop Khrysanthos. The conventual dependencies, with their colourful gardens, accommodate a community of nuns, who sell rose jam, *gliko amigdalou* (an almond preserve), and other succulent local confections.

The iconostasis, incorporating earlier fragments, dates from 1774, and contains mostly 18C icons, but also one of the Baptist of 1611. The principal icon was covered with silver gilt in 1799. The skull of St. Herakleidios is also preserved here. Murals have been uncovered in the aisle.—Adjoining the church is a small domed reliquary chapel containing various sarcophagi and a strange iconostasis composed of four large stone slabs carved with a geometrical pattern of Byzantine inspiration and later covered with plaster. From the floor of hexagonal marble tiles an opening leads down to what was probably a Roman tomb (?the saint's burial place). To the E of the chapel are remains of a mosaic floor.

Hackett, when referring to the saint—who had worked innumerable miracles— reported that in 1769 a young boy of Nicosia racked by 'demoniacal possession' was brought here in the hope that the saint might alleviate his suffering. During Divine Service the boy had convulsions, and vomited forth 'a snake, a span long, and two crabs', which were then hung up in the church 'to confirm the faith of the credulous and to silence the cavils of the unbelievers'.

Immediately to the SW are the ruins of the monastery of *Ayios Mnason*, the church of which was poorly rebuilt in 1774, but incorporates a 5C BC Cypriot capital in its N wall.—A tomb of the Middle Cypriot period was discovered here in 1965, the first of this date to be found in the locality.

FROM EPISKOPIO TO THE MONASTERY OF MAKHERAS (16km). Although the monastery is of no great interest in itself, for those with time, the winding drive through the wooded eastern foothills of the Troödos massif is pleasant, and affords some extensive views. We bear SE through adjacent *Péra*, where a veteran from Mesolongi (1822/26) taught in the first school established here (1861); but being a passionate advocate of Enosis, he was forced to leave by the Turks.—We traverse *Kambia*, 3km to the E of which lies *Analiondas*, apparently inhabited in Roman times, a number of tombs of that era having been found in the district.

To the W is the partially restored monastery of *Arkhangelos Michael*, founded 1769. There are signs of ancient mining near the road from Kambia to (3km) *Kapedhes*, which we by-pass (left), and beyond which the road continues to climb, bearing SW. After 5km we pass the church of *Ayios Onouphrios* (?14C, but burned c 1925 and rebuilt; its interior was redecorated in 1975); a plaque gives further details about this ascetic. We descend to the **Monastery of Makheras** (884m) not far beyond.

It was founded in c 1148 by two monks who had reached Cyprus three years previously, and, it is said, discovered an icon of the Virgin in a cave there. Their successors travelled to Constantinople in quest of funds, and on appealing in person to Manuel Comnenos, the Byzantine Emperor, were granted an extensive tract of mountain and an annual donation from the imperial treasury. Work was commenced on the erection of suitable accommodation for the growing community, which soon gathered a number of aspirants, among them (in 1172) Nilos, who became the first abbot, later Bishop of Tamassos, and then archbishop.

In 1337, according to the story, Alix d'Ibelin, wife of Hugh IV, being of the Latin faith, insisting on entering the *bema* or sanctuary of the church (which was forbidden to women—and still is; cf. Stavrovouni), was instantly struck dumb, and remained so for three years: see *Tokni* for the sequel. In 1393 James I and his court sought refuge here during a period of plague. The monastery was burnt down in 1530 and again in 1892, and in the rebuilding (completed 1900) little of the earlier architectural features were preserved, although some original masonry is seen in the church.

In 1957 Gregoris Afxentiou, second-in-command to Colonel Grivas in the EOKA uprising, died in a nearby hide-out.

The site of the monastery is impressive, together with the views its terrace provides—among them that of distant Nicosia—and indeed, especially when the almond blossom is out (in February) very beautiful. The monks distil an excellent liqueur; overnight lodging for travellers is available. In the *Church* are preserved the original icon (see History), almost entirely covered by late 18C repoussé silver, and the MS of the *Ritual Ordinance* of Nilos, while among a host of crosses, reliquaries, and icons, that of St. George and the Dragon is notable.

From the monastery one may continue to climb S, skirting the E slope of MOUNT KIONIA (1423m; with a meteorological station on its summit), before descending to (8km) *Ayii Vavatsinias* and *Ora* (see p 110).—Alternatively, by bearing NW through the old village of *Lazania* (900m) we approach (5km) **Gourri** (730m), containing some 18C houses preserving good woodwork, seen likewise at **Phikardhou** (to the E), a hamlet which has recently been declared an Ancient Monument, and which is receiving the attention of those responsible for preserving the folk architecture of the island from further depredations. Clitos Jacovides (1913–75), owner of the taverna in Kyrenia frequently alluded to by Lawrence Durrell, was born at Gourri.—From Gourri one may regain the main route by turning left just beyond *Kalokhorio*, with a characteristic belfry, c 7km N.—The road S leads to *Pharmakas*, before climbing across the watershed to *Odhou*, on the S slope of the range: see p 110).

From Anayia our route continues SW.

At 4km a right-hand turning leads to *Ayios Ioannis*, the site of an early Hellenistic necropolis looted by peasants in 1883, although some items, including Graeco-Phoenician jewellery later excavated by Richter, have found their way into the Cyprus Museum, Nicosia. The early 19C church contains an icon of 1540, and built into the churchyard wall is a 14C lion gargoyle, and a head of St. Mark from the ruined chapel of *Akhera*, adjacent to *Meniko*, some distance to the NW; see Rte 8.

A new road by-passes (left) *Aredhiou* (where 15C *Panayia Khryseleousa* contains an icon of the period), and *Malounda*, where there is a badly restored medieval *bridge* on which a defaced Lusignan coat of arms may be seen, and ruined mills further up and down stream. *Panayia Khrysopandanassa* (1763, but in Byzantine style) contains some earlier woodwork, and an ancient cemetery was discovered nearby in the 1960s.

A road climbs 2km S to **Klirou** (1300 inhab.; 455m), an ancient village with many tombs in the vicinity. It was the property of Sir Thomas de Montolif in the 14C and, during the Second World War, was for some time a British Army HQ. *Panayia Evangelistria* stands S of the site of its predecessor, the iconostasis of which (1748) it preserves; it also contains a vindictive rain-*dis*pelling icon covered with silver gilt, which brings bad luck to those who do not bring thanks-giving offerings for rain supplied! Some monastic ruins lie S of the village.—Hence a road leads S to (7km) *Phikardhou* (see above), better approached from *Kalokhorio*, to the SW, and *Gourri*. The main road may be regained W of Kalokhorio.

To the right of the main road lies the village of *Agrokipia*, dating from c 1200, NW of which is the 18C monastery of *Ayios Panteleimon*, with a gabled roof; while 3km due W of Agrokipia lies *Mitsero*, just S of a mining area, where the church contains an apse and iconostasis from an earlier building.

The main road continues to climb S, off which, after c 3km, a right-hand turning leads shortly to *Ayios Epiphanios* (620m), with an over-restored church.

We approach *Apliki* (710m), with a church of c 1760 adjacent to a modern structure and climb over a ridge to *Palekhori*.

PALEKHORI (900m), an ancient attractively-sited village, reputed for its red wine, *loukanika*, and *hiromeri*, straddles the wooded valley of the PERISTERONA, its banks lined with poplars. It was part of the Commandery of the Templars in 1297, and later belonged to the D'Ibelin family. It retains several churches of interest, including *Panayia Khrysopantanissa* in the upper town, 16C but restored in 1863 and further 'modernised' in 1948; it preserves, however, some rare early 17C paintings and a mid-16C icon of the Virgin. The 15C church of *Sotiros* (the Saviour; key from the priest) above the village, preserves *Murals of 1612, and others attributed to Philippe Goul (1466). Nearer the centre are medieval *Ayios Yeoryios*, and *Ayios Loukas* (1925), adjacent to which is the modernised belfry of its predecessor, torn down earlier this century, and described as being 'beautiful' in its time and containing 'extremely interesting frescoes'.

NE of the village (best reached by turning left immediately after following the road over to *Sykopetra*; this jolting and convoluted mountain road is *not* recommended) is the chapel of *Ayii Anargyri* (or SS. Cosmas and Damian), a well-preserved barn-like building of c 1525, near which rise two monoliths, probably no more than the remains of ancient oil-presses.

For the rough but attractive road NW to *Alona* for *Stavros tou Ayiasmati* and *Lagoudhera*, see p 120.

From Palekhori we continue to climb steeply to the SW, crossing the main eastern ridge of the Troödos range with MOUNT PAPOUTSA (1554m) rising to the left and, just beyond the watershed, leave to our right the turning for (5km) *Agros* (see Rte 8) and descend (Views) to **Ayios Theodhoros** (1000m). Here, the much-restored church of *Panayia* contains an iconostasis of 1667 in a perfect state of preservation.

6km **Zoopiyi** (880m), to the right of the road, with two churches—well-sited *Zoodotospygi* (19C) preserving a 15C icon of the Virgin—is one of the main producers of Commandaria wine.

We shortly bear right, by-passing (left) *Kalokhorio* (675m), where *Ayios Yeoryios* (1768) contains murals of interest, and (2km SE) **Louvaras**, one of several hamlets in the area dating from the 13C, where the chapel of *Ayios Mamas* (1454) has a frescoed interior, some of the work attributed to Philippe Goul (and some carelessly restored); note the icons of the Virgin (late 16C) and of Christ (early 17C) and the carved tie-beam.

The road again turns S, descending to *Yerasa*, among its citrus orchards, SW of which, at *Apesha*, reached by a track, are a number of Roman tombs, long ago looted. The road skirts *Paramytha*.

In the churchyard and built into the church wall of adjacent *Spitali* are several Roman cippi. Nearby is a sculpted stone with a hole in the centre, once resorted to by sufferers from malaria, who are said to have been cured by crawling through the aperture after walking seven times around the stone (compare *Patriki*).

2km further E, approached by a track, is the hamlet of *Phasoula*—also reached by a direct and better road from Limassol—to the SW of which, on a hill called *Castra*, are remains of a Roman fort and ancient sepulchres.

We traverse *Ayia Phyla*, now virtually a N suburb of Limassol, where in 1964 a cemetery of c 1600 BC was found, and crossing the by-pass, enter the outskirts of **Limassol** itself; see Rte 10.

8 From Nicosia to Limassol via Peristerona and Agros

92km (57 miles); 16km more to include detours to *Stavros tou Ayiasmati* and *Lagoudhera*.

For the first 8km we follow the by-pass driving SW of Nicosia: see the first paragraphs of Rte 7. The first part of this route is scenically flat and uninteresting until we turn S towards the Troödos range.

On reaching the main road junction we turn right along a new road. The older road turns right further S to *Ayii Trimithias*, where medieval *Ayii Anargyri* (literally 'without fees', referring to SS. Cosmas and Damian, to whom it is dedicated, who did not charge for giving medical attention) was rebuilt c 1900, but preserves the W door of an earlier building, and other fragments.

The road veers N to join what was the main road from Nicosia before the Turkish occupation of 1974 near (4km) **Kokkinotrimithia** (2050 inhab.), a market-gardening centre to the N of the road, and named from the red earth (Gr. *kokkini*) surrounding it. It used to lie on the old Cyprus Railway Line, the bed of which was just S of the main street. To the E of the town is a UNFICYP camp on the site of a British detention camp during the EOKA campaign. On the outskirts is the chapel of *Arkhangelos Michael* (c 1525), a well-constructed stone building incorporating some interesting architectural details.—Some distance to the N lies *Mammari*, named after a Frankish owner, beyond which is the Attila Line.

We turn left, and after 5km by-pass (left) **Akaki** (2150 inhab.), apparently on the site of a castle erected here c 1300 by Henry II of Cyprus, which has two churches of slight interest, one of which is in ruins.

Some 3km SE is **Meniko**, where *Panayia Kyprianos*, rebuilt on the site of a medieval edifice, is dedicated to SS. Cyprian and Justina, martyred at Antioch, whose skulls, later silver-plated, were said to have been buried here.—The area between Akaki and *Avlona* (a Turkish outpost), 4km NW, has been a trouble spot since 1974, and a number of 'incidents' have taken place between UNFICYP and its occupiers.

PERISTERONA (2250 inhab.), now lying to the S of the main road, and named after the pigeons once popular here, was a centre of the peasant revolt of 1426 which proclaimed Alexis 'King'. Our route turns left just short of the town, which may be entered by taking the first right-hand turning off this road, which soon approaches the *Ana Bridge*, probably thrown across the PERISTERONA RIVER in the Venetian era. Watermelons are extensively cultivated here.

Ayios Barnabas and Hilarion, Peristerona

We have a good view across the river (bed) of the five-domed church of *Ayii Varnava** (Barnabas) **and Hilarion**. Although in recent years somewhat over-restored, it dates from the early 10C (with a later narthex), and has been the property of Kykko monastery since 1092. Its barrel-vaulted aisles are divided from the nave by walls pierced by arched openings; there are three projecting apses. Its iconostasis (restored) is dated 1549; a 16C icon of the Presentation in the Temple is of interest, together with an old chest containing a painted scene, said to be of the Siege of Rhodes (1522). The murals which once decorated the church have faded away.

Adjacent to the SW is the village mosque, slightly damaged by arson in 1976.—To the W of the centre is minute *Ayia Varvara* (Barbara), preserving some 16C murals, and an icon of the Virgin of the same period.

For the roads hence to *Kakopetria* and *Pedhoulas*, see Rtes 9A and 9B.

Driving S, we traverse **Orounda**, taking its name from the vetches cultivated here, and also known for its pigs. Across the river is the small and long disused monastery of *Ayios Nikolaos*, with a well-constructed domed church of the mid 16C, repaired in 1733; over the W door is a naïve Lion of St. Mark, probably carved locally.—There are three ruined water-mills to the N.

5km *Kato Moni*, to the E of which is the abandoned village of *Eliophotes*.—We now commence the gentle ascent of the valley, after 12km reaching (right) the turning for *Stavros tou Ayiasmati (the key of which must first be obtained at *Platanistasa*, some 3km further S, reached by bearing left at the next turning off the main road). It is approached by a dirt track curling round the hill slope to the W. The *Church* itself, one of the most attractive on the island, beautifully situated and commanding a fine view, dates from c 1436 and contains an almost complete cycle of 'Byzantine-revival' *Murals* in two tiers, attributed to Philippe Goul, but repainted. Note on the S wall the Baptism of Christ, the Presentation of the Virgin, and St. Mamas riding his lion, among others.

Platanistasa itself (930m) is a pleasant old village, dating from c 1200, but the medieval church of *Ayio Ioannis* (rebuilt 1740) was burnt to the ground on 29 July 1987.

Hence we may climb S to 'grape-bound' *Alona*, its trellised streets festooned with vines; and from there either turn left via *Phterykoudhi* (to the right of the road) and *Askas*, on its promontory (Views) to *Palekhori* (see Rte 7); or climb due S over a shoulder of the hills to gain the Palekhori–Zoopyi road. *Phterykoudhi* (980m), an attractive village, was settled c 1575 after a battle between Venetians and Turks at adjacent *Kalamithasa* in 1570, when the latter village was destroyed; to the E stands *Ayia Pareskeva* (or *Ayia Khristina*; 1411).—The church of *Ayios Ioannis Vaptistis* at *Askas*, of the late Byzantine period, restored 1763, preserves wall-paintings of c 1510 and rarer examples of the early 17C, including one of Dives and Lazarus; also a 16C lectern.

The Pantokrator in the dome of Panayia tou Arakou,
Lagoudhera

The main road climbs SW through the hamlets of *Livadhia* and *Alithinou* to (3km) **Polystipos** (1060m), a pleasant old village set among terraced vineyards, and noted for its hazelnuts and almonds, as are most in this region, known as the PITSILIA. Turning right here we reach a road junction some 2km beyond.

The improved main road continues to ascend, crossing the ridge towards *Khandria* (see below), but the short DETOUR to the domed 12C Byzantine church of the monastery of *PANAYIA TOU ARAKA at **Lagoudhera** should be made first, turning right at a T-junction for the village (1000m). It lies to the right as we approach the village; key adjacent. The building was re-roofed in the 18C, when trellised verandahs were added, and further repaired in 1955.

Its walls are extensively covered with *Murals* of c 1192 (the date of the Painting of the Holy Tile over the door), some of the oldest and finest examples in Cyprus, with noticeably elongated figures, which were restored in 1968–73 by David Winfield. An impressive Pantokrator fills the dome, and among a number of New Testament scenes note the beautiful Dormition of the Virgin (lunette of S recess) and her Presentation (N recess); the Nativity (S side of W vault), Baptism of Christ (recess to left of N recess), and Presentation in the Temple (wall of N recess); Simon Stylites, etc. A double-sided 12C icon is also of interest.

In Lagoudhera itself is a mid 19C church containing icons of the Virgin and Child (c 1560), a triptych of 1593, and a Christ of 1620.

At adjacent *Sarandi*, to the NW, the church preserves an unusual 17C(?) mural depicting the Disciples seated on the ground at the Last Supper.

From here a rough winding road follows the pine-wooded N slope of the range to (6km) **Spilia** (1080m), to the S of which Colonel Grivas had a hideout; a short distance to the N in the hamlet of *Kourdhali* is the monastery of *Panayia Khrysokoudhaliotissa* and church of the *Dormition* (15–16C; restored 1921) of some interest, the latter containing some murals of the period; note also the adjacent hump-backed bridge.—We descend W of Spilia to reach the main road N of *Kakopetria*: see Rte 9A.

Continuing S from Lagoudhera, turn left on reaching the 'main' road running along the S flank of the range, leaving *Khandria* to the NW, and descend to *Agros* (see below), passing (right) the old village of *Agridhia*, with two churches over-restored in 1811.

From **Khandria** (1190m), settled by the Genoese in the 15C, with a background of vine-covered slopes, and a church containing pillars formed by single pine trunks, the road winds W.—Shortly, a left-hand fork leads downhill through the growing village of **Kyperounda** (1650 inhab.; 1135m), where on a hillock a few paces S of the village centre some murals are preserved in the church of *Stavros*. The tower of the church in the main square is pleasantly carved with clusters of grapes.—On the lower slopes are the villages of *Dhymes* (said to have been settled prior to 1200 BC) and more attractive *Potamitissa*, whence minor roads lead to *Kato Mylos* and *Pelendria*, SE and SW respectively.—From Stavros church we may climb to regain the upper road, where turning left we reach the main N–S road at the Karvounos crossroad some 6km S of *Kakopetria*: see Rte 9A.

Agros (1010m), well-situated on the sunny S flank of the range, and surrounded by vineyards, produces succulent *loukanika* and *hiromeri*. The monastery of *Panayia Eleousa Agrou* here was founded by monks from Constantinople in the 9C and was rebuilt some centuries later, although by the end of the 18C it had much decayed. In 1898 a large structure in a Byzantine style was raised on the site. There is another church, dedicated to the Baptist, dating from 1760.

From Agros we turn E to gain the Palekhori–Zoopiyi road (see Rte 7), or we may descend S to **Ayios Ioannis** (880m), with a large modern church containing an iconostasis of 1757 from the previous (deserted) church of 1725. Bearing SW round foothills (Views) we reach *Zoopiyi* (see p 116, and for the remainder of the route to **Limassol**, 22km S).

9   Nicosia to Pano Platres, for Limassol

A. Via Kakopetria

67km (41 miles); the detour to *Asinou* will add 22km to the distance.

For the road to *Peristerona*, see Rte 8. Hence we continue W, by-passing (right) *Astromeritis*, beyond which we veer SW, still roughly parallel to the Attila Line, and at 7km reach the left-hand turning for the recommended DETOUR to *Asinou* church.

Driving due S at this junction, with improving views of the Troödos massif ahead, we leave on our left the village of *Potami*, with a well-constructed church probably of the Venetian period.—At *Vizakia* we bear right below the village, passing (right) the roughly-built chapel of *Arkhangelos Michael* (c 1500), containing some naïve paintings, to **Nikitari**, the modern church of which preserves 'Holy doors' of 1610. The priest (who may be contacted at the café opposite) has the keys to Asinou, and will accompany visitors.—Hence the road leads 4km up the narrowing valley to (465m) the unpretentious church of *ASINOU (more correctly *Panayia Phorviotissa*), with an interior considered by some to be the finest example of a Byzantine church in Cyprus. The main building dates from c 1105, and the domed narthex was added c 1200. In 1300 the barrel-vault was reconstructed and the nave strengthened with internal and external buttresses. Its *Murals*, which cover the interior, repainted in 1333, most of which deserve detailed examination, were cleaned and preserved in 1965–68 under the auspices of the Centre of Byzantine Studies at Dumbarton Oaks (Harvard University), and under the direction of E.J.W. Hawkins and David Winfield.

In the dome of the narthex is the Pantokrator; below which (left) are the Blessed, and (right) the Damned; note the hunting dogs (upper right) as we pass into the nave, in the vault of the W bay of which are (left) the Washing of the Feet, and (right) the Raising of Lazarus. In the vaults of the centre bay are (left) the Crucifixion and Entombment, and (right) the Transfiguration, and Baptism; while over the Sanctuary is the Ascension, and in the semi-dome of the apse the Virgin with the Archangels Michael and Gabriel on her right and left respectively.

A booklet is available which explains in detail the scenes and names of saints, etc. in some 100 other paintings.

The rough roads climbing further into the hills are not particularly recommended, and—as the priest may wish to be returned to Nikitari—the main road may be regained 4km NW of his village at *Kato Koutraphas* (meaning 'one who likes to eat capers'), with a church rebuilt in the 18C preserving W and N doors from an earlier edifice.—Here we turn left some 4km from the point at which we diverged for Vizakia.

A mural in Panayia Phorviotissa, Asinou

After 6km a junction is reached, where a new road crossing into the MARATHASA VALLEY (watered by the Setrakhos) and to *Pedhoulas* (see Rte 9B) bears right.—We follow the improved main road through the district known as the SOLEA (watered by the Evrykhou and Karyotis), after by-passing (right) the village of **Evrykhou** (430m), once the terminus of the Government railway from Famagusta and Nicosia. The small and well-preserved 15C church of *Ayio Kyriakos* contains the altar-tomb of this saint and a 16C iconostasis.

Some 2km to the W is the village of **Korakou**, probably dating from the 15C or earlier. Immediately to the NE is *Ayios Loukas* (1697); while *Ayios Mamas*, also 17C, has acoustic vases built into the apse, and contains a 16C icon of the Virgin.—To the S of Korakou, among orchards, lies **Tembria**, which has been claimed to be the ancient Greek site of *Tembrus*, where enough gold had been buried to support the island for seven years!—Further S, nearer the main road, are remains of an aqueduct, while the old *Khan* is now a Folk Architecture Site, most of the structure, with the exception of the front doors, being original.—Up the side valley to the SW is *Kaliana*, dating from before 1570. The church of *Ayii Joachim and Anna* (16C; restored, and with a new belfry) contains wall-paintings, and some late 16th–early 17C icons.

The new road keeps to the E side of the valley floor, where two interesting churches survive from the monastery of *Podithou* at *Galata*: see below.

KAKOPETRIA (1400 inhab., 660m) is a busy summer resort, and—with the much improved main road—in danger of being over-commercialised. It is nevertheless attractively sited, and reasonably well supplied with small hotels and restaurants (among which the Mylos is well-reputed, particularly for its trout), and it is a good centre for the exploration of monuments in the immediate vicinity. It is no great distance from the Byzantine churches of *Lagoudhera* and *Stavros tou Ayiasmati* (see pp 120 and 119), nor from the summit of the Troödos massif. It was one of the many refuges of the EOKA leader George Grivas.

The somewhat decrepit older village lies further W, on the far side of the river bank, and its 'main street' should be traversed. Its restoration and preservation is continuing.

The adjoining village of **Galata**, immediately to the N of Kakopetria on the 'old' road, should be visited for its churches. It was settled c 1515, and is said to be where Sir Henry de Gibelet kept his hawks. (Martoni records that James I kept 300 hawks of various kinds for the chase.) The first church we come to, *Panayia* (1520), lies to the right of the road leading N into Galata (key at the adjacent garage opposite the Rialto Hotel), and contains murals of the Entertainment of the Angels by Abraham, and of the Sacrifice of Isaac, etc. The priest, who lives near the school, holds the keys to most of the local churches and, if collected by car, will accompany visitors. Passing *Ayia Paraskevi* (1511) we approach the village centre. Behind the modern church stands *****Ayios Sozomenos** (1513), under restoration, with spirited frescoes by Symeon Axenti, a local artist; the exterior wall preserves murals of the Councils of the Church.

Ayios Nikolaos tis Stegis, near Kakopetria

A lane to the NE approaches the site of the monastery of *Podithou*, of which the churches of *****Panayia Eleousa**, and adjacent **Panayia Theotokos** (or **Arkhangelos**), survive. The former dates from 1502; note the round windows of Byzantine origin; also the Virgin and Child in the apse, showing Italian influence, as do others in this church, among them one of Moses, and that of the apocryphal story of

Joachim and Anne.—Above the N entrance of the latter, a few paces to the S, is a painting of the donors by Axenti (see above); those of the empress St. Helena, and of Constantine, her son, are also in evidence.

Lying at a higher level to the left of the road, some 3km SW of Kakopetria, is the important church of *AYIOS NIKOLAOS TIS STEGIS (or *St. Nicholas of the Roof*), with an upper shingle roof (13C) protecting the lower domed and tiled roof (repaired 1955). Fork left after a small dam to a restaurant, and enquire there for the key.

The building dates from the 11C, with a narthex, with its cupola, added in the 12C. Its interior is entirely covered with frescoes of varying dates between the 11C and c 1430, and with others of the 17C or slightly later. Note among the earlier murals the Transfiguration, and Raising of Lazarus, and the 12C paintings in the narthex; a 14C Nativity, the Entry into Jerusalem, and a Crucifixion are also remarkable.

The main road from Kakopetria continues to curve uphill through the thickly wooded upper valley to reach the Karvounos crossroads (1195m).—*Kyperounda* and *Agros* lie to the E: see the latter part of Rte 8.

FROM THE KARVOUNOS CROSSROADS TO THE TRIMIKLINI CROSSROADS (11km). This sub-route is that followed by the 'old' direct road down the valley, now to a great extent superseded by the improved road via *Troödos*: see below. We turn downhill through *Pano Amiandos* (990m), with views to the right of the upper village and the disfiguring asbestos mines on the mountain side; *amianthos* is Greek for asbestos. Its exploitation has now ceased, which is said to have much discomforted the Bishop of Limassol, who had invested heavily in them.—From a point not far S of the village a left-hand turning leads 3km SE to **Pelendria** (1750 inhab.; 865m), in c 1353 the property of Jean de Lusignan, son of Hugh IV. Of its various churches the most interesting is that of *Stavros*, on its S outskirts, a 14C structure with an addition to the N; the whole was carefully restored earlier this century. The interior is extensively covered with murals. Note the screen of Coptic musharaby lattice-work. Some 14C icons are also preserved here, showing strong Eastern influence(?). The large church of *Panayia* (17C), built against the hillside, almost reached by its slate tiles on one side, contains icons which pre-date the building, but they have been over-restored.

The next turning (after 5km) to the right of the main road climbs 3km to the NW to the remains of the monastery of **Mesapotamos** (originally called *Prodhromos*, and founded in the late 14C), rebuilt in 1584 and again in 1774. In 1955 it was a haunt of Colonel Grivas. Some early icons survive in the church, the burial-site of Theophanios (1550), last of the saints of Cyprus, and a former Bishop of Soli.—We reach the Trimiklini crossroad not far S of this turning, passing (left) ruined *Panayia Saittiotissa*, built in memory of an arrow loosed by the Virgin, who, mounted on a white horse, killed a local dragon which once terrorised the district!—The road hence to *Limassol* (35km beyond) is described in reverse in Rte 11.

At the Karvounos crossroads we turn right and continue to climb, by-passing *Pano Amiandos*, on which are centred the open-cast asbestos mines in operation since 1907, which scar the flank of the range.—The road swings abruptly to the right and after ascending for another 7km we reach the crossroads at **Troödos** (1725m), the highest continually inhabited place in Cyprus, being both a summer and winter resort. It is a venue for skiing enthusiasts, the N and S slopes of the mountain enjoying a brief but unpredictable season (January–March). Several *Nature Trails* for walkers fan out from the crossroads.

During the first Turkish occupation it was little visited except by carriers of snow to the capital. Shortly after the British occupation, Sir Garnet Wolseley decided to set up a summer camp here for his troops, which was laid out S of the village, near which a summer residence for the second High Commissioner, Sir Robert Biddulph, was erected. This exotic stone edifice, similar in style to a Scottish shooting-lodge, was built in 1880 under the improbable supervision of the French poet Arthur Rimbaud (1845–91).

Rimbaud, sailing from Alexander, had landed at Lanarca in December 1878, and contracted typhoid while directing labourers quarrying stone near *Voroklini* (cf.). He then visited France to recuperate before returning to Cyprus in 1880 to work on 'le palais du Gouverneur'. In the 1940s a plaque was affixed to the *Government Lodge* commemorating the curious history.

FROM TROÖDOS TO THE PRODHROMOS CROSSROADS (7km). The summit of the Troödos range may be gained by turning NW off the main road here, and shortly bearing left to the peak (MOUNT OLYMPOS; 1952m or 6404ft), the highest point of the island, no longer bare, being crowned by globular radar installations, a TV tower, observation posts, etc. There is evidence of early Greek habitation, possibly a Temple of Aphrodite Acraia, and of a Venetian tower at the nearby settlement of *Palea Khora.*

Not far beyond this approach-road to the summit, a right-hand turning leads to the *Kokkinorotsos Chrome Mine* (copper and iron pyrites).—We continue W through the woods, with occasional extensive *Views to the N, and shortly after passing (left) the Prodhromos Reservoir, descend to crossroads just E of the village, see Rte 9B.—*Pedhoulas* (see 9B) lies on the N slope of the range 3km to the right.—Hence the circuit of the massif may be made by turning S via the monastery of *Troödhitissa* to *Pano Platres:* see Rte 9B.

From Troödos, the new main road descends in sweeping curves (Views) to the SW to *Pano Platres,* for which see Rte 9B; and for the road thence to *Limassol* (42km S), Rte 11 in reverse.—For the road from Platres to Limassol via *Omodhos,* for *Kourion,* or *Kolossi,* see Rte 12; likewise for the various roads descending SW to the coast between *Evdhimou* and *Kouklia.*

B. Via Pedhoulas

80km (50 miles).

For the road to *Peristerona,* see Rte 8; and from there to the turning off the Kakopetria road (and including the detour to *Asinou*), see Rte 9A.

The recently constructed road, which we now follow, connects several tracks and minor roads, most of which climb inland from the coast, the lower reaches of which are now in Turkish-occupied territory. We may now approach the MARATHASA VALLEY from the Solea with ease, by-passing (left) *Linou,* to the N of which lies *Katydhata,* and beyond, the village and mines of *Skouriotissa,* taking its name from the slag-heaps (scoriae), from which copper was extracted possibly as early as 2600 BC. Operations have been perforce temporarily suspended. Gold was once found here. The monastery (restored c 1845) is now of little interest.

We shortly cross the bed of the KARYOTIS and by-pass (left) *Ayios Epiphanios,* birthplace in 1924 of Rauf Denktash, former Vice-President of the Republic, and veer SW, following the old road through woods into the Marathasa valley, its steep slopes thickly planted with olives, almonds and fruit orchards, and there turn left.

5km up the valley we pass (right) the Kalopanayiotis Dam, and by-pass (left) *Nikos,* where the rebuilt church preserves 16–18C icons, before entering adjoining **Kalopanayiotis** (700m), a small spa known for its sulphur springs. It was visited in 1879 by John Thomson, after a four-hour uphill mule-ride from Lefka. From the village centre a lane descends steeply to the valley floor, the ravine now spanned by a modern bridge, to approach the Monastery of *Ayios Ioannis Lamba-distou** (or *Lambadhistis*), well-restored in 1955 (key from a house on the W side of the bridge, or at the monastery itself). The building is entered from the S.

Incorporated under the same steeply pitched roof is the 11C domed church of *Ayios Heracleidios*, an Orthodox church (12C; S), and a late 15C Latin chapel (N). Both the interior walls of the narthex and of the church itself are covered with murals. Note the carved doors and pews, the wax ex-votos, well-preserved icons, and the painting of St. John of 1776. The variety of architecture combines to give the edifice great character, and makes it one of the more rewarding of Cypriot churches to visit.

The keys of local chapels may also be requested, among them *Ayios Andronikos*, just SE of the village, and *Ayios Yeoryios*, with an exceptional icon of the Pantokrator of c 1500.

Approximately 1km further up the valley we turn sharp left. Here a path climbs steeply to the right to a tiny chapel, *Panayia tou Moutoulla** (key from adjacent house), dating from 1279–80, contain-ing an interesting fresco of the donors, and carved doors, and preserving its steeply pitched timber roof below a protective cover.

We traverse the village of **Moutoullas** (780m), and continue to climb steeply through orchards to **PEDHOULAS** (1090m), a summer resort well-known for its Sunday markets and for its cherry-blossom in spring, but of no great interest in itself, and a village in which the passing motorist can easily get lost in its maze of steep streets.—No great distance below and N of the conspicuous dome of its main church is diminutive *Arkhangelos Michael* (1472; key at adjacent house), built by Basil Chamades, and containing frescoes contempo-rary with its erection, including those of the donor and his family, while the Lusignan arms may be observed in the upper part of the iconostasis.—The finely-carved W door of the chapel of *Ayios Yeoryios* is also of some interest.

FROM PEDHOULAS TO KYKKO MONASTERY (14km). From crossroads just above the village we may turn right to follow an improved but sinuous road bearing W along a shoulder of the Troödos range to the **MONASTERY OF KYKKO** (pronounced key-ko). Famous throughout the Orthodox world, with the reputation of being the richest in Cyprus, and which preserves (as is supposed) one of the three icons surviving ascribed to St. Luke himself. Accommodation (some 70 rooms) is available.

It is said to have been founded in c 1100, possibly two decades earlier, by a hermit named Isaiah, who had cured the Emperor Alexios Comnemos's daughter of sciatica, and for his pains was given a precious icon attributed to the apostle St. Luke, known as that of 'Eleousa, the Compassionate'. The monastery has been repeatedly burnt down, the first time in 1365, owing to the enthusiasm of a villager in search of wild honey lighting a fire in the vicinity to scare off the bees. It was rebuilt of wood by Eleanor of Aragón, wife of Peter I, but this tinder structure was destroyed in 1542.

It was visited by Richard Pococke in 1738, who was received here 'with great civility', being immediately served 'with marmalade, a dram, and coffee, and about an hour after with a light collation, and in the evening with a grand entertainment at supper'. Successive edifices were burned down in 1751, and 1831, when its precious MSS were lost, but the icon survived the fires. Abbot Joseph was a victim of the Nicosia massacre of 1821, as the monastery was 'stauropegic', being directly controlled by the archbishop; and it was pillaged that year by the Turks. It was frequently used as a sanctuary, even in this century, and in 1956 its dependencies, being near a mountain hideout of Colonel Grivas, were occupied by the Gordon Highlanders. Michael Mouskos, later President Makarios, was a novice here.

The irregular pile of buildings, roughly triangular in layout, conforming to the site, surround two cloisters. They are of slight intrinsic interest. From the main entrance we turn right in the first cloister to approach the *Church*, the carved marble over the door of which may be a survival from the first building.

The *Icon of the Virgin* cannot itself be seen, being considered too sacred a subject on which to gaze, and is enclosed in a tortoiseshell and mother-of-pearl shrine which stands before the iconostasis. The painting itself, which is said to have been covered since the 16C, is protected by a silver gilt plate stamped with a representation of the portrait beneath, and this cover is presumed to date from 1776. It has, like many others, the reputation of being rain-compelling.

Among other relics are a bronze arm, said to have been that of an impious Turk who, when endeavouring to light his cigarette at one of the lamps illuminating the icon, had this member forthwith withered and transformed into metal by the outraged Virgin; also a 'saw' of a swordfish given in gratitude by a drowning sailor saved by the intercession of the Virgin of Kykko; and a Crucifixion of 1520. One of the bells is said to have been rolled up to Kykko in a barrel from Lefka—an offering from the faithful in Russia. A more recent contribution is a vast and hideous modern chandelier.

The densely wooded and hilly area to the W of Kykko, noticeably uninhabited, is described in Rte 17, but of interest in the immediate neighbourhood, and incidentally providing even more extensive *Views* than from the monastery, is the *Tomb of Abp Makarios III* (1913–77) on *Kykko Hill* (1318m; also known as *Throni*), 2km to the W, and approached by a splendid new road. The late President's grave is marked by a simple black marble slab protected by a stone cupola. On the adjacent summit stands a modern domed chapel.

For *Chakistra* and *Kambos*, 5km and 7km to the N, see Rte 17.

Some 4km S of Kykko is the village of **Milikouri** (775m), probably founded in the 15C. It came into prominence in 1957, when it underwent a 54-day curfew, it being announced that Colonel Grivas was in hiding there, which caused the place to be ineffectually ransacked by British troops. Its *sudjuki* (a sweetmeat of grape-juice, flour, and almonds) should be sampled, while its *zivania* is a marc which is largely exported to Russia. The medieval church was rebuilt in 1811, and contains a good late 17C iconostasis, but the icons were almost entirely ruined by amateur repainting c 1910.—From Milikouri one may follow a very rough track—not recommended for cars—leading down the valley to *Ayios Nikolaos*: see p 137.

Climbing up from Pedhoulas to the Prodhromos crossroads, we pass (left) the Churchill hotel, a pleasant centre from which to explore the area, to approach the summit of MOUNT OLYMPOS by turning left along the road to Troödos: see Rte 9A.—The village of *Prodhromos* (1390m), the second highest in Cyprus, with its Forestry College, provides extensive views over the SW slopes of the Troödos range.

For the main road hence to *Pano Platres*, see below.

An ALTERNATIVE, slightly longer, and more sinuous road is that through *Phini*, running parallel to the main route but further W on the lower flank of the Troödos massif. We climb down to **Lemithou** (1160m), with its so-called 'sacred' olive-groves (whose trees should never be cut) and near the top of the village, the small 16C church of

Ayios Theodhoros (named after the patron saint of Venice until 827, when the body of St. Mark was brought there from the East). It contains some well-preserved murals.

A track descends SW from Lemithou to the villages of *Tris Elies* and, some distance further W, *Kaminaria*. The former was the birthplace of Abp Khrysanthos (c 1720), who held office from 1767–1810, and the site of the martyrdom of St. Charalambos (198), whose relics are preserved in rebuilt *Panayia Eleousa*; that of *Arkhangelos Michael* dates from 1731.—To the right of the track forking right to neighbouring **Kaminaria** is the chapel of *Ayios Vasilios* (St. Basil), containing remnants of murals, as does *Panayia*, on a height above the village (both 16C). 18C icons may be seen in the chapel dedicated to St. Hermolaos, and in early 19C *Ayios Yeoryios*.

Continuing S from Lemithou we traverse orchards and shortly reach *Paleomylos* (1050m), where the small church of *Stavros* (17C) contains some painted woodwork. The road next skirts (right) the village of *Ayios Dhimitrios*, where the early 18C church of the same name preserves an interesting early 16C icon of the Transfiguration.

Leaving on our right the hill of LAKERAS, we bear SE, shortly passing near (right), built around a prehistoric site, the monastery of *Ayii Anargyri* (SS. Cosmas and Damian), deserted this century. The church—said by Gunnis to be haunted—is probably of the late 15C, but with zigzag moulding in its entrance arch. The iconostasis is dated 1697, and some icons and furniture of the 17th–early 18C may be seen, while on the walls are cut the names of earlier visitors, among them that of Rohr, a German traveller, and Porry, the 18C French consul.—2km beyond lies **Phini** (910m), birthplace of Abp Sophronios II (1825–1900), who welcomed the first British High Commissioner to Cyprus in 1878; it is noted for its pottery.— At *Kato Platres*, to the S (915m), also with potteries, and known for its *glyka* (a fruit sweet) we turn left, and ascending through more orchards, climb gently to *Pano Platres*: see below.

The main road follows a bridle path from Prodhromos, completed only in 1902, which skirts the W flank of the Troödos massif, affording panoramic views, and traversing apple orchards. It shortly passes (right) the settlement and monastery of *Trikoukkia* (13C, but rebuilt in 1761), with its much-venerated rain-compelling icon. Here also is a fruit-growing research station. The lowest temperature recorded in Cyprus—5°F (ˉ15°C)—was noted here in December 1941.—After some 3km we turn E and approach the Monastery of **Troödhitissa** (right; 1300m).

It is said to have been founded in 1250 as a shrine for an icon of the Virgin brought hence from Asia Minor, which according to at least one legend was hidden in a cave here from the 8C. The present church is the third constructed on this site and dates from 1731. Several dependencies added in 1780 were destroyed 20 years later in a forest fire. Limited accommodation is available.

The *Church*, with its three aisles, underwent some restoration in the 1960s, and its corrugated galvanised-iron roof has since been replaced by tiles similar to its original covering. The icon of the Virgin was plated with silver-gilt repoussé work in 1799; other relics are displayed near by, including 16C icons, and also a leather belt with silver medallions said to promote fertility in women if worn, with which the enthusiastic monks are keen to encircle the unwary!

Another 5km brings us to **Pano Platres** (1100m), a pleasant resort active through much of the year, and providing attractive views to the S. It had been a place of convalescence for British troops in the late 19C and soon grew in popularity as an escape from the heat of Nicosia; indeed it has been called the 'Simla' of Cyprus. The military chapel was later converted into the police station. With the improved main road from Nicosia via Kakopetria and Troödos (see Rte 9A), and from Limassol (Rte 11) it continues to thrive, being a good centre for making excursions into the neighbouring thickly wooded slopes of the range. Among the more attractive beauty-spots in the area are the *Caledonian Falls*, approached by a path climbing from the main road a short distance NE of the centre.

For the road hence to *Limassol* 42km S, see Rte 11 in reverse; for the road to Limassol via *Omodhos*, see Rte 12, and likewise for the roads leading down to the coast further to the W.

10 Limassol

LIMASSOL, the second town of Cyprus and (since 1974, with the Turkish occupation of Famagusta) the main port, has in the last three decades or so tripled in size, with approximately 120,000 resident inhabitants in 1988 (43,600 in 1960), largely on account of the Greek Cypriot refugees having been settled in the area since the invasion, but also by richer refugees from neighbouring Arab states, which has caused complex social problems. It is largely a mercantile town, and offers very little attraction to the casual visitor, although its Castle, District Museum, and Folk Art Museum are of interest.

It is nevertheless the venue for various Festivals—a Carnival in the spring; an Arts Festival in July; and a Wine Festival in September, etc.—but its citizens are occupied during the rest of the year in exporting a variety of products apart from the fruit and vegetables of the hinterland, in carob-kibbling, distilling, and in general manufacture and commerce. Its inhabitants have a reputation for their sociability, and it is the nearest town to the British base at Akrotiri, whose personnel seek their entertainment here. The more modern town now sprawls well beyond Makarios III Av., built as a by-pass. Another by-pass has been constructed further N, which enables one to continue W on the present motorway without going through the town.

The origin of Limassol (*Nemesos* or *Lemesos*) is obscure, and although ancient tombs have been found in the neighbourhood (including a cemetery of c 1600 BC at *Ayia Phyla*, now a suburb) the settlement was of little importance until after the decline of adjacent *Amathus* (10km to the E) and *Kourion* (c 13km to the W). Among its bishops in the Early Christian period was Leontios (590–668); a later Orthodox bishop was banished hence to Lefkara by the Latins in 1222. Richard I, Coeur de Lion, and Berengaria of Navarre (chaperoned from Sicily by widowed Queen Joanna, Richard's sister) were married here on 12 May 1191. Robert of Turnham and Richard of Camville were then appointed justiciars. It was by then partially walled, and as

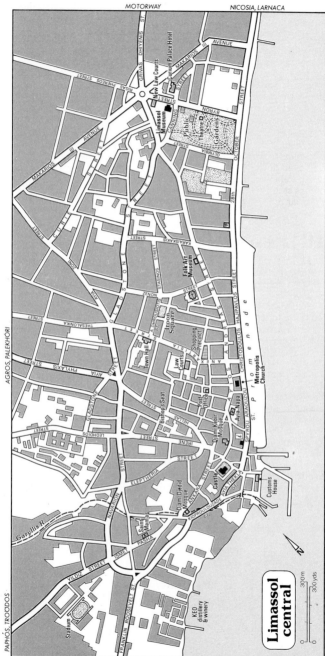

Limassol central

a Crusader base it was attacked by the Saracens. The Emperor Frederick II Hohenstaufen landed here in 1228, en route to Acre (met by Marshal Richard Filangieri and numerous Cypriot nobles, including Jean d'Ibelin), and paused here briefly on his return journey the following year, when his ward, Henry, King of Cyprus, was established and married to a daughter of the Marquis of Montferrat.

Under the Lusignans and the Knights Templar it was further developed, and its vineyards were cultivated by the Knights of St. John. It was from Limassol that in 1303 the last Grand Master of the Templars, Jacques de Molay, was summoned to Paris by Pope Clement V, to be burned at the stake six years later: the order was dissolved in 1312. Limassol was damaged by earthquakes, and in 1373 set alight by the Genoese. During the early decades of the 15C it was repeatedly sacked by Egyptian flotillas, and in 1539 it was devastated by the Turks.

Felix Faber, in 1480, remarked that only 'one wretched church remains standing, without bells... A few Latin clergy still live there, but...their habits are not edifying'; while a certain John Locke, who visited the place in 1553, observed that the 'towne is ruinated and nothing in it worth writing [about], save onely in mids of the towne there hath been a fortresse, which is now decayed, and the walls part overthrowen'. He also noticed a great number of locusts. Thirty-six years later Villamont described its poor single-storey houses as being 'built chiefly of earth covered with rushes', all the previous habitations having been destroyed in the serious earthquake of 1584. A contemporary traveller confirms that the doors of these humble abodes of the Greeks were so low that one had to stoop to enter them: 'a device to prevent the Turks bursting in and stabling their horses in private houses'. And yet these Turks apparently wore roses, violets, and other flowers in their turbans!

It had little changed by 1815, when Turner described it as 'a miserable town, consisting of 150 mud houses, of which 100 are Greeks, and 50 Turks; yet of the fifty shiploads of wine which Cyprus exports annually, twenty are on an average despatched from Limassol'. Its wine and carob exports grew considerably during the later 19C, and the town prospered. A new pier was completed in 1881, when its population was c 6100 (4057 Greek Cypriots; 1612 Turkish Cypriots). Several important buildings were destroyed by a flood in 1894. In more recent years a new port and ship-repair yards have been constructed to the SW of the centre.

George Grivas Dhigenis (1898–1974), the EOKA—and later terrorist—leader, died and was buried here.

Tourist Offices: 15 Spyrou Araouzou St, at the W end of the Promenade, and just E of the town.

At the W end of the recently widened but otherwise unprepossessing *Promenade* are warehouses, a pier, and the *Customs House*, and a few paces N of the latter, set in a garden (in which a mosaic from a Roman villa at Alasa has been relaid), is the ***Castle**, the principal antiquity of the town, recently adapted to house the **Cyprus Medieval Museum**.

The present edifice dates from the early 14C, although its W wall was in part the E wall of the earlier Byzantine fortifications, on the ruins of which it was built and in the chapel of which, in 1191 Richard I and Berengaria may have been married. The latter was then crowned Queen of England by John Fitz Luke, Bishop of Evreux, in the presence of the Archbishops of Apamea and Auch, the Bishop of

Bayonne, Guy de Lusignan (afterwards Lord of Cyprus), Bohémond III (Prince of Antioch), and Raymond III (Count of Tripoli), among others.

The central pillar supporting the vaulting of the Great Hall collapsed and part of the castle was demolished in 1525. After 1570 it became a Turkish redoubt, and a number of changes were made to its internal layout. It later served as a gaol (until 1940) and as HQ of military forces. In 1950 the vaults were strengthened, and it has since undergone further restoration.

A street in Limassol, photographed in 1878 by John Thomson

Steps ascend to the N entrance. To the right of the entrance vestibule is the *Great Hall*, from the far corner of which spiral stairs lead onto the roof (Views), from which one may descend by another stair past two floors of cells. From the lower floor steps lead down to what was probably a former chapel.

A fine collection of tombstones, plaques, sculpture, and ceramics, notably of the Lusignan and Venetian periods, has been installed, together with arms, Islamic inscriptions, etc.

A few paces to the NE of the castle is the *Djami Kebir Mosque*; another mosque stands at the W end of Ankara St, in what was once the Turkish quarter of the town, overlooking the usually dry bed of the GARYLLIS.

A short distance E of the former is the W front of **Ayia Napa**, an ungainly edifice completed in 1903, which replaced a rustic church of 1738, the walls of which were apparently covered with murals. A number of icons survived, but the interior of the modern building is garish in the extreme. The churchyard contains the tomb of Esther Harriet, infant daughter of the eccentric Reverend Joseph Wolff and his wife Georgiana (daughter of Lord Orford), who visited Cyprus in 1828.

Skirting the church, we may take the next right-hand turning to regain the PROMENADE and turning left, very shortly reach—in an alley adjacent to the *Continental Hotel*—the *Metropolis Church* (or *Ayios Andronicos*), built in 1870 in a Byzantine style. The chapel of St. Mamas preserves a late 17C carved and gilt iconostasis.

ANEXARTISIA ST, the next but one on the left, is the main thoroughfare of the old town, with a new shopping precinct on the right, while further to the N somewhat squalid streets, also on the right, lead to disreputable HEROES SQUARE.

We may follow Ayios Andreas St, the first on the right off Anexartisia St, to reach, on the left, just beyond Zenon St, at No 253, the **Folk Art Museum**. Several rooms display collections of Peasant Costume (waistcoats and breeches), Bride's chests and trousseaus; embroidery; jewellery; jackets ornamented with felt and gold thread, and blouses; furniture, carved woodwork, and tools; a section is devoted to spinning and weaving, and another to ceramics, etc.

The street continues NE to a road junction, where one may bear right along Canning St, skirting shady *Public Gardens*. On the N side of the street stands the *District Archaeological Museum*, opposite the entrance to which is the *Curium Palace* hotel.

The ***Limassol District Museum**, set back from the road, preserves in its garden a *Sundial* belonging to Kitchener.

R1 Axeheads and implements of the Neolithic and Chalcolithic I period, and sherds and tools from Sotira and Erimi; idols and querns (Neolithic II and Chalcolithic); Bronze Age ceramics, including a fine rectangular bowl; Late Cypriot and Mycenaean pottery; Cypro-Geometric ware; Cypro-Archaic ware; imported jugs decorated with subsidiary figures; Hellenistic and Graeco-Roman ware; a range of pottery from 3000 BC to the 13C AD from the Limassol area; from Amathus (12C BC–4C AD); and from Kourion (2300 BC–4C AD); a series of six amphoras (from 2300 BC) and three *dinos*.

R2 Statuettes, lamps and glassware; terracotta figurines (note ear-perforations), and chariots; cylinder-seals, etc.; jewellery from 17C BC–4C AD; shell necklaces, ivories, and picrolite objects; glass, alabasters, lamps, and limestone statuettes. Note the poppy on a ring of pottery.—Two cases display coins found in the district, including that of the Emperor Caracalla (AD 211–17) showing the Temple of Aphrodite at Palea Paphos (see also p 149) and gold coins of Heraclius and his son Constantine (c 613–39). Other objects include razors and fibulae; a bronze bull, bronze mirrors, and a strigil or skin-scraper; and a collection of amulets.

R3 Two capitals from Amathus (6C BC), and one of the Hathor type (Cypro-Archaic II); statues of the Egyptian god Bes and of Artemis-Hekate (325–150 BC); lower part of a cross-legged statue from Amathus; bearded head from Phasoula (4C AD); funerary stelae, including that of Theotime, daughter of Apollonios (2C BC), with two rosettes; two cippi; a round marble table from Kourion on a limestone base from Amathus; a headless statue of Zeus holding an eagle (4C AD); terracotta busts, including sphinxes supporting cups; a bull-masked figure; sarcophagi; etc.

The Promenade can be regained by turning down Byron St, skirting the Public Gardens, in which there is a small *Zoo*.

A short distance SW of the town—to the left of the Akrotiri and Paphos road—is the *KEO Distillery and Winery*, which may be visited during normal working hours.

For roads from Limassol to Larnaca, see Rte 3; to Nicosia, Rtes 6, 7, 8, and 9, all in reverse; for Paphos, Rte 13.

11   Limassol to Pano Platres, for Nicosia

Approximately 40km (25 miles). An alternative but slower road is
that via *Omodhos*, described in reverse in Rte 12, a possible return
journey.

Driving NW from Limassol, we follow part of the old Military Road,
recently improved, which passes near the site of a former British
Army camp at *Kato Polemidhia* (now a suburb of Limassol), c 2km
NW of which are the ruins of a mid-14C Carmelite church (*Karmi*).
We later cross a ridge to meet the 'old' road up the Kouris valley
just N of *Khalassa*. Near this village, also known as *Alasa*, is a late
Bronze Age site, now covered by the waters of a reservoir.

We soon get a good view ahead of the Troödos range, and
by-pass (left) **Monagri**, whose villagers were Linobambakoi (see
Glossary) in the 16–19Cs. The church of *Ayios Yeoryios* (16C,
largely rebuilt in 1872) preserves some paintings in its vault.—To
the NW, right of the road, stand the relics of a small monastery
dedicated to *Arkhangelos Michael*, possibly dating from the 12C,
and rebuilt in the 1780s. One wall is painted.—To the S near the
river is the restored monastery of *Panayia Amasgou* (early 16C),
with paintings of the early 12C, early 13C and 16C, cleaned by
Dumbarton Oaks in 1969–72.

4km further NW is **Silikou**, where the last of the Lusignans is said to have
hidden to avoid detection by the Turks in 1570. Of the many ruined chapels
in the vicinity, one dedicated to the Baptist had (according to Gunnis)
adopted a curious custom of rolling children suffering from malaria up and
down the floor by the altar three times, to effect their cure. Silikou was a halt
on the 'Military Road' constructed by the British in 1879–80, which led from
Polemidhia Camp to the camp at Troödos.

5km *Trimiklini*, which we next traverse, has a church of 1744, N of
which we bear left, leaving the old road ascending to the Karvounos crossroads and directly to *Kakopetria* to our right; see p 124 in
reverse.

The left-hand turning at the crossroads leads due W.—After 3km a lane leads
left to the hamlet of *Kouka*, said to date from as early as the 8C if not before,
where the cruciform domed church of *Stavros* is said to contain as a relic the
dust (sawdust?) from the *suppedaneum* (or foot-support) of the (? True) Cross,
when it was sawn into pieces by order of St. Helena.—*Perapedhi* (760m) lies
to the left 1km beyond this turning, a village dating from the 16C or earlier,
still dominated by its old wine factory (1891), in use during the season. It is
also reputed for its apples. *Ayios Nikolaos* (1796) contains a 16C icon of the
Virgin.
A road descends a rocky, wooded gorge to the S, in which (right) stands
the re-roofed church of *Ayia Mavra, a 15C monotholos with a later narthex,
containing naïve wall-paintings of some interest. The holy well here is said to
have gushed forth at a crevice in the rock through which St. Mavra disappeared when fleeing from her father and husband on the night of her
enforced marriage, the cliff opening in answer to her despairing supplication
to the Virgin.
The road goes on to **Kilani** (825m), an old village where in 1191 Richard I,
Coeur de Lion, destroyed a camp of Isaac Comnemos. In the 17C the Orthodox bishopric was briefly here during the temporary decline of Limassol. In
1690 Mehmed Boyajioglu, who had led a rebellion against Kapudan Pasha
for almost seven years, was eventually caught here. Kilani was the birthplace
of Kyprianos (the 18C historian and archimandrite: his History was published
in 1788), and of Abp Paisios (died 1768). It had a reputation in the 18C for its
silk scarves and veils.—A road continues SW to (3km) **Vouni**, a well-sited

village of old red-roofed stone houses.—3km SE of Kilani is *Lophos*, an old village of steep cobbled streets.

From the Trimiklini crossroads we climb NW on a much improved road, by-passing (left) *Moniatis*, and after 6km bear abruptly left to enter *Pano Platres*: see p 129.

For the roads hence to *Nicosia* via *Kakopetria*, and *Pedhoulas*, see Rtes 9A and 9B in reverse.

12 Pano Platres to Limassol via Omodhos

44km (27 miles)

Descending through *Kato Platres* (see latter part of Rte 9B) at *Mandria* (left) we bear right for (3km) **Omodhos** (800m), lying amidst its vineyards, probably founded c 1150, and in c 1400 owned by Sir John de Brie, Prince of Galilee. (An improved road from Mandria leads W to *Ayios Nikolaos*; see below.) There is an old, now restored, wine press here. The village is reputed for its lace.

The Byzantine church of the famous **Monastery of Stavros**, which stood in the middle of the village, was later replaced by a new edifice, rebuilt on a larger scale in c 1930.

The iconostasis of 1817 contains an icon of St. Philip (1773), whose skull in its reliquary (depicted on the icon), is kept in the apse together with other relics, including yet another splinter of the True Cross, and the hempen *Ropes* that bound the hands of Christ, incorporated within two large crosses of silver-gilt repoussé work. On the N exterior wall of the church is an inscription over the grave of a Major Henry Rooke, who died here in 1811.—The two-storey dependencies of the monastic enclosure house a poor 'Folk Museum'; but note the ceiling and a room devoted to the guerrilla activities of members of EOKA. The woodcarving in the *Synod Hall* (1812) is also of interest.

The road now climbs along the flank of a ridge, after 2km passing (right) a turning descending to *Vasa* (690m), an old village founded c 1250 or earlier and at one time belonging to the Hospitallers. In the centre are ruins of a Venetian watch-tower near which villagers found some Venetian swords, which they gave to Rupert Gunnis when he visited the place in 1933; they are now in the Cyprus Museum, Nicosia. Outside the village is the small domed church of *Ayios Yeoryios* (15C), while to the NE stood the monastery of *Pente Litharia*, probably of the same period.

A lower road from Omodhos traverses the village of *Potamiou*, in which *Ayia Marina* (1551) is crowned by a central octagonal dome. Just S of the village are the ruins of *Ayios Mnason*, reputed to be built on the site of that Cypriot saint's tomb (cf. Tamassos).

Upon reaching the main road to *Limassol*, bear left.

For roads leading W and then SW towards the coast from this junction, see below.

After 2km a right-hand turning leads S to **Pakhna** (1350 inhab.; 700m), surrounded by stone-walled vineyards, in and near which are a number of ruined chapels.

From here the road continues S via *Prastio*, near which is the curious barrel-vaulted church of *Panayia* (early 18C), abutted by two domed 14C chapels.— Further S, beyond *Evdhimou*, is the coastal road: see p 146.

The road now traverses **Ayios Amvrosios**, from which a minor road ascends left to (5km) *Vouni* (see Rte 11).

The next track to the left leads to *Ayios Therapon*, where a hard *haloumi* cheese is produced.

We shortly pass (left) the church of *Stavros* (15C), deserted and decaying, with a brick-built apse. To the E is the abandoned village of *Pano Kividhes*, which has been replaced by a new village of the same name, through which we also pass, and beyond which the road descends rapidly towards the bed of the KOURIS at (9km) *Kandou*.

Before entering Kandou a right-hand turning ascends 5km to **Sotira**, where the church of *Metamorphosis* (rebuilt 1553) contains an ornate iconostasis and icons of St. George (17C) and of the Virgin (early 16C, but damaged). On the hill to the W, approached by a track circling to the N, is a Neolithic II site of square-walled habitations excavated in 1947–54, producing 'combed ware' pottery. Unlike *Khirokitia*, the dead were placed in adjacent pit-graves not below the floors.

The Turkish Cypriot community of **Kandou** abandoned the village in 1974 and its houses were occupied by Greek Cypriot refugees the following year. In the neighbourhood are three chapels: *Panayia Khrysopolitissa* and *Ayia Marina*, both 15C, are S of the village and contain old murals; *Ayia Napa* (16C) also with murals, but decayed, lies on the far bank of the river.

We meet the main coast road just S of *Kandou*. Immediately before reaching the junction a right-hand turning leads past the ruins of *Pamboula* to the village of *Episkopi*, on the far side of which is the Museum (see Rte 13).

The left-hand turning at the junction leads past (left) *Erimi* and further E, *Kolossi* (see Rte 13). It then skirts the N boundary of the *Western British Sovereign Base Area* to approach the W outskirts of **Limassol**; see Rte 10.

From the road junction 5km S of *Omodhos* three other roads descend towards the coast. To follow any of these, fork right to by-pass (right) *Mallia*, amongst its vineyards, to reach another junction.

FROM MALLIA TO KOUKLIA VIA DHORA. The left-hand fork here leads to (6km) *Dhora*, beyond which the road deteriorates. **Dhora** (620m) has two churches: well-built *Ayia Marina* of 1598; and, on a hill to the S, *Panayia*, built on earlier foundations. According to legend, when the villagers pulled down the old church to erect another nearer the village, whatever they built during the day was destroyed during the following night by the Virgin, so that they were obliged to rebuild it on the original site. A famous rain-compelling icon of the Virgin is preserved here.

A minor road leads 6km SW to the village of **Pano Arkhimandrita** (400m), to the S of which, on a track to the lower village, is the hermitage of *Ayii Pateres*, possibly a former Roman rock tomb and containing some frescoes. In a niche of the N wall are some bones said to be the remains of 318 saints slaughtered here by heathens when they landed on the coast at *Pissouri* after escaping from persecution in Syria, but no historical record of the event has survived.—*Kouklia* (see p 147) lies some 11km further SW.

FROM MALLIA TO THE COAST BEYOND NIKOKLIA VIA PRETORI AND KEDHARES. This road (off which the third turns) forks right at the junction just W of *Mallia*, and climbs N to **Arsos** (790m), known for its dark red wine. On the outskirts is an ancient church, rebuilt, containing 17C icons. Relics of the 6C BC have been discovered in the neighbourhood.—The road continues to climb, then curves down through *Ayios Nikolaos*, just N of which stands *Arkhangelos Michael* (13C): until c 1928 it had both Latin and Orthodox altars; in the apse lies a large decorated marble slab; there is also a marble font.—Now bearing SW, the road shortly by-passes (right) **Pretori** (650m), said to be named after Prator, a Roman general who owned a villa here; its church contains a once-venerated icon of the Virgin (16C), covered by silver-gilt repoussé work.—The junction at which the third road diverges is reached after 1km: see below.

We traverse **Kedhares**, beyond which we pass (right) *Ayios Antonios* (17C; restored), with a steeply-pitched roof; its icons are preserved in the more modern church.—The road now descends steeply into the DHIARIZOS valley, shortly crossing the river, and bears left through the hamlet of *Kithasi*. The valley narrows, with huge rocks overhanging the ravine.

On the far side of the riverbed, at the settlement of *Prastio*, is a deserted late 15C church, its walls formed from unhewn rocks, as are those of the smaller church of *Ayios Elias* on the W bank of the river. Also on the far bank, SW of the settlement, at the edge of an olive grove, is the ruined monastery of *Ayios Savvas tis Karonos*, its church rebuilt in 1502, restored in the first half of the 18C, and recently repaired. Some of the carved stonework, both of the church and of the monastic dependencies, is notable, and the unrestored icons are in a reasonable state of preservation.

We soon reach *Mamonia*, where in 1308 John de Dampierre, Constable of Cyprus, died.—6km beyond, on the far bank, lies *Souskiou*, where the modern church preserves an important icon of Christ (c 1520).—The main Limassol–Paphos road is reached after a further 5km, beyond *Nikoklia*, a hamlet named after Nikokles, King of Paphos c 320 BC. Its church (1768) contains a number of icons contemporary with its construction, while adjacent lie a marble Corinthian capital and column, probably from *Palea Paphos*, to the S on the far bank of the Dhiarizos: see p 147.

FROM PRETORI TO THE COAST VIA ARMINOU AND KELOKEDHARA. The third road, descending right at the junction just before *Kedhares*, shortly veers W to cross the DHIARIZOS before climbing in steep zig-zags to *Arminou*, once inhabited by Armenians. The church of *Stavros* (c 1750) contains a silver-gilt plaque of Christ on the Cross, said by the locals to have come from *Souskiou* (see above) on its own accord, causing some friction between the two villages.—A right-hand turning just beyond Arminou leads across to (4km) *Ayios Ioannis*, on the steep W slope of the ridge, and abandoned by its Turkish Cypriot community in 1975. In the valley below is the rebuilt *Medieval Bridge* spanning the ROUDHIAS.—We approach *Mesana*, to the SE of which, amongst vineyards at the foot of the valley by the river, lies the monastery of *Ayios Yeoryios* (late 15C), containing some well- preserved carving, and unrestored 16C icons.—**Salamiou** is shortly reached, to the E of which stands *Panavia Eleousa* (16C; repaired 1916), retaining some early 17C icons.

The road now crosses towards the W slope of the ridge through (5km) **Kelokedhara**.

To the NW, in the valley of the XEROS POTAMOS, stand dependencies forming three sides of a square, of the monastery of *Santi* or *Sindi*, founded c

1500. The large church of *Panayia Eleousa*, with a hexagonal dome and square apse, is well-preserved. In local legend it is associated with ruined *Ayia Paraskevi*, on the far side of the stream.

The road goes on through (5km) *Stavrokono* to join the coast road 9km beyond.

13 Limassol to Paphos via Kolossi, Kourion, and Kouklia

71km (44 miles).

Although the direct route to *Kolossi* by-passing Ypsonas is frac-tionally shorter, the pleasanter approach is that bearing SW from Limassol via the *Phasouri Plantations* and along a eucalyptus and cypress-shaded road. **Ypsonas** (3050 inhab.) is named after the gypsum (Greek *gypsos*) found there.

After passing (left) the *KEO Distillery* (which may be visited during working hours) we reach a road junction, and the main approach to the *New Port.*—A left-hand turning further W leads to the extensive beach known as the *Lady's Mile*, E of the *Salt Lake*; see below.

The plantations which the road now traverses, in some places through a tunnel of trees, were established in the early 1930s by the Cyprus Palestine Plantation Company on land reclaimed from a marshy district to the N of the Salt Lake. It is now largely devoted to the cultivation of citrus fruits and sultana raisins, while honey is also produced. Visits to these farms may be made, preferably by prior arrangement with the Tourist Office.

We eventually reach a T-junction just within the AKROTIRI or WESTERN BRITISH SOVEREIGN BASE AREA. The left-hand turning traverses the AKROTIRI PENINSULA, where in the 19C wild-boar hunting was a popular sport, and shortly skirts the W edge of the **Salt Lake** which, like that at Larnaca, is a stop for migrant birds, in particular flamingos. At the lake's SW corner the road climbs gently SE past the village of *Akrotiri*.

The next left-hand turning (a rough track) leads (c 2.5km) to the remains, amid vineyards and citrus plantations, of the monastery of *Ayios Nikolaos*, better known as that of **St. Nicholas of the Cats**. It was founded c 325 by Basilians. According to Cypriot tradition, St. Helena of the Cross was responsible for introducing felines to combat the reptile population, as at *Stavrovouni*, and as companions for the monks in preference to catamites. The present stone-vaulted building dating from the 13–15C, was abandoned soon after the Turkish occupation of 1570, and mutilated. It has now been restored. Note the four carved shields on the marble lintel of the N entrance.

Immediately to the S is the runway of the RAF airfield.

The main road continues through the extensive cantonments of the base area to CAPE GATA (to the SE), the southernmost point of the island, with a lighthouse, and named after the cats of the monastery. To the SW is CAPE ZEVGARI, and the *Princess Mary Military Hospital*. In the cliffs to the E, towards Cape Gata, 125 chamber tombs and 57 sarcophagi have been counted. Relics of 8th millennia habitation—the oldest on the island—have been discovered on the peninsula, together with remains of the pigmy hippopotami.

The castle of Kolossi

The right-hand turning at the above-mentioned T-junction leads in 3km to the **Castle of Kolossi**, with its conspicuous four-square keep, one of the more interesting and attractively sited monuments of its period in Cyprus.

It was the camp of Isaac Comnenos which Richard I, Coeur de Lion captured here in 1191, but no fort was then described. The Knights Hospitaller were granted land in the area by Hugh I in 1210, and presumably built the first fortifications. After the fall of Acre in 1291, the headquarters of the Order of St. John of Jerusalem were moved to Limassol, and shortly afterwards to Kolossi. It was also briefly, until 1308, in the hands of the Knights Templar but their properties were then confiscated and the Order was abolished (see Limassol History). Although the headquarters of the Hospitallers were again transferred in 1310, this time to Rhodes, a Commandery remained at Kolossi, which was confirmed as their headquarters in 1380.

The fortress controlled some 40 villages; and there were minor Commanderies at *Templos* or *Temblos* (SW of Kyrenia) and at *Phinikas* (E of Paphos). These well-irrigated estates were particularly rich in madder, sugar-cane plantations, and vineyards; and the produce of the latter is still known as 'Commandaria' wine. Although much damaged, the castle was successfully defended against the Genoese in 1373 and 1402, but its lands were ravaged in the Mameluke raids of 1425–26. The fortress was largely rebuilt in the mid 15C by the Grand Commander, Louis de Magnac, who was succeeded in 1468 by John Langstrother, an Englishman (who was eventually beheaded by Edward IV after the Battle of Tewkesbury). Kolossi later passed into the possession of the Cornaro family, and the titular rank of Grand Commander of Cyprus remained with them until 1799, although the estate fell to the Turks in 1570.

John Locke, an English traveller visiting the island a few years before the Turkish occupation, refers to the pickled 'beccaficos' which the knights introduced to the Venetians as a great delicacy, large quantities being exported (cf. Paralimni). The Turks carried on the adjacent 'sugar-factory', but business declined with the rise of the West Indian industry. In 1750 Alexander Drummond was incensed at finding the great gate of the castle 'buried in some vile houses, so that I could not see it'; but the fortress was still in use as a farm building in the second decade of this century, and the battlements were only restored in 1933.

The entrance to the enceinte is by the Guardian's lodge, from which we approach the E entrance of the *Keep* of three storeys surmounted by a crenellated terrace. Note the machicolations, and coat of arms above the entrance on the E side, believed to be that of Louis de Magnac (see History), set below the royal quarters of Jerusalem, Lusignan, Cyprus, and Armenia, and flanked by those of Jean de Lastic and Jacques de Milli, Grand Masters of Rhodes from 1427.

On the interior wall (right) is a damaged mural of the Crucifixion. The first floor consists of two intercommunicating vaulted chambers set N–S, while those of the second floor are set E–W. Note the fireplace in the far room of this upper floor, which is decorated with chain and leaf motifs; also the side seats of the windows built into the massive walls. The spiral staircase ascends to the roof (*Views*). The basement consists of three chambers, set E–W.

To the right of the exit is an area formerly occupied by store-rooms, stables, and other dependencies. In the far corner of the enceinte are remains of a round tower beside which is a postern gate. The well-head and semi-circular tower to the E are relics of earlier fortifications.—Of interest is the *Sugar-factory*, with five large vaults, and also the mill-race. Note also the double wall on the W side, with staggered arches; the attractive oculi on the gable; and the heavily buttressed E wall.

On approaching the village of *Kolossi* (2350 inhab.), to the N, we pass a small chapel (left), and turn left on meeting the main road from Limassol.

On the E outskirts of (2km) **Erimi**, to the right of the road, is the site of a Chalcolithic settlement where circular stone huts were excavated in 1933 to a depth of nine successive occupation layers. The neighbouring churches of *Panayia Khrysopolitissa* (15C) and ruined *Ayios Yeoryios* (16C) are of slight interest. We cross the river KOURIS and bear left, but those wishing first to visit the *Museum* at Episkopi before exploring the site of Kourion (see below) should turn right, then immediately left, and follow the sign-posts.

Episkopi (2550 inhab.), was once walled, and in the 7C was the seat of an Orthodox bishop, hence its name. In the 13–14C it was owned by Jean d'Ibelin, Count of Jaffa, and by the Cornaro family. The principal church (*Ayia Paraskevi*), recently rebuilt, contains a 17C icon; that of *Panayia*, used by the Turks as a grain store until 1974, preserves some murals; near it are the ruins of *Ayios Antonios*, of which the double lancet windows of the apse remain. *Ayios Yeoryios* (15–16C), until recently the village mosque, with a minaret, has had its murals whitewashed.

A number of excavations are taking place in the area, including those at the site of *Phaneromeni*, between the village and the W bank of the Kouris, where a Middle to Late Cypriot settlement and cemetery have been uncovered; among the artefacts found there are numerous pottery vases of unique shape and decoration, and probably of a local type.

The **Kourion Museum** occupies the house of the late George McFadden, the American archaeologist who initiated systematic excavations at Kourion in 1933, and started the collection in 1937.

The W wing contains terracotta figurines, votive figures and figures of horsemen; terracotta lamps (5–2C BC); bronze strigils, mirrors, and arrowheads; picrolite and faience seals and scarabs, and cylinder seals of Late Cypriot III date from *Kalorziki* (c 1km SW); coins; limestone heads, and carved couples; a 2C AD marble head of Aphrodite from Kourion; a sculpted Boy on a dolphin; Bacchus, Melaeger, and other statues, and pottery, including White Painted ware, Black-on- Red ware, Cypro-Archaic I Red Slip ware from Episkopi, and Cypro-Geometric I Bichrome dishes from Kalorziki; a marble statue of Hermes Pastor, dated 2C AD; and a 5C BC syllabic inscription referring to a prince of Kourion.

The E wing contains material from the *Sanctuary of Apollo* and from the sites of *Bamboula* (just NE of the village) and *Phaneromeni*. This includes 7–6C BC terracotta chariot models from the sanctuary; faience vases; a six-sided picrolite seal; dedicatory inscriptions—one of which records a building at the sanctuary by Trajan; gold ornaments and ivory objects; 14C BC Mycenaean pottery from Bamboula; and Early Cypriot II and III Red Polished ware from Phaneromeni. Note also a marble lion fountain (Roman) and a medieval marble lion from the Baths of the Sanctuary of Apollo.

S of the main crossroads in the centre of the village is a group of ruins known as the *Serayia*, relics of a 15–16C sugar-mill, including part of a chapel with a side aisle on the S, with an *opus sectile* floor, and marble reliefs from the Kourion basilica. Hundreds of cone-shaped clay pots were discovered here in 1979, used in the manufacture of sugar from crushed cane.

On leaving Episkopi, the once substantial church of *Panayia Khrysanyiotissa* is passed on the right. To the left, below the limestone cliffs of Kourion, is the chapel of *Ayios Hermogenos* (or *Ermoyenis*), possibly from the Byzantine era, and containing the tomb of that saint; surrounding it is a Roman necropolis, extensively plundered.

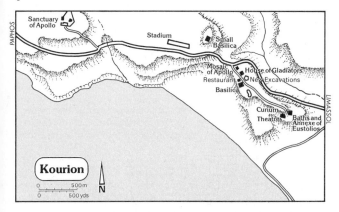

The road now climbs to the cliff top, in part artificially scarped, to the entrance (left) to the *Acropolis* of **KOURION*, one of the most important and spectacular ancient sites in Cyprus. It commands from its height a panoramic sea view.

Although the district has been inhabited since the Neolithic (see *Sotira*, 6km N; and *Erimi*, 3km NE), and during the Bronze Age at nearby *Phaneromeni*, the first settlement in the immediate area was probably on an eminence near the Temple of Apollo, c 2km further W. It is likely that this site was populated by Dorians from Argos in the Peloponnese in 1595 BC, and it was possibly named after Koureus, son of a Greek immigrant. The Greek city played an important part in the rebellion against the Persians in 498 BC, but by changing sides at a crucial moment it helped the Persians to take Salamis and thus gain control of the island. Conversely, Pasicrates, the last King of Kourion, supported Alexander the Great by leading his fleet against the Persians at the siege of Tyre (332 BC).

Kourion retained its prosperity under the Romans, and was referred to by Strabo, who mentions the adjacent promontory from which they hurled those who had the temerity to touch the altar of Apollo. Its citizens later accepted Christianity, and after destructive earthquakes in the 4C AD, a basilica was erected. Arab raiders attacked the town in the 7C; and the bishop transferred his residence to neighbouring Episkopi, as it became known, and Kourion soon declined into insignificance.

In 1876 it was the site of one of General Luigi Palma di Cesnola's excavations. He claimed to have discovered, close to the theatre here, the superb hoard of gold and silver objects known as the Curium Treasure, which was later sold to the Metropolitan Museum, New York. This caused endless controversy, for it was then argued that the treasure was the proceeds of his ransacking of tombs throughout the island during the previous decade; and that the area said to have been dug over by the American consul had in fact been undisturbed. Excavations have continued sporadically since: see individual sites.

Immediately to the left by the main road is the *Achilles Mosaic*, near which the Paphos Gate must have stood. It is part of the pavement of what was once the colonnaded portico of an important building, and depicts the legend of Achilles, disguised as a maiden, accidentally revealing his identity to Odysseus; a smaller mosaic in an adjacent room represents Ganymede being carried off to Olympos by an eagle.

To the left a few paces further along the road is the so-called *House of the Gladiators*, in the courtyard of which is a colourful mosaic showing two gladiators in combat.—Slight remains of a *Roman Aqueduct* may also be seen nearby. (Should these two sites be closed, interested visitors should request the loan of the keys from the site Guardian, whose lodge is a short distance further S.) To the right is a Tourist Pavilion and car park.

Immediately to the right of the main enclosure are the extensive ruins of an Early Christian *****Basilica**, probably erected in the 5C, and the 'cathedral' of the early bishops of Kourion. It is abutted to the N by a *Baptistery* of the 6C, excavated by A.H.S. Megaw, a former Director (1935–59) of the Department of Antiquities of Cyprus.

Steps descend between two columns placed between the two buildings. To the left is the *Basilica*, some 70m long and 40m wide. The roof of the nave and two aisles were originally supported by two rows of 12 granite columns on marble bases and with marble capitals. There is a single apse, just below which are four bases of columns which presumably supported a baldachin over the altar. Traces of mosaic pavement can be seen, but much of it has been ploughed up. The aisles are flanked by stone-paved corridors, while to the W, beyond its narthex, is a forecourt and hexagonal water-tank.

The buildings to the W, including those surrounding the adjacent atrium entered from the narthex, may well have been those of the *Bishop's Palace*.—The atrium of the Baptistery, the remains of which are better preserved than the Basilica, is surrounded by marble colonnades, but only one column with its capital has survived. This also has a hexagonal water-tank or phiale in its centre. The remains of several smaller columns seem to indicate the existence of an upper colonnade. Evidence of an earlier structure has also been found, suggesting that the Christian edifice was constructed largely from the ruins of an important pagan building, possibly thrown down in the earthquakes of 332 and 342.

Two steps ascend to the main *Baptistery*, likewise with a nave, two aisles, and an apse. In a recess of the S wall there is a small marble-sided cruciform basin for baptismal immersion.

The earthquakes (see above) destroyed a large public building to the left of the entrance lodge, which is now being excavated. The outer back wall of dressed limestone blocks and some inner divisions have been unearthed, and the structure was possibly connected with the public baths of Kourion, later abandoned.

Several large cisterns have also been found, and the colonnaded building is now thought to be the stoa of a Roman *forum* of the second half of the 2C AD. Further N is a shell-shaped niche among several larger niches which together with other features identify it as a *nymphaeum* (45m long and 15m wide), dating from the 1C AD to the 7C. A spirally fluted column of grey marble has also been uncovered.

Kourion, the theatre

The road continues on to the *Theatre*, the *Baths*, and the so-called *Annexe of Eustolios*. The superbly sited **Theatre* was excavated in 1949–50, and partly reconstructed since 1961. It comprises a curved auditorium seating 3500, entered through five gangways approached by a vaulted corridor running round the back of the theatre. The original orchestra was circular; behind the present semi-circular orchestra are the foundations of the scene-building. It is probable that the original small theatre on the Greek model (late 2C BC) was adapted during the Roman period, and enlarged to its present dimensions in the 2C AD. The scene-building was again re-modelled, and part of the outer wall buttressed. The theatre was abandoned in the 4C, and subsequently served as a quarry.

Since its recent restoration it has been the venue of public performances of music and drama during summer months, for details of which enquire at Tourist Offices.

Immediately to the NE, and at a higher level, is the complex known as the ***Annexe of Eustolios**. Palatial in size, and originally built as a private villa, it was probably later used as a place for public recreation. It post-dates the abandonment of the theatre, and its mosaic floors were not completed until the early 5C AD, by which time Christianity was established in the city.

Floor mosaic in the Annexe of Eustolios, depicting Ktisis or the Founding Spirit, personified as a woman holding a measuring rod

From its W entrance we cross the vestibule, to the left of which lie servants' quarters. The mosaic floor contains a welcoming inscription. Beyond is a rectangular garden courtyard, around three sides of which ran a portico and mosaic pavement. Fragmentary inscriptions refer to Eustolios (the builder), and Apollo (the former patron of the site), while another specifically refers to Christ. Note also the fish and birds.

(Form F. 19.)

F

№ 279919

IMPORTANT
Please keep
your ticket

REPUBLIC OF CYPRUS

Department of — Antiquities

*The Museums and Ancient Monuments
(Admission Fees) Regulations, 1950*

ADMIT ONE TO KOURION SITE

Valid for one visit on...

Price 50 cents

Steps to the N of this court ascend to the **Baths**, the central room of which has a mosaic floor of four colourful panels—one depicting a partridge and another a bust of Ktisis, a female figure personifying the 'Founding Spirit', holding an object similar to a standard measure, and almost exactly the length of a late Roman foot. The apse-like sections to the N and E are *frigidaria*, with a shallow foot-bath preceding each. To the W is the *tepidarium*; and beyond, the *caldarium*, preserving built-in basins, and heated by hypocausts. The firing chambers and air ducts have also survived. To the N is a large water-storage tank, presumably supplied by the above-mentioned aqueduct near the custodian's lodge.

Other excavated areas of ancient Kourion—the Stadium, and the Sanctuary of Apollo—lie c 1km and c 2km W of the Acropolis, and N of the Paphos road, which we now follow.

The **Stadium**, partially uncovered in 1939 and 1947, is recognisable by its U-shaped plan, and by its entrance gates, one on each side and one in the centre of the rounded end. It dates from the 2C, but was abandoned in the mid 4C. A section of seating, which would have originally accommodated c 6000 spectators, has been reconstructed, comprising seven rows raised above the track.—A small late 5C *Basilica* has been excavated c 200m E of the stadium.

A sign-posted track shortly leads right, off the main road, to the **SANCTUARY OF APOLLO, or more correctly of Apollo Hylates, God of the Woodland (in this case of not unattractive scrub forest). The existing remains were almost all erected c AD 100, and were destroyed by earthquakes, probably in the mid 4C; several walls have been re-erected, having been found lying flat on the ground as they had fallen. These had themselves replaced structures laid waste by an earthquake of AD 76–77. Artefacts discovered there prove that the cult of Apollo had been celebrated here from as early as the 8C BC.

The partially restored Sanctuary of Apollo

A path leads W from the Guardian's lodge to the enclosure by the site of the *Paphos Gate*. To the left of this entrance a broad flight of steps ascends to a building consisting of two long chambers thought to have accommodated either visitors to the sanctuary or their votive offerings.—To the right, behind a long Doric portico, only part of it preserved, is a series of five large rooms separated from each other by corridors. Each room has a raised dais on three sides, divided from the central paved area by Doric colonnades. The central room has been partially restored. Similarities in the design of this so-called *South Building* with that to the NW suggest that they may have had the same function. According to an inscription, two of these rooms were erected in AD 101.—From almost opposite the Doric portico a street leads N towards the remains of the Temple of Apollo, to the right of which was a *bothroi*, or pit, into which any excess of votive offerings was discreetly placed in order to provide room for later contributions; an accumulation of terracotta figurines and pottery from the 5C BC was discovered here when it was excavated.

The small *Temple of Apollo* (early 1C AD), now partly restored with the help of the Leventis Foundation, is preceded by a monumental flight of steps and a portico, and it was here that rituals dictated by the cult took place: it was the altar here that Strabo himself referred to when stating that those who dared to touch it were forthwith flung from the cliffs of Kourion.—Retracing our steps, we pass (left) the *Archaic Precinct* in which votive offerings, antedating those in the *bothroi*, have been uncovered, including a bronze belt fragment worked in repoussé, representing two lions devouring a griffin, and ascribed to the 6–5C BC. The buildings here may have accommodated the officiating priests, and the treasury.

Regaining the main paved area, we descend a flight of steps (left) on the site of the *Kourion Gate*. To the right is the *Palaestra*, tentatively dated to the Augustan period, but erected above mid 4C walls. A small stone cistern lies in the near corner of the colonnaded courtyard here, in which athletic visitors might indulge themselves in sweaty games before taking their baths. The adjacent complex of *Baths* lies just to the N, which, following the normal plan, consists of *frigidarium*, *tepidarium* and *caldarium*.

The main road continues W, and we shortly enter the *Episkopi Cantonment*, forming the W end of the WESTERN BRITISH SOVEREIGN BASE AREA (and containing its HQ), and descend in sweeping curves to skirt 'Happy Valley', with its polo fields, playing fields, and stadium.

A tunnel here penetrates the E slope to reach the beach, golf course, Inter-Service Yacht Club, and other amenities.

Climbing out of the valley, after 5km we reach crossroads some distance to the N of the village of **Evdhimou**, once walled and of importance as the centre of Lusignan and Venetian provinces. According to Mariti it was one of the four cities built for Arsinoë by her brother Ptolemy Philadelphus. Until 1974 it was almost entirely a Turkish Cypriot village, and built into the walls of its principal mosque are stones from an ancient church on this site. The Mamelukes landed with over 3000 troops on the coast here in 1426.—5km further N lies *Prastio*; see p 135.

Anoyira (470m), 3km NW of Evdhimou, has a Chalcolithic II cemetery site, and several ancient churches on the right of the approaching road. Among them is the deserted late Byzantine monastery of *Timios Stavros*, in which some tombs are preserved; opposite the church are the foundations of a small Roman temple. Further N is recently demolished *Ayia Varvara*, also of the Byzantine period, and *Arkhangelos Michael* (1794) containing a women's gallery among other features and an unusual sundial on the S wall, probably from an earlier edifice.

To the N of the main road lie three villages—*Ayios Thomas*, *Plataniskia*, and *Alekhtora*—recently abandoned by their Turkish Cypriot communities and resettled by Greek Cypriot refugees—which stood on an older road. The last named was of some importance in medieval times judging by the number of ruins in the vicinity, the best preserved of which is *Ayios Kassianos*, c 2km to the NE, where a 4C German saint of that name is said to be buried.—*Ayios Yeoryios*, on the road to Pissouri, once contained murals, but these have been destroyed by smoke from shepherds' fires lit in the interior.

After 3km we pass (left) *Ayios Mavrikios*, set amongst vineyards, probably a Latin chapel dedicated to St. Maurice; and then a lane leading S to PISSOURI BAY (now being developed as a small resort), flanked by precipitous CAPE ASPRO. The main road climbs, off which a left-hand turning ascends to **Pissouri** itself, perched on a cliff at an elevation of 245m, and commanding extensive views.

We shortly pass (left) the rock-hewn chapel of *Ayios Elias*, in which some wall-paintings survive, before beginning the long descent towards a barren flat-topped limestone hill, behind which we turn to reach the sea, passing (right) the approach to a Tourist Pavilion providing a pleasant sea view. Beyond are the rocks of *Petra tou Romiou* on the edge of a small pebbly beach celebrated in legend as the birthplace of Aphrodite (see below). The scrub woods on the hills to the N are called RANDI FOREST.

After 6km the road veers inland, and we see on a height (half-right) the prominently sited *Royal Manor*, or *Covocle*, behind which, approached by the next right-hand turning, is the village of **Kouklia** and the site of **PALEA PAPHOS**, so-called *Palea* (old) to distinguish it from New or *Nea Paphos* some 16km NW—now *Kato Paphos*; see Rte 14. A new approach road leads right immediately on turning off the main road, ascending towards the Covocle.

First inhabited c 1500 BC, the site was later occupied by settlers from the Aegean, and became the capital of one of the first Cypriot kingdoms, and as such it was attacked by the Persians in 498 BC. It was for centuries renowned as the centre of the Cult of Aphrodite, the foundation of her temple being ascribed by Pausanias to Agepenor, a hero of the Trojan War, likewise the traditional founder of Nea Paphos. Another tradition holds that Cinyras, king of Cyprus and father of Adonis, the handsome youth beloved of Aphrodite, was responsible. Cinyras was also an ancestor of the Cinyrades, the theocratic priests presiding over an orgiastic cult resembling that of the Phoenician Astarte, whom the Greeks identified with Aphrodite Anadyomene.

Aphrodite, the goddess of love, generation, and fertility, is said to have been born from the sea-foam off the rocks known as *Petra tou Romiou* (see above) and conveyed gently in a shell to the shore by the moist breeze of Zephyr, as since frequently described and depicted by poets and painters (Botticelli's 'Birth of Venus' being perhaps the most famous example).

Her votaries worshipped her in the form of a cone-shaped aniconic stone (now in the Cyprus Museum, Nicosia), and numerous fragments of smaller marble cones were found when the site was explored in 1888. The original appearance of the temple is as shown on the silver Cypriot coins of the time of Vespasian, contemporary with the earthquake of AD 70, after which it was much altered. During the Middle Ages the site was quarried for its stone to construct a sugar-refinery, parts of which still survive.

The cult was formally abolished in the 4C by the Emperor Theodosius, but its extraordinary fame continued to give rise to many prurient stories. Von Suchen (mid 14C) refers to pagan pilgrimages to the shrine, where 'all ladies and damsels before their betrothal yielded themselves to men; for in Cyprus above all lands men are by nature most luxurious', echoing Martial's verdict *Infamem ninio calore Cyprum*—'infamous through too much heat...'.

William Turner, who, visited the site in October 1815, observed that the village was 'nothing but a mass of ruined churches and houses, of which the latter about thirty are inhabited, half by Turks and half by Greeks', who with good stone houses, were undoubtedly happier than those of Larnaca and of the capital, whose homes were only of mud, while of the churches 'one only remains sufficiently entire to be still used'. The Temple, luckily hardly touched by Cesnola, was first systematically excavated in 1887, by the British School at Athens Expedition, and the site has been excavated intermittently since: by the British Kouklia Expedition in 1950–55, and by a Swiss-German group since 1966. Many of the artefacts unearthed are displayed in the Museum housed in the Covocle.

Other excavations have been conducted more recently at the necropolis at *Skales* (c 1km SE), where several chamber tombs have yielded numerous artefacts ranging in date from the 11C BC to the Hellenistic period.

The ancient remains on the site of Palea Paphos are not sufficiently obvious to be of any great interest other than to the professional archaeologist. They are spread over a wide area, and a lively imagination is required to conjure up an idea of its past importance. The main site, that of the *Sanctuary of Aphrodite*, lies immediately S of the present village on a promontory now dominated by the Covocle. A necropolis has also recently been discovered, containing numerous tomb gifts of the 11C BC.

The medieval manor or **'Château' de Covocle* is partly a fortification of the 13C, but this was largely destroyed by the Mamelukes in 1426. The N wing and gate tower, the W wing, and half of the E wing date from the Turkish period, when it was used as the manor of a large farm or *Chiftlik*.

The 'Château' de Covocle

Its name may be derived either from 'covouculeris', a Byzantine word for the bodyguard of rulers, who were sometimes rewarded by the gift of a country-house; or from the Greek for sepulchre or pavilion.

From the present courtyard (at a higher level than the medieval one) a flight of steps descends to a large cross-vaulted *Hall* (over 30m long and 7m wide), lighted by small pointed windows. The re-roofed upper storey, commanding a fine view, has rectangular windows, and is approached by an exterior ramp.

It has been restored to house the re-organised **Palea Paphos Museum**, with good displays of material found in the area, including terracotta figurines; ivories; White Painted ware from Skales; Hellenistic and medieval pottery and glass; mosaics (that of *Leda and the Swan*, the original of which is in the Museum at Nicosia, was recovered in London after having been stolen from here by art thieves); a 12-sided colonnette with incised letters filled with bitumen (550–500 BC); the painted wing of a marble sphinx (6C BC); stone mortars and pestles; a shell necklace with picrolite pendant (Chalcolithic I); a limestone head with a wide necklace, and four rings in each ear; weapons found in the Siege Mound (see below); a stone bath; a limestone relief of the Annunciation from the Katholiki church; and also a large conical stone, similar to that appearing on the silver Cypriot coins of the time of Vespasian, found on the site of the Sanctuary of Aphrodite here; and an epigraphical collection.

This **Sanctuary** comprises a courtyard flanked N and S by two open stoas or halls, with foundations near the latter of a colonnaded central hall. To the E are various chambers between which lay the E entrance, probably vaulted.

Further E is the *Katholiki Church* (formerly *Panayia Khrysopolitissa*, and earlier called *Panayia Aphroditissa*), where until comparatively recently young mothers offered candles to Panayia Galatariotissa (the milk-giving Virgin) at a conspicuous stone set in the old temple wall—the last trace of the ancient fertility cult (see above).

S of the S stoa stand huge Cyclopean blocks (up to 4.8m long and 2.11m high) forming part of a Late Bronze Age wall known as the *South Wing*, but no decision has been reached about the precise origin and purpose of this structure. The whole area has been much disturbed over the centuries in the interest of a complex of buildings erected in medieval times as a factory for the refining of cane sugar, controlled by a royal official from the Covocle.

Some 40m W of the South Wing lies *Site C*, a Roman Peristyle House of the 1C AD, with later reconstructions. Its E foundations lie on a bothroi, from which numerous votive gifts in the form of terracotta figurines, including goddesses with uplifted arms, and fragments of pottery (mostly Archaic and Classical), some retaining their original polychrome decoration, have been unearthed.—Further NW, on the ruins of other Roman houses, are the remains of Byzantine *Ayios Nikolaos* (16C), destroyed by fire in the 18C.—*Site F*, a Late Roman building with a plain mosaic floor, lies to the NE of the main temenos.—In 1978 a large square capital with stepped sides, typical of Late Bronze Age sanctuaries in Cyprus, was discovered by chance in the yard of one of the village houses.

Other sites in the immediate area include: *Site A* (to the right of the road leading uphill to the NE of the village), comprising the fortified *North-East Gate* on the slope of Marcello Hill, and adjacent **'Siege Works'**. The former was first erected c 700 BC, later strengthened, and Guard Rooms were added in the 4C BC.—Immediately to the E is the *Siege ramp* built by the Persian army when attacking Palea Paphos in 498 BC, which was mined by the defenders, who dug three rock-hewn tunnels beneath the city wall in an attempt to topple the wooden towers used by the enemy. Several hundred fragments (columns, altars, stelae, etc., and a finely sculpted head of a Priest King of Paphos) from an extramural sanctuary have been uncovered, which had been used to build up the ramp. Almost 500 bronze and iron arrow-heads and spear-points, and a Greek bronze helmet, have also been unearthed in the immediate area. The Paphians, in rebuilding the fortifications at a later date, erected a revetment wall around the siege ramp, including it in their defences in preference to removing the pile, leaving it as an undisturbed site for archaeological excavation. It has since been partially reconstructed behind a modern retaining wall.

Some distance to the S, and approached by passing *Site G* (probably part of the city wall), is *Site B*, overlooking Palea Paphos. Here stand the remains of a large and important building of the 5C BC, abutting the city wall, and constructed of blocks with fine ashlar facing. The size and form of the small rooms and narrow corridors (of Persian type?) suggest that it may have been the residence of the Persian commander after the siege.

Hence we may return to Site A, and to Kouklia.

Regaining the main road, turn right across the DHIARIZOS, and 2km beyond, the XEROS POTAMOS.

The road soon by-passes (left) *Mandria*, where, above the W door of the church, is a curious marble capital and female head, assumed to come from an earlier Latin convent further S. To the SW is the chapel of *Ayios Evresis* (or *Arkona*), incorporating marble columns and other material from an earlier site. Between the chapel and the sea lies an ancient quarry, its rocks pierced by numerous vaulted tunnels.

At **Timi**, passed to the right, is the former Byzantine church of *Ayia Sophia*, long used as a mosque (until 1975) and its frescoes have been covered by layers of whitewash. The local cheese and sausages (loukanika) are reputed.

For the sub-route from Kannaviou via the *Monastery of Khrysorroyiatissa* to Timi, see pp 168–9, in reverse.

To the left is the approach road to *Paphos Airport*, inaugurated in December 1983.

3km beyond Timi we cross the POTAMOS TIS EZOUSAS at **Akhelia**, in the medieval period a centre of the sugar industry. Two churches of that period remain. *Ayios Yeoryios* is a 16C basilica restored in 1742–43, when its narthex was destroyed, probably in an earthquake. Most of its magnificent woodwork was removed and sold at auction in London c 1900, but its late 16–17C icons remain. *Ayios Theodosios* is a cruciform building of perhaps the 12C, barbarously modernised in 1932, but containing some 15C murals; its altar is made from a piece of Roman marble.

Some 2km to the S is restored *Ayios Leondios*. Roman columns and capitals which once littered the site are now in the Paphos Museum.

We approach **YEROSKIPOS** (2650 inhab.) its name a corruption of 'Hieroskepos', the Sacred Garden of Aphrodite. There are remains of a small Roman temple near the church, but the town itself dates mainly from the Byzantine era. According to Von Suchen, who visited the place in 1340, the legendary vineyards of Engadi were located in the vicinity; but they have not been identified with any certainty, and a similar claim has been made for a district N of Paphos. The town is reputed for its *Loukoumi* or Turkish Delight.

Yeroskipos was the home of Andrea Zinboulaki, a youth whose intelligence prompted Sir Sydney Smith, when there in 1800 (see Paphos History), to appoint him British Vice-Consul, and he thereafter took on his protector's name, calling himself Haji Smith.

By turning left in the village centre, we shortly see the picturesque silhouette of the five-domed Byzantine church of ***Ayia Paraskevi** (the only other five-domed church surviving in Cyprus being in *Peristerona*). It is an interesting and attractive building, originally cruciform in plan, but enlarged by the addition of a nave and aisles in the 19C, and by an ugly excrescence in 1931. It contains remains of 14C murals, below which is a 12C Dormition of the Virgin and, in the central cupola, some 9C paintings. The most famous of its 15C icons is that of the Virgin, with a later Crucifixion on the reverse.

A short distance to the E is the *House of Haji Smith* (see above), now containing a ***Museum of Folk Art**. On the ground floor is a collection of domestic and farming implements, including looms, bread-boards (or rather planks with saucer-shaped depressions), cotton-crushers, sieves of silk, a spinning-wheel, threshing boards, a pair of eel-catching tongs, etc.—The upper floor contains a colourful collection of Cypriot costumes: silk shirts, waistcoats (*ghilekko* and *zimbouni*), pantaloons, etc., and a painted bride's chest or *sandouki*. There are also collections of decorative pottery and carved gourds (one depicting an elephant; another the bombing of a warship in 1940); a Cypriot lute manufactured from a pumpkin gourd; and a painted clock belonging to Michael de Vezin (died 1792), a former British consul at Larnaca.

Continuing W, the suburbs of **Paphos** are entered shortly, soon passing (right) the *District Museum*: see below.

14 Paphos

PAPHOS (with a combined population estimated at 22,900 in 1988; 9100 in 1960; now swollen considerably by tourists during the season) is the name generally given to the twin towns of *Ktima*, the upper and newer part, and *Kato Paphos*, formerly known as *Nea Paphos*, the lower area, nearer the port, containing the main archaeological sites. It has often been confused with the earlier Mycenaean foundation of *Kouklia-Paphos* or *Palea Paphos*, the centre of the celebrated cult of the Paphian Aphrodite, which lies some 16km SE: see Rte 13. Paphos has also been mis-pronounced in recent centuries as *Baffo* or *Basso*, among other names.

The new town, the capital of the District of Paphos, with a 'classical' *Town Hall* surrounded by gardens, lies on a plateau some 45m above sea level. It also contains, on the Limassol road, the Paphos Museum, with an interesting collection of finds from the ruined Roman city and the 'House of Dionysos', and a Byzantine Museum.

Tourist Office, 3 Gladstone St, in the upper town. Its *Airport* lies to the S, beyond *Yeroskipos*.

A road, the continuation of Gladstone St, only 'metalled' in 1891–92, leads down to the fishing port, which has grown rapidly in recent years with the opening of several luxurious beach hotels, while a rash of bars and restaurants have appeared in addition to those formerly skirting the harbour. Note that a number of new hotels have sprung

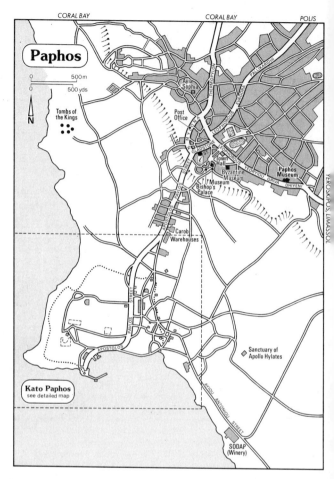

up a considerable distance E of the port and main monuments, and a precise understanding of their position should be ascertained before booking.

It has been claimed that 'New' Paphos was inhabited in the late 15C BC by settlers from Syria or Lebanon; or to have been founded by Agepenor, leader of the Arcadian contingent to Troy, who was wrecked here in c 1184 BC. It is more likely that it was formally founded by Nikokles, the last King of the Paphian Kingdom, towards the end of the 4C BC, when an earlier Greek settlement on the site was walled. As the most westerly port of Cyprus, it was developed as a commerical base and a ship-building centre, using timber from adjacent forests, issued its own coins and, under the Ptolemies, it replaced Salamis as the island's capital.

In the prosperous Roman period (58 BC–AD 395) it was known as *Augusta Claudia*, with the later addition of *Flavia*, and among its proconsuls was the orator Marcus Tullius Cicero (51–50 BC). Sergius Paulus, a later proconsul, was converted to Christianity by the Apostles Paul and Barnabas (a native of Cyprus) in c 45 AD, and traditionally it was here that St. Paul received his 39 lashes (but see below, and Salamis). It later became the seat of a bishopric, one of three of the Orthodox rite, and in 1220 of one of four Dioceses of the Latin Church. But in 15 BC, and c AD 200, and again in 332 and 342, it was damaged by earthquakes, and with Constantia—as Salamis was then called—being again chosen as the capital, devastated Paphos rapidly declined. Although only a provincial backwater, in 648 it suffered the first of a number of sporadic depredations by Arab corsairs, and its population abandoned the port, seeking safety in the less vulnerable upper town, which probably dates from this time.

Among crusaders who died here were Guelph, 4th Duke of Bavaria (1101), Erik the Good, King of Denmark (1103, of fever), and Amadeus, Count of Savoy (in 1148). Paphos was briefly under Genoese rule (1372–74); but in 1460 it was captured by James 'the Bastard'. According to Pero Tafur, a Catalan noble who visited the place in 1436, the port was very unwholesome, and on the very day he arrived, both the bishop and two of his esquires had died. Another traveller described it in 1480 as 'but a miserable village', its harbour abandoned and its churches in ruins. In 1608 it was the centre of an unsuccessful revolt against the Turks led by a Venetian, Victor Zembetos. Of its remaining fortifications only the castle at the harbour entrance, destroyed by the Venetians, was rebuilt by the Turks.

In 1799 Sir Sidney Smith established an Agent here to attend to the provisioning of British men-of-war (see *Yeroskipos*), and (according to the Reverend Edward Daniel Clarke, who visited Cyprus in 1801) also removed some inscribed marbles hence. At this time the population of Paphos and Ktima had shrunk to about 1000, but by 1881 it had grown to 2204 (of whom 1318 were Turkish Cypriots and 870 were Greek Cypriots). Its harbour, by then silted up, was dredged in 1908 and improved in 1959. In 1953 the town experienced another slight earthquake. It was here that Abp Makarios sought safety during the coup d'état of 1974, before being flown to London.

The upper town contains comparatively little in the way of old buildings, although the *Mosque of Djami Kebir* (1584), towards its NW end, may have been erected over the ruins of an earlier Christian church. The *Bishop's Palace* and adjacent 'cathedral' are of little consequence.

To the SE of the town centre, flanking the Limassol road, is the **District Museum*.

The position of the objects displayed is likely to change when the new extension is inaugurated.

R1 at present contains: Late Cypriot Base Ring and White Slip wares; stone mortars, and Mycenaean stirrup jars (Late Cypriot II); medieval Cypriot pottery and glass (12–16C); heads of terracotta votive figurines and statuettes (Cyprio-Archaic and Classic), Chalcolithic picrolite idols; and a mould for a male face; Middle Cypriot Red Polished ware; Black-Figured and Red-Figured vases from Polis (6–5C BC), including one of a sculpted female head; flasks from the Kissonerga site and ceramics (including 13C maiolica) from the Saranda Kolones site, and from Skales (11C BC); surgical implements of the 2–3C found under the Annabelle hotel; an early Hellenistic crouching lion; Roman pottery vessels, glassware, and terracotta lamps; Cypro-Archaic Black-on-Red ware, including a jug with a cow-like spout; Neolithic tools, picrolite figurines, some from Kithasi (Chalcolithic I), and Bronze weapons. Cases contain jewellery dated from the 15C BC to the 6C AD, coins and coin-moulds of the Hellenistic mint of Paphos (6–5C BC), and Roman coins, one depicting the Temple of Aphrodite at Palea Paphos. Also displayed is an iron lampstand from Marion (5C BC).

RR2–3 contain a limestone grave relief (4C BC); a Hellenistic sarcophagus with a corbelled lid, from Peyia; a worn marble torso of Aphrodite (Graeco-Roman) from Nea Paphos, found in the sea; another of Aphrodite, armed; other statues from the Villa of Theseus; and a relief of a reclining river-god.

R4 contains marble statuettes, including two goddesses in black and white marble (Roman, from Nea Paphos), and of Asklepios; and display cases containing: Roman glass, and from the Hellenistic period (from Pano Akourdalia) lamps, including two large 'double lamps' of the Roman period; marble eye-balls; various spherical votive objects; metal, marble, and bone artefacts; clay 'hot-water bottles', moulded to the shape of hands, feet, and other parts which their heat might soothe; pottery of the Hellenistic and Roman periods from—among other sites—the 'House of Dionysos' (see below); terracotta figurines of dogs and stags; masks; a 6C marble panel from Ayios Georghios, Peyia; imported Byzantine glass, and ceramics (12–13C); and a collection of Renaissance sculpture.

A **Byzantine Museum** may be visited at No. 26, 25th March St, which skirts the Public Gardens to the W of the District Museum.

Among the more notable icons on display are: a Pantokrator (1565); St. Nikolas (1520); St. John the Evangelist with donors (1562); Archangel Michael (15C); St. Paul (16C); St. George Pervoliatis (16C); St. Catherine (17C); Birth of the Baptist (from Kedhares; 17C); and also some Holy Doors from Arminou (18C), and several other 16–17C paintings of Christ, the Virgin and Child, St. John the Baptist, Archangels, and Nativities.

An additional collection of icons may be seen in a building flanking Andreas Ioannou St, adjacent to the Bishop's Palace. Notable are those of Ayia Marina (13C), with St. George (14C) on the reverse (from Ayia Maria Philousa, Kelokedara); a Soldier, with the Virgin on the reverse (both 12C); a 16C series devoted to the Life of the Virgin; and 16–17C examples, among them the Baptist, a Christ, the Virgin 'of Kykko', and St. George 'of Burgos'.

Of slighter interest is the nearby private *Collection of George S. Eliades* at 1 Exo Vrysis St, which comprises miscellaneous collections of coins; costumes; stone axe-heads (Chalcolithic period); a Roman basalt quern; an 18C bride's chest; an amphora from Lefkoniko (9C BC); and farm implements and kitchen utensils. In the garden are two tombs of the 3C BC.

From the main 'square' in the town centre by the old buildings of the Police Station, Gladstone St (with the *Tourist Office* at No. 3) descends steeply, and continues as Kato Paphos St (or Apostolos Pavlos St) towards the port. Passing (left) carob warehouses, and the rock outcrop known as *Petra tou Digheni* (of Dighenis), we reach crossroads: the right-hand turning leads N to the so-called *Tombs of the Kings* at Paleokastro; see below.

We shortly reach the line of the Roman **City Wall**, which we pass at the site of the *North Gate* (see Pl. p 159 for its approximate position around the ancient enceinte).—To the left is a rocky eminence known as the FABRICA HILL, below which are a number of rock-cut chambers, including one called *Ayios Lambrianos*. Entered by a flight of steps, some have vaulted roofs and plastered walls, and they probably date from the early Hellenistic period. Another similar chamber lies immediately W of the main road at its junction with a minor lane. The hill should be ascended for the view from the summit, undoubtedly the site of a temple.

Having first enquired at the Museum as to the possibility of access, it is convenient to visit from here the nearby series of rock-cut underground domed chambers leading off a vaulted passage. They date from the late 4C BC, and may be the site of a sanctuary, although previously identified as the *Garrison's Camp*. A short distance beyond these is another series of rock-cut tombs, the antechambers of two of which are decorated with painted geometrical or architectural patterns.

A few paces beyond the chambers under Fabrica Hill we pass a tree (left), every branch of which is covered with fluttering strips of cloth left as votive offerings by visitors to the adjacent catacombs of *Ayia Solomoni*. One chamber of the catacombs, converted into a chapel in the early 12C, was once known as that of the *Seven Sleepers* (or Seven Maccabees); its frescoes were damaged by graffiti at an early date. A further flight of steps descends to a holy well.

The next lane to the left leads to the slight remains of the so-called 'Hellenistic' Theatre (c 300 BC), the upper part cut into the rock, and the rest only partly excavated.

Beyond this intersection, we pass (right) the SW angle only of the former 14C *Latin Cathedral*, which stands out like a tower. Its most famous incumbent was Jacobo Pesaro, who held the see from 1496–1502, when he became Admiral of Pope Alexander VI's fleet fighting against the Turks.—A lane here leads right to the main *Theatre*, see below.

The next lane to the left passes (right) a boat-building establishment, and (left) an octagonal domed *Mosque* (formerly a ?12C church), with a damaged minaret, opposite which are the domes of (?Frankish) *Baths*; others may be seen a short distance to the NE.—A little further E is (left) **Ayios Yeoryios**, containing the tombstone of a member of the Beduin family. Bearing half-right from here, we approach domed *Ayios Antonios*, another diminutive building preserving a Byzantine N aisle, recently restored for the use of the Church of England.

Some distance N of the former are the ruins of 15C *Ayia Marina*, adjacent to the site of the NE gate of the walled city.

Approximately 1km to the E, but at present in private hands and not easily accessible, is the late 4C BC *Sanctuary of Apollo Hylates*, with two underground chambers, the inner one circular and domed.

From Ayios Antonios we turn W past the site of the E gate of the enceinte, and (left) *Panayia Theoskepasti*, erected on the site of the original church, which according to tradition, was miraculously veiled by a thick mist which saved it from being sacked by Arab raiders in the 7C, but not from the attentions of later builders.

We shortly reach an area of intensive excavation, overlooked to the

N by 15C **Ayia Kyriaki** (or *Khrysopolitissa*), an earlier Latin church
converted to the Orthodox rite, and Byzantine in form, to which a
belfry has been added. To the left of the road approaching from the W
are several tombstones, and the site of a Gothic *Franciscan church*, on
the N side of which are relics of zigzag moulding. Several column bases
survive, and also the lower part of the triple apse. Ayia Kyriaki itself
stands on the site of the N aisle of an earlier and more extensive
*Basilica** (over 50m long), originally of seven aisles, reduced to five in
the 6C, part of the apse of which remains, while two of its monolithic
granite columns abut the church. Numerous columns and capitals of
green and white *Cipollino* marble (from Karystos in S Euboea,
Greece) lie around, and a considerable area of late 4C mosaic
pavement has been exposed, both in the basilica and W of the
narthex, where the E and S porticoes of an atrium have been
discovered, together with a central fountain, and several more
columns and finely-carved capitals. To the S of the basilica stood the
Bishop's Palace, with deep vaulted basements, while a ramp descended from dependencies to the atrium. Several other features will
come to light, no doubt, once the present road across the site has been
removed, and the surrounding area excavated further.

It was a column jutting out of the ground just W of the basilica which was
previously railed off and pointed out as the 'Pillar of St. Paul', where, according
to an untrustworthy legend, the apostle was bound and lashed prior to
converting the Roman governor Sergius Paulus to Christianity.

The main road may be regained by following a lane to the W.

From this point a road leads W, shortly passing (right) the
extensive site of the *Frankish 'Crusader' Castle** also known as
Saranda Kolones (so-called from its numerous granite columns, some
40 of which previously lay scattered over the area). It was once

Ayia Kyriaki, Paphos

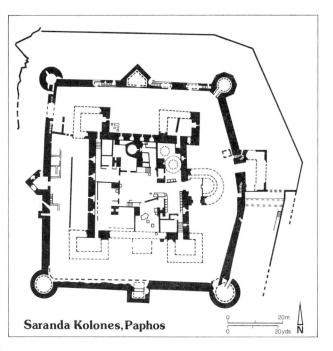

Saranda Kolones, Paphos

0 — 20 m
0 — 20 yds
N

thought to be the Temple of Aphrodite, but has since proved to be the remains of an important fortress, formerly called the 'Byzantine' castle. Excavations commenced in 1957 confirm that it was constructed during the early years of the Frankish occupation, but it had only a short life, being destroyed by earthquakes in 1222.

It consists of a square keep with four projecting towers, one at each angle, and is surrounded by a strong outer wall (3m thick) and ditch. While the present entrance is on the W, the original entrance was on the E, approached by a bridge across the ditch, and through a D-shaped gate-tower of which only the basement survives. The keep itself was built around an open courtyard, in which stood massive piers from which vaults supporting an upper storey once sprang. The exterior wall was defended by eight towers or bastions of differing form, including a pentagonal one containing a postern gate; a number of staircases led down to sally-ports opening into the ditch. Note the horse-troughs on the interior walls of the keep.

The counterscarp wall has now been exposed by the excavators, but the upper facing blocks have largely been removed.

Continuing W, a right-hand turning leads past an *Asklepieion* to the restored **Roman Odeion**; its 14 rows of seats (behind which ran a corridor) have unfortunately been stripped of their stone facing by earlier quarrying. Below the central axis of the auditorium is a subterranean tunnel. The semi-circular orchestra pit and stage have also been uncovered. To the E stood the *Agora*.

Saranda Kolones, Paphos

To the NW is a *Lighthouse*, and further N there are extensive remains of the ancient town **Walls**, together with a ramp and a rock bridge leading across the recently excavated 'moat', flanked by an eroded cliff.

Immediately W of this approach road there is a temple site, and beyond it the protective roof of the ***House of Dionysos**, so-called from the frequent representation of that god in the mosaic pavements of the building. The site had been exposed by ploughing, and excavations began in 1962, which revealed the remains of an extensive c 3C Roman villa comprising 22 rooms disposed around a peristyle atrium. Although little remains of the walls, probably shattered by earthquakes, the floors are substantially intact, and in 14 of the rooms the colourful mosaics may be seen in an extraordinarily good state of preservation.

Steps ascend to a viewing platform, which extends around and across the site. The subjects of the mosaics are mainly mythological, including Apollo and Daphne; Pyramos and Thisbe; Dionysios and Ikarios; and Poseidon and Anymone, among others. Some of the rooms are paved with mosaics displaying a variety of geometric designs. Three sides of the atrium are decorated with hunting scenes (note the moufflon, leopard, bear, boar, and tiger). Also remarkable are the Triumph of Dionysios, a panel of vintage scenes surrounded by a beautiful and delicate rinceau pattern, a representation of Ganymede and the Eagle, peacocks, musicians, etc.

An important discovery was made while the foundation trenches for the shelter were being dug: a panel of Hellenistic mosaic pavement in small black and white pebbles —the second known pebble mosaic of this type in Cyprus—was uncovered 1m below the level of the Roman mosaics. It consists of the mythical sea-monster Skylla, from the body of which spring the upper part of a female figure (with pink hair) and the fore parts of three dogs, the whole flanked by dolphins. It has been reset in a nearby room which previously had no mosaic floor.

A turning S leads past (right) the *Meteorological Station* to the recently excavated **'House of Aion'**, a new building but incorporating original features, including a large panel composed of five sections depicting mythological subjects, and the***Villa of Theseus**—the latter excavated by a Polish mission. The villa, a building occupying an area of c 9600m^2, and probably the official residence of the Roman governor of Cyprus, was erected on an earlier Roman and Hellenistic site. From cat-walks an area of over 1400m^2 of exposed mosaic pavement can be viewed under its protective roofs. Scenes and designs include a circular mosaic of Theseus and the Labyrinth (adjacent to which are some murals), and a depiction of the Life of Achilles (surrounded by lions, tigers, leopards, etc.).

Excavations continue to the W, where the **'House of Orpheus'** contains a further remarkable series of mosaics, being prepared for display at the time of writing. These include one of Hercules and the Lion of Nemea, an Amazon holding her steed by the bridle, and Orpheus and the Beasts (measuring 4.25 x 5.10m).

A turning to the E leads to the port, passing (left) the foundations of a 5C basilica dedicated to *Panayia Limeniotissa*.

On reaching the quay, one may turn to the right past several restaurants, the *Customs House*, and warehouses (one of which is now the headquarters of a turtle-breeding project), to reach the partially moated ***Fort of Paphos**, at the base of the ancient breakwater (on which are the slight ruins of a second fort). It was erected on the ruins of a medieval castle of 1391, which had replaced an earlier tower. The castle was blown up by the Venetians, and the W tower was rebuilt by the Turks in 1580–92, as recorded in an inscription over the entrance. During the British occupation it was used as a salt store, and only in 1935 was it declared an ancient monument.

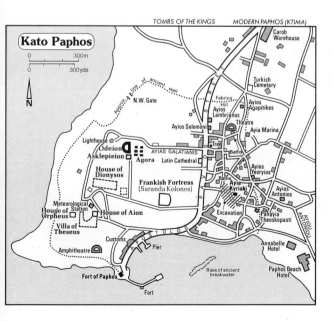

In 1815 William Turner, when referring to this fort, gave an interesting description of a problem not infrequently encountered by curious travellers—not only in Cyprus—and still occurring in the late 20C. Turner showed his *firman*, or permit, to the Agha 'which, as he [the Agha] could not read, he handed to his secretary, who went right through it. The Turks have built a mean insignificant castle on the beach at the Marina; and he, supposing it was this I came to see, hummed and hawed, said I should have done well to bring an order from the governor at Nicosia, and (by the suggestion of his secretary) added that my firman only said I was to pass through Cyprus, and not to inspect it. To this I answered that of course my object in passing through was to see; that I would not give a para to see the castle, which was as wretched a building in the way of fortification as I ever remembered to have set my eyes on. That my only object in visiting the Agha was to pay him a compliment, as I was only come to see the antiquities which he could not prevent me from doing, or if he did try to do so, I should then know how to act: he replied that he had no intention of preventing me, and we left him'.

From the vaulted central hall, beyond which are small courtyards, one may enter rooms on either side, off which are cells once used as prisons, with dungeons below. Steps lead to the roof, providing panoramic views.

At a short distance NW of the fort is an oval depression assumed to be the site of yet another *Theatre*, but this has not yet been confirmed by excavation.

To the SE, beyond the end of the breakwater, are the submerged remains of its ancient extension towards the *Moulia Rocks*. (They may be explored by under-water enthusiasts.) Relics of an inner mole—in fact an extension of the city wall—lie NE of the present breakwater.

Between the road skirting the harbour and the *Annabelle* hotel, some distance to the E, there is a built tomb; and a rock-cut chamber tomb may be visited *in situ* below the hotel by applying to the reception desk. Other excavations are under way immediately to the W of the hotel.

From the SE end of the outer harbour—beyond the SODAP winery—a 'Processional Way' once led from a point of disembarkation towards *Palea Paphos* (c 14km SE; see p 147).

The ***Tombs of the Kings**** (incorrectly named, but so-called from their imposing character) are approached by a road leading NW of the Fabrica Hill. They lie to the W of the Guardian's lodge, but, being subterranean, are hardly noticeable until reached. They date from the 3C BC and there are well over 100 in all, scattered over an extensive area known as *Paleokastro*.

The more impressive of those so far entirely excavated are rock-cut tombs arranged round an open peristyle court approached by steps cut into the rock. The peristyle is of the Doric order, and the rock face is also decorated with a façade of Doric columns, and an entablature of triglyphs and metopes; others are cut square. Some of the tombs were probably re-used during the Early Christian period, on the evidence of some crosses carved on the rock. A recently excavated area is located around a hillock to the SW of the entrance.

The approach road has been extended to skirt the coast, meeting the main road further N between *Kissonerga* and *Coral Bay*; see below.

15 Paphos to Coral Bay and Ayios Yeoryios

20km (12 miles).

Driving due N from the upper town of Paphos, fork left after c 1.5km (but from the *Tombs of the Kings*—see above—the new road leads directly to *Coral Bay).*

The right-hand fork off the old road leads in 7km to the monastery of *Ayios Neophytos* (see Rte 16) via **Emba** (1200 inhab.), a village continually inhabited from at least the 12C, and mentioned as being the point of embarkation of Peter I in 1362, but this is more likely to have been from *Lemba*, to the NE; see below.

Emba has a reputation for its wild flowers, particularly in April, while in spring the rocks near *Ayios Yeoryios*, S of the village and E of the road, are a mass of cyclamen. The barrel-vaulted church of the Byzantine period has been largely rebuilt, and contains two layers of frescoes, the later of the 16C. The main two-domed church of *Emba* (12–13C; repaired 1955), with a narthex which was added in 1744, is dedicated to *Panayia Khryseleousa*. Its frescoes were ruined by a local dauber in 1886, except for the Pantokrator on the dome, which was out of his reach and remains untouched except by smoke. A well-painted Venetian coat of arms can be seen, together with a two-panel icon of the Apostles (early 16C). A gospel (Venice, 1539) is also shown, in a condition any bibliophile would be ashamed to display.—The road next climbs to (3km) *Tala*, with well-sited *Ayia Ekaterini*, a domed Late Byzantine building with an added narthex, and containing remains of frescoes on its W wall.—An Early Cypriot cemetery was discovered in 1963 some 5km to the NW at *Spilia tou Mavrou*.

A brief DETOUR from the main coast road may be made by forking left almost immediately after bearing left through **Khlorakas** (1450 inhab.), a market-gardening centre.

Here, in November 1954, Colonel Grivas surreptitiously landed from Greece to lead EOKA guerrillas against the British, a quantity of arms having been previously unloaded. More arms and equipment were recently found here.

To the left of the S entrance of the village lies the toy-like Byzantine church of *Ayios Nikolaos*, its murals smoke-blackened, while adjacent to the large modern church is 13C *Panayia Khryseleousa*, ruined by amateur attempts to restore its paintings.

On regaining the main road, we traverse *Lemba*, the centre of an area intensively occupied in the 3rd millennium BC, as confirmed by recent and progressing excavations at the local sites of *Lakkous*, further N; *Mosphilia*; and *Mylouthkia*, where 28 graves and 11 circular stone buildings have been uncovered. By following the seaward road and turning right, a track leads shortly to a site on which several *reconstructions* of Chalcolithic buildings have been erected.

Kissonerga has a modern church preserving four icons of 1775 from its predecessor, and a holy well resorted to in the past for the relief of female ailments. We shortly approach the shore and cross the river XEROS.

Maa lies to the W of the next crossroads, the site of recent villa development overlooking a bay S of the adjacent and once secluded **Coral Bay**, so-called from its pinkish sand formed by minute fragments of coral. It was in the *Cave of Ayii Phanentes* (Discovered Saints), to the E of Maa, that the fossil bones of pigmy hippopotami were found by the credulous inhabitants of Kissonerga in medieval times, and assumed to be those of early Christian martyrs.—Of more interest is the Late Bronze Age fortified settlement of **Palaeokastro**, sited on the rocky headland between the two bays, just W of a restaurant, with a rock wall cutting off the peninsula. Several seasons of recent excavation have confirmed its violent destruction c 1200 BC.

From the aforementioned crossroads, the main road continues N to (3km) **Peyia** (1200 inhab.), attractively sited on a hillside, and probably founded by the Venetians, although claims are also made for a Byzantine foundation. We turn abruptly W here before bearing NW parallel to the coast, with pine and juniper forests on the hillslope to the right, to (7km) the site of **Ayios Yeoryios**, with the ruins of a 6C *Basilica*, in fact three superimposed churches, discovered in 1951. These ruins, and those of another 11–14C edifice with mosaics and adjacent baths, await further excavation, but the site may be visited by applying to the resident guardian. Note the finely carved marble capitals. The modern church was erected in 1928.

A good road climbs N and then E from Peyia, providing fine sea views, to *Kathikas*; see Rte 16.

It is possible to descend to a small harbour, in the vicinity of which there are some twenty rock-cut tombs. The whole area of CAPE DREPANUM was the site of a Roman city, but its extensive ruins have still to be systematically excavated.

Offshore lies the island of YERONISOS, rising abruptly from the sea, on the S side of which are remains of a Neolithic settlement; on the W are remains of Roman buildings, now the haunt of pigeons.

From the junction just short of Ayios Yeoryios the right-hand road continues to hug the coast, but although improved, it is still very rough in places as it winds through the scrub-covered, uninhabited tract of the AKAMAS PENINSULA, and peters out c 8km S of CAPE ARNAUTI. A track leads right off this road to the *Avgas gorges*, the more impressive of which is the more northerly.

After 6km the main road passes CAPE LARA, and some 11km further N we reach the ancient settlement of *Ayios Konon*, with a rebuilt church named after a 1C martyr. The area, not easily accessible, appears to have been a Hellenistic-Roman town and necropolis, still to be thoroughly explored. The ruins of a Byzantine church may be seen among the pines not far inland, and some marble mooringcolumns are still visible along the shore.

It is hoped that this district will shortly become a protected natural reserve, in spite of opposition by the Bishop of Paphos, who wished to exploit his property there; otherwise it may soon become as irremediably spoiled as has been the area around *Cape Greco*; see Rte 2.

16 Paphos to Polis

34km (21 miles).

We climb NE from the centre of Paphos, with pleasant retrospective views, to (5km) crossroads, immediately to the right of which lies

Mesoyi (300m), its springs supplying Paphos with water; its other products are wine and hemp.—Adjacent is *Mesa Khorio*, just S of which stands the medieval chapel of *Ayia Marina*, the dust from the floor of which, according to a local superstition, will reconcile a man with his nagging wife if collected and sprinkled (surreptitiously) in his own house!

The left-hand turning leads past (left) *Trimithousa* to (4km) the **Monastery of Ayios Neophytos**, providing extensive sea views. The buildings, including recent additions of little architectural interest, are well-sited on the leafy valley side.

The founding hermit, born in 1134 near Kato Lefkara, cut a cave in the rock in this secluded site with his own hands, and by c 1200 a community had grown up around it. St. Neophytos was the author of a number of works including Ritual Ordinances concerned with early Greek monasticism, theological treatises, and an historical commentary on Cyprus at the time of Richard I, Coeur de Lion's occupation, uncomplimentary to that crusading king. The monastery became stauropegic in 1631.

The monks have recently opened a workshop for the restoration and binding of ancient MSS.

The earlier dependencies in the courtyard date from the 15C. A flight of steps ascends to the *Church* of three aisles with a barrel-vaulted roof supported by columns, the capitals of which are carved with acanthus leaves. Remains of 16C murals may be seen in the apse, and of an earlier period in the N aisle vaulting. Some early icons are preserved, and in a wooden sarcophagus the saint's bones, removed from his tomb in 1750; his skull is contained in a silver reliquary.

A few paces to the N of the main building are the three contiguous caves forming the saint's retreat, now conveniently provided with easier access, and comprising a chapel, its walls and vaults covered with paintings contemporary with its excavation; his private cell, in which is an empty tomb (also his bed?); and a sanctuary.

The main road continues NE from the Mesoyi crossroad, after 3km by-passing (right) **Tsadha** (600m), with a church rebuilt in 1908 containing an interesting icon of the Virgin (c 1540).—Some 2km to the SE lies the monastery of *Stavros Mythas*, once a residence of the bishops of Paphos, the doors of which show strong Gothic influence.

The road now descends the N flank of the watershed, and after 5km reaches the right-hand fork for *Polemi, Kannaviou, Stravros tis Psokas*, and *Kykko*: see Rte 17.—We shortly traverse **Stroumbi**, rebuilt here in a somewhat functional style after the upper village had been seriously damaged in the earthquake in 1953. It is reputed for its wine.

FROM STROUMBI TO POLIS VIA DHROUSHA (23km). From the road junction just beyond old Stroumbi take the left fork, which leads through a number of small villages on the crest of a range of hills forming the backbone of the AKAMAS PENINSULA, many of them exchanging their Turkish for Greek Cypriot communities during recent years. The road provides some good plunging views of the coast to the W, and later, to the N. We first reach **Kathikas** (645m), only connected by road to Stroumbi in 1903, and curiously named after the Greek for 'chamber-pot'; it is a centre of grape and sultana production.—The road W, later descending to *Peyia* (see Rte 15), provides extensive sea views.—3km *Pano*, and *Kato Arodhes* (the medieval name of the place being Rhodes, for it was once the property of the Knights Hospitallers of St. John of Jerusalem, whose headquarters were in Rhodes from 1309 until 1522). We approach *Inia*, once known for its embroidery, immediately NE of which is **Dhrousha** (630m), originally settled by Greeks from Arcadia.—**Kritou Terra** lies 2km to the E, N of which is *Terra*, which has been continuously inhabited since at least the Roman period; a Roman milestone has been incorporated into the façade of one of its houses. It was the birthplace of Haji Georghakis Kornesios (cf. Yeroskipos.).

There are several ruined churches in the vicinity, the most interesting of which is that of **Ayia Ekaterina**, best approached by a path leading NE for 2km from the N end of Kritou Terra, although the church overlooks the main Paphos-Polis road. *Check first regarding access.* It is a large three-aisled medieval structure with a triple-domed narthex, on the S wall of which there is a fresco of St. Catherine. As the church was known as the 'seven-domed' it seems likely that the main apse, crossing, and the ends of each aisle were also formerly domed.

The much-improved main road, providing several spectacular views over *Khrysokhou Bay*, descends from a junction NW of Kritou to (8km) *Prodhromi*, adjacent to *Polis*: see below.— An ALTERNATIVE but rough track leads W from Dhrousha through the hamlets of *Phasli* and *Androlikou*, both abandoned by their Turkish Cypriot inhabitants; the mosque of the latter contains fragments of the earlier church of *Ayios Andronikos*. We may turn NW here through **Neokhorio**, on the N slope of the Akamas peninsula, and descend to the coast between *Lachi* and the *Baths of Aphrodite*: see below.

The main road N from Stroumbi now descends the widening KHRY-SOKHOU VALLEY, leaving to the W *Theletra*, formerly known for its embroidery. Its church was erected in 1755, but its icons and iconostasis come from its predecessor.—The main road descends further in a sweeping curve past (left) **Yiolou**, scene of an EOKA ambush of a British Army convoy in 1958; it has an early 19C church.—We pass near (left) the monastery of *Ayii Anargyri* (SS. Cosmas and Damian), with a tiny church of 1649, adjacent to a Neolithic site.

To the W, beyond the hamlet of *Miliou*, are the twin hamlets of *Pano* and *Kato Akourdhalia*, with a 16C church, the murals of which are now whitewashed over. Gunnis mentions that the house of an eccentric Englishman who lived here in the early 19C was pointed out to him.

6km. On the hillside to the left lies *Kholi*; early 16C *Arkhangelos Michael*, partly a medieval watch-tower, contains icons and murals contemporary with its construction.

We shortly traverse *Skoulli*, and the larger village of *Khrysokhou*, abandoned by its Turkish Cypriot community in 1975 as were a number of other villages overlooking the valley to the SE (best approached by the road from Polis to *Lyso*: see below).

3km. **POLIS** (1000 inhab.), a small place of slight intrinsic interest but of growing importance, is the main town in this corner of the island and a citrus centre. It is now cut off from direct communication from Morphou and Nicosia.

To the SE on an eminence stood the city of **Marion**, said to have been founded in the 7C BC by Athenians. It was an important copper-mining centre, but was destroyed in 312 BC by Ptolemy I. Some decades later a new town was built adjacent to the W, and named *Arsinoë* after the sister of a later Ptolemy (Philadelphus, 285–47 BC). It was called Polis in the Lusignan period, when the Orthodox see was suppressed, although the present Bishop of Paphos still bears the title of Bishop of Arsinoë.

The whole area is surrounded by a necropolis, the tombs of which have yielded abundant artefacts to various excavators, particularly of imported pottery of Attic type. Over 400 tombs were opened by Richter in 1886. Those near Arsinoë are mainly Hellenistic; those further E are more frequently of the 6-4C BC.

Cotton was the main crop during the Middle Ages, but it is now mainly a citrus-growing region and is also rich in olives, wheat, carobs, walnuts, and almonds. The Turkish Cypriot population of Polis and adjacent Prodhromi moved to the N of the island in 1975.

A pleasant short EXCURSION may be made from Polis to the so-called **Baths of Aphrodite**, 9km to the W. Crossing the POTAMOS TOU STAVROU TIS PSOKAS, immediately W of the town, we by-pass the suburban village of *Prodhromi* and turn NW through *Lachi*, a tiny fishing and especially sponge-fishing port. Remains of an ancient jetty lie below the present water-level.—Shortly beyond, we fork right, passing through attractive wooded country skirting KHRYSOK-HOU BAY, with the ridge of the **AKAMAS PENINSULA** approaching the coast to the left, to reach (right) a Tourist Pavilion overlooking the bay, with its remarkably clear water, and providing a splendid view E and NE towards *Pomos Point*. A few minutes' walk along a path to the left brings us to a dank grotto among bamboos and ferns, the legendary spot where the goddess Aphrodite took her bath before marrying Akamas. Chalcolithic artefacts were found between the bath and the sea in 1960.—The right-hand track climbs parallel to and some distance above the sea through a still unspoilt land and sea-scape (at present a military area and occasionally out of bounds), to (6km) the **Fontana Amorosa** (so-called by Ariosto in 'Orlando Furioso'), now but a muddy pool.—CAPE ARNAUTI lies c 3km further NW.

Alexander Drummond visited this area in the mid 18C but had not the curiosity to taste the water of the long-famous *Fountain* of Love (sometimes confused with the *Bath* of Venus Genetrix or Aphrodite, the water of which is less palatable), for—as the British consul sagely observed—the effect 'upon old people like me, is said to be that of making the spirit willing while the flesh continues weak...'. A nearby fountain was said to have the reverse effect! It was near here that Rizzo di Marino was captured in 1488 after the failure of his plot to topple the Venetians by the assassination of Caterina Cornaro's uncles at Famagusta. He was strangled in Venice.

A second EXCURSION (45km there and back) is that along the coastal plain on the E side of sickle-shaped KHRYSOKHOU BAY to (22km) *Pakhyammos*, beyond which it is at present not easy to pass, the adjacent village of *Kokkina* being in Turkish hands. (8km E of this enclave is the Attila Line.)—Driving NE from Polis, after 5km we leave to the right the village of *Argaka*, with a church rebuilt in the late 19C containing some disastrously 'restored' icons.—At c 5km **Yialia** lies a short distance inland below the NW foothills of the Troödos range, here the least inhabited part of the island. The village is known for its early vegetables and fruit, including bananas. Its houses straggle up the valley among orange-groves, in which lie the slight ruins of a rare circular church, probably of the Latin period, and known as *Ayios Cornuto* or *Monastir*. Enlart considered it to be the remains of a Byzantine church of trefoil plan. It was sacked in 1461 but contains remains of ?15C murals.

Kato Yialia, c 2km inland from which is the hamlet of *Ayia Marina*, in a district which has been largely replanted since the forest was destroyed by fire in 1975.

The main road approaches *Nea Dhimmata* and, after winding above the more broken coast, **Pomos**; some 5km SE, beyond *Pomos Dam*, are the remains of the monastic church of *Panayia Khrysopater-itissa*, an early 16C barrel-vaulted building to which a raised narthex was added in 1816; it contains an icon of 1542.

Beyond Pomos the road rounds POMOS POINT to (5km) *Pakhyam-mos*, the last village before the Turkish occupied 'pocket' around *Kokkina*, which became swollen with Turkish Cypriot refugees, who were supplied by sea and by UNFICYP-escorted road convoys.

(It was here in August 1964 that Grivas made an unprovoked attack on Turkish Cypriot villages, precipitating a retaliatory Turkish airforce raid which soon stopped the fighting.)

The region E of the enclave can be visited by following tracks from either Pomos or Pakhyammos, but the deserted villages are of little interest, for in the whole of the hilly and isolated district of TILLYRIA the only church of any importance is *Panayia* or *Galoktisti*, isolated in a valley 1km E of *Khaleri* (or c 1.5km SW of **Kato Pyrgos**). It is a small thick-walled Byzantine structure divided by a heavy arch and with a dome over the W end. According to legend, milk instead of mortar was used in its construction, and expectant mothers used to resort to an icon of the Virgin there.

Until recently the area was the haunt of Linobambakoi (see Glossary).

—*Vouni*, in the Turkish occupied zone, lies 8km due E of *Pyrgos*; see Rte 19.

FROM POLIS TO LYSO (11km) FOR STAVROS TIS PSOKAS, some 13–16km beyond. While not the easiest route (most of it being along rough tracks) it is passable, and traverses some beautiful forest tracts; it is as well, however, to confirm in advance whether accommodation is available at the *Forest Station* (see p 167) if you intend to stay the night in this wilderness.—We fork left off the Paphos road immediately S of Polis, and gently climb SE to **Steni**, near which lie the ruins of the 13C monastery of *Khrysolakourna*, once of importance, the church of which was remodelled and heavily buttressed after an earthquake in the 16C. Its last abbot was hung by the Turks in 1821. Scattered marble fragments remaining in the area might indicate the existence of an earlier temple here.—A short distance beyond lies *Peristerona*, where the ugly modern church preserves some early icons of its predecessor, several badly repainted.—*Trimithousa*, to the S, saw the commencement of the revolt in 1833 of Giaur Imam, a local resident, whose followers controlled Paphos for several months.

Lyso (545m), the largest village in this fig-growing district, commands impressive *Views to the NE over KHRYSOKHOU BAY. Medieval *Panayia Khryseleousa*, possibly a Latin church originally, retains some Gothic capitals and arcading, and coats of arms on its N and S doorways; regrettably, some of its icons have been repainted. There are a number of rock-tombs in the area, while to the SE is the abandoned Turkish Cypriot village of *Melandra*, of ancient origin, with two deserted medieval chapels.—One may return to *Polis* along a rough track from Lyso via *Pelathousa*, where medieval *Ayia Ekaterina* was converted into a mosque, while *Panayia Khorteni*, to the NW, is another domed Byzantine building preserving its founder's tomb and some frescoes. Other old tombs in the area contain the remains of early copper-miners.

A rough winding track leads NE and then E from Lyso, after c 6km reaching crossroads; continue straight ahead here, through the forest, to approach **Stavros tis Psokas** (see below), although the winding forest road appears to be never-ending.... (Avoid this route—and those along other forest roads—towards dusk, or after heavy rain.)

17 Paphos to Kykko via Kannaviou and Stavros tis Psokas

66km (41 miles).

A slow and tiring route, the first part of which has been improved, but one which traverses some of the most attractive and isolated regions of the island. *The distances measured on these mountain tracks are approximate. They should not be attempted in bad weather, for unless there is good visibility, the road loses most of its charm.* Accommodation should be booked at *Stavros*, or at villages further E such as *Pedhoulas* or *Kakopetria*.

A slightly shorter and more direct route can be followed from Kannaviou to Kykko via (6km) *Pano Panayia*, and thence E and NE to (21km) *Kykko*: see below.

Those with a base at Paphos can make a circuit (68km) by bearing E beyond (25km) Kannaviou to *Panayia Khrysorroyiatissa*, and thence S and SW to regain the coast at *Timi*, SE of Paphos: see the sub-route described below.

Forking right 5km beyond *Tsadha* (see Rte 16) the road climbs to **Polemi** (455m), once famous for its topaz crystals (known as 'Baffo—or Basso—diamonds'), but now better known as a grape-packing centre; it was damaged in the 1953 earthquake. The church of the Nativity, or *Christou*, of Byzantine origin, and considerably enlarged in 1723 when the S aisle and narthex were added, contains some 17C icons and an elaborately painted panel in the Italian Renaissance style.— 5km *Ayios Dhimitrianos* (565m) with a well-placed church of 1794, much rebuilt since, has a number of Roman tombs in its vicinity.

From here roads lead N to neighbouring *Milia*, *Lasa*, and *Dhrinia*, among other villages, some with a reputation for their embroidery; the latter has a church of 1755 on an earlier site, restored in 1842.

The road descends to (3km) **Kannaviou**, an attractive hamlet on the POTAMOS TIS EZOUSAS. We follow the valley for c 1.5km, before forking left off the main road, which crosses the river to *Asproyia*, *Pano Panayia*, and the monastery of *Panayia Khrysorroyiatissa*: see below.

At c 1km we reach a bifurcation, and may take either road: the right-hand track follows the lower valley most of the way.

The *Forest Station* of **Stavros tis Psokas** (780m) was established in 1884, and has since been the headquarters of the Paphos Forest District, which controls some two-thirds of the island's forests. On their arrival the British found these in an appalling condition, but Winston Churchill (then Under-Secretary of State for the Colonies), when visiting Cyprus in 1907, prudently arranged for the provision of additional funds for re-afforestation, and the forests have since grown and flourished very considerably, partly due also to A.H. Unwin's enlightened policy (in the late 1920s and early 30s) of condemning the ravages of insatiably nibbling goats, which had largely stripped and destroyed the vegetation.

The area is also the natural habitat of the *ovis ophion*, the Cyprus *moufflon*, which is a strictly protected species of mountain sheep only just saved from extinction. A herd is kept in an adjacent enclosure, but they are shy creatures and are not always to be seen. They were at one time hunted with leopards, of which James I kept 24 for this purpose.

Accommodation is available at the 'Rest House'. The monastery here was abandoned in 1850. In 1974 the Turkish Air Force inexcusably set alight some 260km^2 of forest in Cyprus (some 20 per cent of the total), much of it on the N slopes of the Troödos range near here, but re-afforestation is well under way.

From the Forest Station we climb NE, soon turning right for 5km to reach crossroads (or rather, tracks). The left-hand turning leads directly towards *Kykko*; the right-hand track descends into the *Cedar Valley*; the central track, and recommended to all but the faint-hearted, ascends to the summit of **Mt Tripylos** (1362m), commanding panoramic *Views*, among them plunging views S over the *CEDAR VALLEY. The track then descends: turn left on meeting the lower road. The area is largely populated by the indigenous *cedrus brevifolia*, unique to Cyprus and now *strictly protected*, as well as the more common Troödos pine (*pinus larico*).—Follow the valley side until meeting the direct road, and turn right for c 2km to reach the improved road from Kykko leading to the comparatively unspoiled villages of *Chakistra* and *Kambos* (5km and 7km, respectively, N of Kykko) on the slope of the range and on the road descending to Turkish occupied *Karavostasi* (16km NE, on Morphou Bay).—Turn right here for (3km) *Kykko*: see Rte 9B.

Chakistra (790m) is surrounded by cherry and almond trees and has a church containing very crudely restored icons; *Kambos* (645m) is noted for its cultivation of oregano (the medicinal plant used in cooking) and for a liqueur made from the terebinth (*pistacia lentiscus*), and has a large church (restored 1881) with an ugly white belfry.

An ALTERNATIVE route may be taken by turning E a short distance beyond Kannaviou, and climbing to (3km) *Asproyia* (630m), in the neighbourhood of ancient iron-mines, where *Ayios Epiphanios*, with a steeply-pitched roof, was largely rebuilt in 1723; it preserves an icon of the Pantokrator dated 1523, and another of the same period.— Beyond lies **Pano Panayia**, the birthplace of Makarios Mouskos (1913–77), as Makarios III, Archbishop of Cyprus from 1950, and first President of the Republic of Cyprus from 1960.

A track at the entrance to the village climbs left, and by forking right after c 2km we reach the valley of the ARGAKI TON VRYSHON after another 5km. Here we may bear either left up the valley to (8km N) the *Cedar Valley* (see above) and there turn right; or alternatively, turn right down the valley for 3km, and then fork left for *Kykko*, c 12km NE; see Rte 9B.

Travellers wishing to return to the coast from Pano Panayia should continue on the main road, which shortly reaches (right) the important *MONASTERY OF PANAYIA KHRYSORROYIATISSA (830m; 'Our Lady of the Golden Pomegranate'), commanding fine panoramic *Views. The *Church*, containing a well-carved iconostasis, and built within the triangular cloister, was repaired in 1955.

It is said to have been founded by a monk named Ignatios in 1152, but the present church dates from 1770, erected during general rebuilding and restoration of the entire monastery by Bp Panaretos, when a silver-gilt case (1762) was made for the Icon of the Virgin and set in a heavy frame in 1786. This icon was particularly resorted to by criminals and condemned persons. The original copper-plate (1801) depicting the icon made by the famous Cretan icon-painter John Cornaro is also preserved here. Other dependencies were erected by Abbot Joachim in the early 19C. Visitors are hospitably accommodated. The monastery is reputed for its wine.

We shortly pass on the left (1km) the attractively-sited but disused monastery of **Ayia Moni** (under restoration), its dependencies forming three sides of a courtyard. It is one of the earliest Christian remains in Cyprus, dating from the 6C, if not earlier, and constructed on the site of a Temple to Hera. The apse of its predecessor was preserved when the church was rebuilt in the 17C (restored 1885). Note the boldly carved acanthus leaf design below the semi-dome; also the small chapel behind.

We traverse **Statos**, immediately beyond which, off the left-hand fork, a by-road climbs to the high-lying planned village of *New Statos-Ayios Photios* (c 925m), commanding extensive views. The lower road by-passes *Ayios Photios* itself (725m), with a church of c 1570, repaired in 1835, preserving a medieval bronze cross above its W door.

The next left-hand turning leads shortly to **Galataria**, said to be named after

Galatarka, a woman whose sheep produced an inordinate amount of milk; its church, *Panayia Galaterousa* (literally, bearer of milk), is a pleasant stone building of 1768 containing some good early icons (15–16C).—To the SE is the chapel of *Ayios Nikolaos* (1550), built against a conspicuous rock, and containing smoke-blackened murals.

At *Khoulou*, a hamlet due W, the church of *Ayios Yeoryios* (1480) has been virtually reconstructed. Khoulou was the birthplace, c 1350, of Joanna L'Aleman, Peter I's mistress.

The road continues to follow the ridge between the valleys of (right) the POTAMOS TIS EZOUSAS, and (left) XEROS POTAMOS, providing entensive views, and traverses **Pendalia**, above which are some ancient tombs in a cliff. Its church contains an interesting but 'restored' icon of the Virgin and Child, on the reverse of which is Elijah being fed by ravens.—We next descend to (5km) *Amargeti*, with a prominent church, near which in 1887 D.G. Hogarth excavated a small Temple of Apollo (or Melanthius?) and uncovered numerous terracotta and stone statuettes.—After *Eledhiou* and adjacent *Axylou* (440m), the burial-place of a least three 4C Cypriot saints, the winding descent is continued through *Nata* (210m), and after another 5km **Anarita**, known for its *halloumi* cheese (produced by thyme-fed sheep and goats).—A short distance S is the ruined church of the Byzantine monastery of *Ayios Onesiforos*; the saint, according to tradition, was born at Constantinople, and was at one time an admiral in the service of the Byzantine Empire.

At *Timi* (see p 150), turn right to regain *Paphos*, c 8km NW; see Rte 14.

PART II

18 Nicosia: Northern Sector

For the History of Nicosia, see p 88.
The estimated population of the N sector of the city is 37,400.

The main entrance to the Turkish-occupied part of the Walled City (see also Rte 5C) is the *Kyrenia Gate* (see p 99), just W of due N, and almost facing the new *Turkish Embassy* and adjacent *Atatürk Cultural Centre*.

We follow Kyrenia St to the S past (left) the entrance to the **Mevlevi Tékké**, once the monastery of the 'dancing' Dervish sect, founded in the 13C but suppressed by Kemal Atatürk in 1925. The building (early 17C) has since 1963 been a **Museum of Turkish Cypriot Arts and Crafts**.

Dervishes dancing in the Mevlevi Tékké

Around the wooden floor on which the dervishes ecstatically whirled (above one end of which is a musicians' gallery) there are cases displaying musical instruments (among them a *canon* and an *ut*); costumes (including a *bindalli* or wedding-dress); decorated socks; purses; embroidery; tobacco-pouches; glass; metalwork; calligraphic court records; and a collection of dolls wearing Turkish Cypriot costumes.

Adjacent is the *Mausoleum of the Sheiks*, containing 16 tombs (apart from others underground), among them that of the last sheik, Selim Debe (died 1954). In the garden, among other Turkish tomb-stones, is the white marble sarcophagus of Augustino Carlini (died

1553), a member of the Supreme Council which governed the island during the Venetian occupation.

The street shortly approaches the triangular ATATÜRK SQUARE (previously Qonaq or Konak Square), to the right of which are some old brown-stone arcaded and verandahed government offices, law courts, and the Post Office. In the centre of the square stands a grey granite column (probably from Salamis), which was once surmounted by the Lion of St. Mark; it was overthrown in 1570 and not re-erected until 1915. Coats of arms of Venetian families may be seen around its base.

The tower of a subsidiary palace of the Lusignan kings and later of the Venetian governor stood just to the W, until needlessly demolished at the turn of this century.

Bearing half-left, we pass (right) a hotel, behind which stands the *Saray* (or *Serai*) *Onou Mosque*, to reach an intersection of narrow streets.

Some distance to the W in Mufti Ziya Eff St stands the **Arab Ahmed** (or **Arabahmet**) **Mosque** (1845; restored 1955), built on the site of an earlier church.

Among the paving-stones are the tombs of Francesco Cornaro and of Louis de Nores (1369; in plate armour). A hair from the Prophet's beard is preserved here, and is shown to the Faithful once a year. In the graveyard, below a monument erected in 1927 by Sir Ronald Storrs, lies Kiamil Pasha (1833–1913), the anglophil Grand Vizier of the Ottoman Empire intermittently from 1885, who was born at Pyroi, between Nicosia and Larnaca.

Victoria St leads S from the mosque—passing (left) the attractively restored **Mansion of Dervish Pasha** in an adjoining street, which since 1988 has housed an *Ethnographic Museum*. Notable are the *divans*, and its cool blue and white decoration. Victoria St continues towards the *R.C. Church* near the *Paphos Gate* (see p 98), now S of the Green Line.

To the left, in a side alley, stands the **Armenian Church** dedicated to the Blessed Virgin Mary (*Sourp Asdouadzadzin*), originally a Benedictine convent (13–14C; dedicated to N.D. de Tyr). It was ransacked in 1310 during a revolt. It was later handed over to the Armenian community, which had existed in that quarter of the town since Byzantine times (there were c 2400 Armenians in Nicosia and its suburbs in 1960). The Gothic character of the original is perhaps best seen from the unfinished cloister, containing some interesting tombstones (many traced by Major Tankerville Chamberlayne in his 'Lacrymae Nicosiense', Paris 1894); a number of other tombstones lay below a carpet in the interior until removed in 1962. At present access to the church is restricted, it being very near the Green Line.

Turning E just short of the above intersection and following Mousa Orfanbey St, we pass (right) the entrance (below the present street level) of the old portal of the church of *St George of the Latins* (14C); it was later coverted to Turkish baths known as the **Büyük Hamam**.

Leaving the *Iplik Bazari Mosque* on our left, we reach the corner of the *Kumarcilar Khan ('of the gamblers'; also known as that 'of the itinerant musicians'), a late 17C caravanserai or inn, now

restored and providing offices for the Turkish Cypriot Antiquities
Department. It contains a central courtyard of two storeys, the pillared
upper floor supported by Gothic arches, and the roof covered by flat
domes.

The Büyük Khan under restoration

A few paces S stands the NE buttress of the larger *Büyük Khan
('the great inn'), an entrance of which is on its W side. It is still in the
process of a thorough restoration, although renovated once in 1955. It
preserves octagonal stone chimneys, and in the centre of the
courtyard a small domed octagonal *mescit* or mosque, supported on
marble pillars. It opened as a caravanserai in 1572, but during the
early period of British rule, until 1893, it was used as Nicosia's Central
Prison. There is a long-term project to turn it into a Museum.

On regaining the street abutting the E wall of the khan, take the
next left-hand turning and follow Arasta St to the *Selimiye Mosque,
so-designated in 1954 in honour of Sultan Selim II (1566–74) in whose
reign the Turks captured the island, and previously known as the
Cathedral of St. Sophia or *Aysofya*. It is the principal monument of
Nicosia—in spite of its fallen state— its twin minarets forming a
prominent landmark in the centre of the walled city. Architecturally—even when stripped of those human features abhorrent to
the Faithful—it remains one of the more imposing relics of Christendom in the Near East, although the more complete façade of its com-
panion at Famagusta is more aesthetically pleasing. Nevertheless, its
present unkempt state, both internal and external, leaves much to be
desired.

Work on the present cathedral began in 1209, under Abp Thierry, a Parisian,
although fragments of a slightly earlier and probably temporary structure are
discernable in the N doorway. The edifice was eventually consecrated in 1326,

but the W façade, largely due to Abp Eustorge de Montaign (1217–51) and to the munificent patronage of Louis IX of France in 1248, may not have been completed for another three decades; the towers remained unfinished. In 1373 it was pillaged by the Genoese, and by the Mamelukes in 1426, and suffered damage in the earthquakes of 1491, 1547 (after which the upper part of the clerestory at the E end was rebuilt by the Venetians), and 1735. Hugh II was buried here in 1267. In 1570 or very shortly after, it was converted into a mosque. The interior was gutted of all Christian emblems by the Turks, and the bones of those buried there were scattered and their tombstones re-used to pave the floor. The two tall minarets were added later. (In Greek *Ayia Sophia* means Divine or Saintly Wisdom, and has no connection with any female named Sophia.)

The Selimiye Mosque, formerly the Cathedral of St. Sophia (photographed in 1878 by John Thomson)

The building measures 38m by 66m. The balance of the unfinished W front, with its decorated portals—the central one almost twice the width of its companions, and surmounted by its great W window—is spoilt by the superimposition of the incongruous minarets. Note—in the central portal—the small sculpted figures picked clean of the plaster with which they were once covered by the Turks, above which only two censing angels remain; and the elaborate floral decoration, including the clematis, as an architectural motif on the N doorway. The roofs, supported by buttresses, are flat terraces.

The interior of the building, which has fulfilled the function of a mosque for over 400 years, may be visited, but travellers are reminded to remove their shoes before entering and to observe silence if any formal worship is taking place.

The plan consists of a nave and aisles of five bays, terminated by a semi-circular apse encircling both nave and aisles. The massive cylindrical pillars have been whitewashed and their marble Byzantine capitals painted dark green, red, and yellow (as noted by the

Archduke Louis Salvador of Austria in 1873, who considered such daubing abominable). The four columns in the apse are probably from Salamis. Martoni (1394) mentions that the whole of the vault from the choir arch to the high altar was painted with 'fine blue and gold stars'—more likely golden stars on a blue base. Note that the carpets—few of which are remarkable—are placed diagonally, to face in the direction of Mecca; a grandfather clock also indicates Mecca time. The *Mihrab* stands in the S Transept, once the Lady Chapel (founded by Hugh III in 1270), while above the N Transept is the Women's Gallery. Adjacent is a small chapel, once the Treasury. In what was once that of St. Thomas Aquinas (the second on the S side: the saint had dedicated his *De Regimine Principium* to Hugh III) are a number of Christian tombstones.

Opposite the N door of the cathedral, with marble columns, and surmounted by a rose which has been filled in, stand relics of the Latin Archibishopric, of which only a door, two small windows, and various coats of arms remain.

Immediately S of the W Front is the partially ruined **Bedestan*, long used by the Turks as a grain store and covered textile market (whence its name); it is in fact part of two abutting churches, the W ends of which have been destroyed. The N façade contains three portals, the E doorway being a stone copy—but of inferior workmanship and smaller in scale—of the marble portal of the cathedral. Above the lintel is a panel on which six Venetian coats of arms are carved (one defaced), in the centre of which is the figure of a saint, assumed by some to be St. Nicholas 'of the English'. A small tracery 'rose' decorates the upper part of the gable. Note also the external iconostasis, probably brought here from elsewhere, which is embellished with a small sculpture of the Death of the Virgin.

The S half of this building is the older church, consisting of two aisles and two apses: note the shields on the capitals of the central line of pillars. A carved portal from the W end was removed in 1906 to the gardens of Government House (see p 92). Two aisles were added in the 16C, one ending in a three-sided apse, and surmounted by an octagonal cupola. The vaulting at the W end of this nave may have been restored (badly) after an earthquake.

A number of medieval tombstones have been collected together here, many of them from the *Ömerye Mosque* (see p 102). Its proximity to the mosque caused the Muslim community to reject a plan (1879) to renovate and convert the Bedestan into an Anglican church.

Bearing round the S side of the Bedestan, we cross diagonally NE between the cathedral apse and a restored building of the Venetian period (probably the Chapter House; the rich mouldings of its windows repaired) to reach the small domed **Library of Sultan Mahmud II**. It was founded early in the 19C and contains gilt woodwork in the Turkish 'Empire' style, and a collection of Turkish, Arabic, and Persian books, including a few rarities.

Just to the E stands the *Jeffery's Museum*, incorporating a Flamboyant Gothic window from the Lusignan palace (see p 171), and containing a small lapidary collection. It is named after George Jeffery, who was responsible for the conservation of the island's monuments in the early years of this century.

Kirlizade St leads N, shortly passes (right) the **Haidar* (or Haydar) **Pasha Mosque**, once the Church of St. Catherine, and apart from the cathedral, the most important surviving Gothic structure in Nicosia. The façade of this late 14C building in the Flamboyant Gothic style, in which windows were pierced during the Turkish period, preserves two doorways: that on the W has a broken marble lintel decorated with a rose supported by two dragons(?), three times repeated; that to the S is a heavier portal surmounted by a lintel on which are three defaced shields, above which is a graceful window. Note the unusual buttresses. N of the apse is the sacristy, its vaulting supported by corbels of carved heads, which have surprisingly survived. Long derelict, the building has been recently restored.

Flamboyant Gothic window from the Lusignan palace, now in the Jeffery's Museum. See plate on p 89

Captain (later Field-Marshal) Horatio Herbert Kitchener (1850–1916), who from 1878 was responsible for the first survey of Cyprus, lived in 1880–83 at No. 1 Haydar Pasha St, adjacent.

Further N, on the left, after passing a restored Turkish house and a Turkish tomb—one of three in the vicinity—are the slight remains of the *Yeni Cami Mosque*: only the staircase with its turret, above which a minaret has been added, remains from the medieval church (14C?), superseded by the mosque in 1571. The rest of the building was torn down by one of the more insatiably rapacious governors during the mid 18C in a futile search for buried treasure.

From here the *Atatürk Square* can be regained by retracing one's steps to the Cathedral-Mosque. The alternative is to thread through a maze of alleys (indicated on the Pl; pp 100–1) to the *Kyrenia Gate*, passing near the former church of *Ayios Loukas* (c1758), long derelict but now restored.

19   Nicosia to Morphou, Soli, and Vouni

61km (38 miles).

For the road to (19km) *Skylloura*, see the latter part of Rte 22, in reverse.

FROM SKYLLOURA TO KALOKHORIO (13km). The road due W ascends through *Ayia Marina*, just to the W of which is the ancient Byzantine settlement of *Floudi*, now in ruins.—Further W is the monastery of *Ayios Yeoryios o Rigatos* (15C, and often restored since), with an extensive necropolis adjacent.—NE of Ayia Marina is the abandoned monastery of *Prophitis Elias.*—The road traverses the hamlet of *Dhyo Potami* before entering *Kalokhorio*, see p 189.

The main road from Skylloura bears SW to (8km) *Philia*, and then NW through (3km) *Kyra*, where *Panayia Khryseleousa* (16C; restored 1879) has fine fluted columns by its W door.—*Morphou* is 6km due W.

To the S of Kyra is *Masari*, a poor hamlet in an attractive setting on a riverbank; *Ayios Antonios*, barrel-vaulted, had frescoes, long-since whitewashed over. To the SW of the church, near the Attila Line, are the villages of *Kato Kopia* (also *Katokopia*) and **Argaki**, with a 16C or earlier church, rebuilt c 1885, preserving a Baroque iconostasis and some poorly restored contemporary icons.—*Morphou* is 5km NW of the latter.

MORPHOU (6650 inhab. in 1960; now estimated at 11,200) was probably settled by Greeks, and in the Byzantine era was the centre of the Akrides or 'coast-watchers'. Its inhabitants were active during the revolt of the peasant 'king' Alexis in 1426. In 1974 it was occupied by the Turkish army and has since been called *Güzelyurt*. A concrete mosque has been built in front of the Byzantine church.

In the Lusignan period its main crops were sugar and cotton, and later flax, but these have been largely replaced today by citrus production, strawberries (two crops annually), vegetables, and cereals. In 1907 it was connected by rail to Nicosia and Famagusta, which eased the export of its produce. It was described by Drummond in the mid 18C as 'a very cheerful place'; the rebuilding of its church of Ayios Mamas, containing fragments from other ancient buildings, and the saint's tomb, had still not been completed at that time.

The **Monastery of Ayios Mamas**, in which is preserved the tomb of St. Mamas (see below), is of Byzantine foundation, probably replacing a Temple to Aphrodite. Rebuilt in the 15C, the church was again much remodelled from 1725, when the central dome was added; and in c 1779, when further monastic dependencies were erected, using some columns and capitals from the former church. A number of details survive from the 15C Flamboyant Gothic structure: the N and S doorways, the nave columns, the two marble columns of the W window, and the shrine of the saint. The W door is covered with graffiti, including that of the French consul M. Porry (1738), and an inscription (1753) recording the visit and cure of a man from Moscow. The modern wing was the residence of the Bp of Kyrenia.

The impressive iconostasis is a mixture of styles and periods, including four marble columns with Gothic capitals, the lower panels dating from c 1500. (These latter are some of the more interesting remaining on the island of the Venetian period, with Venetian coats of arms at the corners, once painted, and decorated in high relief.) The gilt and painted woodwork of the iconostasis and of the baldachin above the altar are both late 16C; the altar itself is supported by five marble columns, two with Byzantine capitals. The only old icon remaining is one of the Virgin, dated 1745. The painted pulpit is dated 1761.

The *Shrine of St. Mamas* is in a recess below Gothic arches on the N side of the church. A white marble Byzantine (Roman?) sarcophagus is built into the thickness of the wall, so that it can be seen from both sides. This sarcophagus, containing the saint's relics, was opened by the Turks after their first occupation, who expected it to contain treasure, and the holes they made are still pointed out, through which, it is said, sweat miraculously issued.

Living as he did in a mere cave, St. Mamas felt it was unjust that he should be expected to pay the oppressive taxation of the Byzantine rulers, and refused. He was arrested and taken to Nicosia. During the journey, as the party was passing through a wood, a ferocious lion—unknown in Cyprus (although tame hunting leopards were owned by the Lusignan kings)—sprang out to attack a lamb gambolling in the path ahead. St. Mamas held up his hand, and the lion stopped in its tracks, wagging its tail in token of submission. The saint, tired of walking, picked up the lamb, and to the astonishment of his guards, mounted the lion and, on reaching the capital, so entered the duke's throne-room. The sight so amazed the duke that St. Mamas was forthwith absolved from paying his taxes. His candid defiance and the subsequent miracle gained him the admiration of the Cypriot peasantry, and he was long venerated.

Adjacent to the monastery is a small **Museum**, devoted to the Archaeology and Natural History of the area, including some Middle or Late Cypriot period ceramics from Toumba tou Skourou; some terracotta figures; and also artefacts imported from Anatolia.

6km to the NW lies *Syrianokhori*, probably settled—as its name suggests—by Syrian mercenaries in c 1200. The marshes adjacent to MORPHOU BAY once provided good snipe-shooting.

Leading SW, the road by-passes (left) *Nikitas* and after 6km traverses *Prastio*, the centre of a rich agricultural area, with a late 18C barrel-vaulted church. The monastery of *Ayios Nikolaos* (1828) on its outskirts is of slight interest; that of *Baraji*, to the N, is of the same period.—Continuing SW, the road passes through *Ghaziveran* and (6km) **Pendayia**, an important town in medieval times and earlier; to its N lie the ruins of *Ayios Yeorios*, surrounded by Roman tombs, while in the churchyard of the adjacent monastery of *Xeropotamos* lie a number of Corinthian capitals and other relics from *Soli* (see below). To the S are the ruins of the Byzantine monastery of *Ayii Seryios and Bacchos*. The golf course of Pendayia dates from 1912.

From Pendayia a road leads SE to (5km) **Petra**, on the Attila Line. It was once the personal property of Peter II, who in 1375 gave it to Sir Thibald Belfarage for his services against the Genoese. Its main church of *Metamorphosis* (Transfiguration) has been entirely rebuilt. It nevertheless preserves early icons, the most important being the untouched Virgin and Child of c 1500. Domed *Ayios Vasilios* had its frescoes whitewashed over when converted to a mosque.—To the N is the ugly village of *Elea*, with a medieval church abandoned in c 1930, adjacent to which is a Venetian fountain.—3km to the W of Petra is *Kalokhorio*, on the railway line from the Skouriotissa Mines (see Rte 9B); 3km beyond is *Lefka*, see below.

At 6km SW of Pendayia, after skirting the S shore of MORPHOU BAY, the road leads to **Karavostasi** (or *Xeros*), a large unattractive village which until the recent occupation was the main port for loading copper from the Skouriotissa Mine, worked out by 1976. In 1441 Helen Palaeologina landed here to marry John II, becoming a somewhat tyrannical queen; it is said of her that she bit off the nose of her husband's mistress, Marietta of Patras (mother of James II, 'the Bastard' and last King of Cyprus).

3km SE is the large village of **Lefka** (3680 inhab. in 1960), which was once one of the principal baronies of the kingdom, and a centre of the peasant uprising of 1426 (cf. Morphou). Surrounding the place is a Hellenistic and Roman necropolis dating from an earlier period of exploitation of the copper mines in the area. Bronze Age artefacts have also been found.

The mosques of *Koprulu Haci Ibrahim Aga* and *Orta* are said to stand on the sites of ancient churches. A Rococo tomb of a pasha (c 1820) can be seen in the graveyard, and inscribed cippi abound.

Ambelikou, 3km to the SW of Karavostasi, is surrounded by Roman tombs, and Chalcolithic remains have also been excavated. A Corinthian marble capital from Soli and other fragments may be seen there.

Immediately to the W of Karavostasi is the site of *SOLI.

The original city of *Sillu* was founded here in c 700 BC as one of the ten Hittite Kingdoms of Cyprus. A century later, when Solon was visiting King Philokypros at nearby *Aepia* (see *Vouni*), the Athenian statesman suggested ways and means of defending the place, which in c 498 held out for four months when besieged by the Persians. (This provided a slender foundation for the tradition that *Sillu* changed its name to Soli in honour of Solon.) Soli was a flourishing centre for the export of copper during the Roman era, and is reputed to have had the first public library on the island. Its theatre was probably constructed in the 2C AD, and its basilica in the 5C. It was a residence of the Orthodox Bishop of Nicosia during the Latin domination (c 1222), although by that time the town was virtually abandoned, and had been since Arab raids in 632.

It was briefly visited by Pococke in 1738, who could make little out of the ruins, already used as a quarry and which in the later 19C were plundered of much of their remaining masonry for the construction of Port Said and the Suez Canal.

The Swedish Expedition of 1930, led by Einar Gjerstad, excavated the theatre, and in 1932 laid bare the temples of Isis (50 BC), Aphrodite (250 BC; the Aphrodite of Soli can be seen in the Cyprus Museum, Nicosia), and Serapis (or Mithras; AD 550). Concurrently, they explored the small island of Petra tou Limniti offshore to the W of Vouni, and found Neolithic implements and pottery. Further archaeological expeditions were busy in the area from 1965 until the Turkish invasion.

It is convenient to visit first the *Theatre*, the highest of the sites on the gentle hill slope, and cut into the rock. The auditorium had a diameter of some 52m. It has been much restored, but provides a pleasant view N across MORPHOU BAY.—Further down the slope, to the right, are the remains of the *Basilica*, including a number of mosaic floors.— To the W is the site of the *Agora*, which was being excavated prior to the Turkish occupation.

Upon regaining the coast road, bear W through the village of *Potamos tou Kambou*, a site reinhabited during recent years by refugees from *Galini*, inland to the W. A headless marble statue (probably from Soli; 2C BC) has been built into the church apse at Galini.

Some 3km W of Potamos, after climbing inland, a steep track leads right to approach the hill-top plateau which provides the imposing site (with extensive views) for the ***Palace of Vouni**.

Excavations here in 1928–29 did not reveal anything earlier that the 5C BC, and it is therefore inferred that it was not Vouni, formerly identified with Aepia, which was superseded by Soli (both names mean hill or hill top). It has been suggested that Aepia may have been Evrykhou, SE in the Solea valley. Solon is supposed to have recommended that the site be moved to Soli, nearer the sea and with a better water supply. The building of the palace followed the restoration of a pro-Greek dynasty by Kimon after the fall of the city of Marion, present-day Polis (see Rte 16), but it was burned c 380 BC, and shortly after attacked by Soli, and destroyed.

The main entrance (later blocked) of the palace is approached from the SW, leading into the megaron. Off the megaron are the state apartments, with a flight of seven steps descending to a peristyle court, surrounded by rooms. Below the court is a cistern, and on the seaward side of the well-head stands a stone stele designed to support a windlass.

From the NW corner of this area one may visit the *Baths*, with a vaulted furnace, to the S of which is a *Service Court*, off which store-rooms open.

Returning to the megaron, we pass the site where the Vouni treasure was found; to the NW is a further series of rooms, some with cisterns beneath, and others with store-rooms for amphorae, etc. The new main entrance was made at the NW corner of this building.

Below the palace, to the N, is an open-air temenos, where a deposit of sculptures was found. In an adjacent room are four altars, two circular, and two semi-circular.—To the S, at the summit of the hill, are the slight remains of a *Temple to Athena*, of the third quarter of the 5C BC.

On descending to the main road one may continue W to (3km) *Limnitis*. Neolithic remains have been found on the islet of *Petra tou Limniti*, offshore to the NW.—3km inland is the village of *Loutros*, said to have been first inhabited by settlers from the Aegean island of Tilos, brought here in c 350 by St. Helena, the mother of Constantine.

A short distance further W is the Attila Line, cutting off communications with *Polis*, while inland rise the sequestered hills of TILLYRIA, the NW foothills of the central Troödos range: see also p 165–6.

20   Nicosia to Kyrenia via St. Hilarion

32km (20 miles).

The road leading NW from Nicosia passes (right) the suburb of
Trakhonas, where an interesting medieval church was destroyed
and replaced by a modern building in 1916, and traverses the
suburb of *Orta Keuy* (Ortaköy), with a medieval bridge, and *Geunyeli* (Gönyeli), the scene of some ugly inter-communal incidents
in past decades. The road starts to climb the foothills of the Kyrenia range, with the peaks of PROPHITIS ELIAS (888m) slightly to the
W, and to the E the peak of TRYPA VOUNO or MOUNT ALONAGRA
(935m).

From Orta Keuy the 'old' road to Kyrenia forks right to (8km) *Kato* and *Pano
Dhikomo*, noted for their handloom weaving.
    At 7km a road leads left to the village of *Krini* and, further W, *Pileri*
(345m), with a large medieval cistern and arched water conduit cut into the
mountainside; to the S is the ruined hamlet of *Bilesha* (or *Pleshia*), with
remains of a church.

The main road passes (left) near *Aghirda*, close to which a battle
was fought in 1232, when the Lusignans defeated the Longobards;
in the past it had the reputation of being the haunt of high-
waymen, being conveniently placed at the entrance of the pass to
Kyrenia.
    The next left-hand turning climbs steeply to the main entrance
of the *CASTLE OF ST. HILARION—'a picture-book castle for elf
kings', in the words of Rose Macaulay, a wild and dramatic maze
of fortifications, vaulted chambers, and crumbling towers, sprawl-
ing over the towering mass of splintered rocks which here forms
an eyrie commanding the range, and offering plunging views of
the coast below. The summit lies at 732m (2400 feet).

It is named after a 10–11C monastery that once stood on the site—also
known as *Didymos* (twins) after two small adjacent crags—which had been
the abode of an anchorite called Hilarion who had sought refuge here from
the Holy Land (not to be confused with St. Hilarion the Great, who died near
Paphos in 731). The site was partially fortified prior to its eventual surrender
by Isaac Comnenos to Richard I in 1191. It was strengthened in the 1220s,
and was the refuge of Jean d'Ibelin and the boy-king Henry I when the
Emperor Frederick II Hohenstaufen attempted to take over the island. In
1229 Frederick's supporters were in turn besieged in the castle by D'Ibelin
and Philipo di Novarra, who was wounded. Philipo, of Lombard origin and
also known as Philippe de Novare, died c 1265; he spent most of his life on
the island and was the author of a history of the war, continued by the
'Gestes des Chiprois' of Gérard de Montréal.
    Three years later, by the timely defeat of Richard Filangieri and the Lom-
bards by D'Ibelin at Aghirda (SW of the Kyrenia pass) on 15 June 1232, the
castle was saved, and the 'Imperial' forces, retreating on Kyrenia, were
forced to capitulate the following April. It was embellished during the 14C,
and was frequently the summer residence of the Lusignan court. Hugh IV
retired here in 1348 to avoid the plague. Young Peter II sought safety here
with his uncle John, Prince of Antioch, during the Genoese invasion, and it
was here that the grim episode occurred in which John, persuaded by his
sister-in-law Eleanor of Aragón that his Bulgarian mercenaries were planning
to assassinate him, precipitated them one after the other into a dizzy abyss.
    The castle was slighted by the Venetians after 1489 in spite of its strategic
importance. It communicated by flares at night with Kyrenia and Buffavento,
and through the latter with Nicosia and Kantara.

Passing through the outer gate, abutted by the restored gate-house, and (left) the barbican, we enter the LOWER WARD, in which the garrison and their mounts were quartered, and the site of cisterns.

The path ascends to the left, passing (right) *Stables*, and continues to climb to an upper gate-house, and threads a tunnel beyond, to enter the MIDDLE WARD. To the right stands the Byzantine *Church*, once domed, and restored in 1959 to prevent the collapse of its vaults. It dates from the late 10C. To the N are steps descending to a vaulted passage and hall, probably serving as a refectory. To the right is a vaulted loggia or *Belvedere*. Adjacent were the kitchens, while the NE section of the building provided palatial accommodation for the royal family before the erection of more extensive apartments in the Upper Ward. Part has been converted to house a restaurant and bar, and commands good views.

Hence we continue the steep climb by a winding path and flights of steps, passing (right) another large cistern, to approach the UPPER WARD, entered through a Frankish arched gate set into the Byzantine wall and overlooked by a tower. To the right were the kitchens, while on the W side of the enceinte are the ruins of the *Royal Apartments*, built above another cistern. One window, known as that of the Queen, retains some tracery and side seats, and provides an extensive view towards Cape Kormakiti. Steps ascend to ramparts to the S, on the wind-blown crest of which is the *Summit* (*Views). Before making the descent, the agile may climb to *Prince John's Tower*, isolated in the centre of the fortress, with sheer precipices on three sides, and said to be that from which the Prince of Antioch hurled his Bulgarians (see above).

Having descended from the castle and regained the main road, we pass on the right a direct road to *Bellapais*, 5km E (see Rte 21), and climbing down the N flank of the range, with splendid views to the E, we veer N, by-passing the village of *Thermia*, with an old church, to enter **Kyrenia** itself, see below.

21 Kyrenia and Bellapais

KYRENIA (3500 inhab. in 1960, including 2371 Greek Cypriots, 695 Turkish Cypriots, and 195 British), the capital of its District and the main town on the N coast of the island, with its rapid growth during the last 40 years, has lost much of its once tranquil character. Its present estimated population is 6900. Over three decades ago Lawrence Durrell had already noted alarming symptoms of a change in atmosphere, but its horseshoe-shaped harbour, flanked by several restaurants, is still comparatively unspoilt; the Castle is of consider-able interest, and it remains a convenient centre from which to explore the beautiful N side of the Kyrenia range.

As *Cerynia*, it was an Achaean Greek settlement in the 10C BC; as *Corineum* it was a Roman town; and in the Christian era it became an Orthodox see. Although walled, it was, with most other coastal towns, looted by the Arabs. Its castle, on the site of an earlier Byzantine fort, was the residence of the Lusignan kings, and in 1374 it was attacked by the Genoese. In 1570 it surrendered to the Turks without a shot being fired. The port was known as *Gerinia* (or *Gerines*) during much

Kyrenia from the air, with the castle in the foreground

of the Turkish occupation. The Turks themselves retired to the castle at night, leaving the town in the hands of the largely Greek population. In 1631 it was reported as being 'chiefly ruinous'; by 1814 only about 15 families lived here.

Communications with Nicosia were improved in 1880 by the construction of a new road via Dhikomo, and another further W through Geunyeli in 1902. The population rose from 1200 (half Greek and half Turkish Cypriots) in 1881 to 2900 in 1946. The small harbour—the only one of any consequence on the N littoral—was improved in 1886–91, and in the 1950s a breakwater was carried around to the E of the castle, the main N entrance being then closed. From the turn of the century Kyrenia became increasingly a place of retirement for British Colonial officials among others, and here the

(NEW HARBOUR)

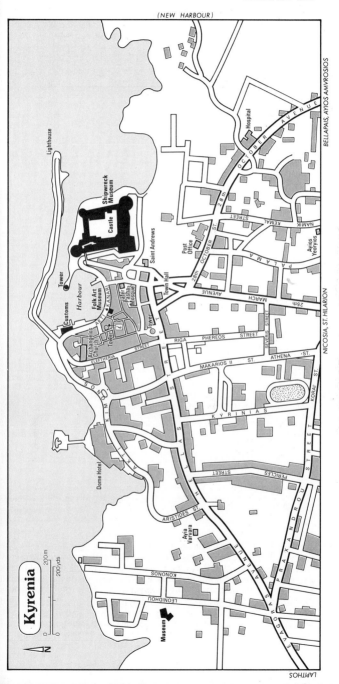

Kyrenia

N

0   200 m
0   200 yds

Lighthouse

Tower

Harbour

Castle

Shipwreck
Museum

Saint Andrews

Customs

Folk Art
Museum

Cafer Pasha
Mosque

Town Hall

Archangelos
Church

Tower

KANARI

i

ELEFTHERIA

KIM

SON

Dome Hotel

HELLAS   STREET

KYRINIAS

RIGA PHEREOS STREET

MAKARIOS II   ST.   ATHENA   ST.

SEVERIS STREET

STREET

Hospital

OCTOBER   AVENUE

26th

NAMIK   KEMAL   STREET

Post
Office

26th OCTOBER   ST.

Ayios
Yeoryios

PALAMA

25th   MARCH   AVENUE

KORAI   ST.

PERICLES   STREET

PRAXANDROU   AVENUE

EVAGORAS

ARISTIDES   ST.

Ayia
Varvara

SONONOS

LEONIDHOU

Museum

BELLAPAIS, AYIOS AMVROSIOS

NICOSIA, ST. HILARION

LAPITHOS

British colony lived 'what appeared to be a life of blameless monotony' (in the words of Durrell, who himself first settled here in 1953). The *Dome Hotel* and its bar flourished.

There was general looting of private property during the Turkish occupation of 1974. By 1986 only ten per cent of the c 2500 permanent British residents remained. Meanwhile Turkish Cypriots from the Limassol area had been resettled in the district, and 'colonists' from the mainland have also landed here. A new harbour is under construction to the E of the port. The old upper town, previously known as the Turkish sector, was called *Regiatiko*. The present Turkish name for the whole town is *Girne*.

An attractive **Museum of Folk Art** has been opened in a building overlooking the Harbour, containing a wine-press, looms, a Bride's Chest (sandouki) among other furniture, and fabrics from the Karpas. Note the brazier, a bed alcove, and a collapsible bed with carved posts. A short distance to the E stands the imposing *Castle, approached by a bridge on the site of an earlier draw-bridge.

The original Byzantine fortificiations must have been constructed, perhaps around a Roman fort, prior to the 11C. It surrendered shortly after being attacked by Guy de Lusignan in 1191, and it changed hands frequently during the period 1228–33, when Frederick II Hohenstaufen was attempting to control the island, finally falling to D'Ibelin in April 1233. It was considerably remodelled in the 1290s, and then used as a State prison; in 1349 King Hugh's two sons were held there in punishment for attempting to visit Europe! In 1368, during the absence abroad of Peter I (one of the two princes), his mistress Joanna l'Aleman was mewed up here—not unreasonably—by his queen, Eleanor, in one of her many fits of jealousy. Under the future James I it successfully resisted, in 1373–74, all Genoese attempts to take the fortress, and after the king's coronation in 1385 the castle became his favourite residence, and further improvements were undertaken. The royal family took refuge here in 1426, when the Mamelukes briefly overran the island, as did Carlotta and Louis de Savoy in 1460, when invested by her step-brother James, the Bastard. It surrendered four years later when the occupants were threatened with starvation.

The Venetians did much in the way of reconstructing and adapting the stronghold. The W wall was entirely rebuilt in 1544, and massive towers were raised at the NW and SE angles, and in 1560 the huge rectangular SW bastion. It is possible that the fortifications surrounded an inner harbour, which was filled in during this period. It was surrendered to the invading Turks under Sadik Pasha without a fight in 1570, however, on learning of the fall of Nicosia. In 1765, following the revolt of its commandant Khalil Agha, its walls successfully resisted being stormed, but it surrendered after being blockaded.

It was again used as a prison during the British occupation, and was later converted into police barracks. In 1950 it passed into the hands of the Department of Antiquities. It was largely restored in 1955, when it was again occupied by the military, being garrisoned by British security forces and used for the internment of members of EOKA.

On entering the castle bear right, passing (right) steps descending to a *Water-gate*, and (left) a passage leading to a 12C Byzantine *Chapel* (with a restored dome). A *Gate-house*, embellished with a medieval coat of arms, placed there in recent times, leads into the main courtyard; note the tomb of Sadik Pasha (1571), the Turkish naval commander. Steps ascend (right) to *Royal Apartments*, below which is an undercroft, and oubliettes. Continuing the circuit of the walls in an anti-clockwise direction, we pass the Byzantine SW Tower, just beyond which a passage descends to the SW bastion at a lower level. Adjacent is the SOUTH WARD (excavated in 1952–53), the exterior entrance to which is flanked by carved lions, probably Roman. Another passage leads down to dungeons below the SE Tower.

Abutting the E wall are several large halls, two of which now house the *'**Kyrenia Ship'**, wrecked in c 300 BC and found at a depth of some 18m c 1km offshore to the NE, from which position it was removed in 1969 by the University of Pennsylvania Expedition, being the oldest vessel ever to have been raised from the sea bed. The hull—of Aleppo pine sheathed with lead—was then reassembled and immersed in a preservative before being displayed, together with part of its cargo and ballast consisting of plates, oil jugs, jars of almonds, amphorae, etc. A replica of the ship, may be seen, together with photographs of the diving and salvaging operations. The exhibition had been virtually completed just prior to the Turkish occupation.

To the NE is another tower, horseshoe-shaped, and with an undercroft. The * Views of the Kyrenia range from the battlements are superb.

Making our exit from Kyrenia we climb SE, either traversing or by-passing (left) Kazaphani, with its unusual Late Byzantine church (Panayia Potamitissa), containing decayed frescoes and a well-preserved medieval wall-tomb.—Regrettably, the extensive Early Bronze Age necropolis of Vounos, remotely sited on the hillside between Kazaphani and Bellapais, has been systematically looted, and numerous tombs have been rifled.

Bellapais in 1878, photographed by John Thomson

5km. **BELLAPAIS** (220m), with the ruins of its magnificently sited abbey, for which it was long famous, sprang into prominence, as Bellapaix, with the publication in 1957 of Lawrence Durrell's 'Bitter Lemons'. The author had lived in a rehabilitated Turkish house in the village in 1953–55, and in his description of the buying of the house his keen sense of humour is seen at its best.

Here he wrote 'Justine', while amongst his visitors and guests were Patrick Leigh Fermor, Patrick Balfour (Lord Kinross), John Lehmann, George Seferis, Sir Harry Luke, Rose Macaulay, and Freya Stark.

Although much is hidden by the luxuriant vegetation, the village has lost its once unsophisticated character with the commercialisation of the area, which has likewise deprived the square to the S of the abbey of much of its charm. The village hardly existed until the Turkish invasion of 1570, when it grew with the influx of Greeks from Kyrenia and with the female offspring of the philoprogenitive monks (see below).

It has been suggested that the site was originally the Orthodox Bishop of Kyrenia's residence and refuge from Arab raiders during the period 648–965. The name 'Episcopia', by which the abbey was earlier known was later corrupted to 'Lapais' or 'de la Paix', and in the 16C to Bellapais.

The abbey was founded c 1200 as a house of Augustinian canons by Aimery de Lusignan, that Order previously having custody of the church of the Holy Sepulchre until the loss of Jerusalem in 1187. They were accompanied, or soon followed by, white canons of the Order of St. Norbert, and from 1206 adopted the Norbertine or Premonstratensian rule under Thierry, second Latin Archbishop of Nicosia. Their white habit gave the abbey still another name—the *White Abbey*—by which it is referred to in 15–16C documents.

It grew in size and importance largely due to the pious patronage and generosity of Hugh III (died 1284), who is possibly buried here. In 1373 its wealth (including a fragment of the True Cross bequeathed in 1246) attracted the rapacious propensities of the Genoese, who proceeded to appropriate most of its portable treasure. Its pretentions were such that it frequently came into conflict with the Archbishop of Nicosia, where the mitred Abbots (with the privilege of carrying a gilded sword and of wearing golden spurs when riding) also maintained a town residence. During the years 1354–58 King Hugh IV lived in the abbey, to which he had added suitably royal apartments.

By the mid 16C the strict rule of the community had sadly deteriorated: many of the monks had wives (some as many as three!), 'and the revenues are assigned to their children so that the brethren live in great penury'—so stated one official report. By the time it had been sacked by the occupying Turks in 1570, there was little to recommend it but its site; nevertheless it was still described as 'most magnificent' by Pococke in 1738, and it was visited in 1750 by Alexander Drummond, who was equally impressed by its 'palatial stile'; but when Captain Kinneir passed this way in 1814 he observed cows grazing in the outer court.

Much of the building had been used as a quarry for the construction of adjacent village houses, and in 1878 the British Army callously cemented over the floor of the great hall in the expectation of turning it into a military hospital. The ruins were repaired in 1912 under the supervision of George Jeffery; but when he requested an increase in the contemptible budget given for the preservation of the island's monuments, in particular for the consolidation of the dormitory, he was told by the Philistine authorities (according to Sir Harry Luke) that its stone 'would come in handy for road-metal'. It did not even do that: the weathered sandstone proved far too soft.

The ***Abbey** is built on a rock escarpment, the N edge of which drops vertically for over 30m. The main entrance is from the SW through a gateway where there was previously a drawbridge. Opposite this stands the 13C *Church*, its flat roof supported by four pillars. By the entrance to the Cloister, stairs ascend to the dormitory. To the E of the *Cloister*, embellished by four Cypresses, is the square *Chapter-house* with its vaulting once sustained by a single central marble column; adjacent is the *Undercroft* of the dormitory, with remains of its plain barrel vault, and a damaged rose window at its N end. At the NW corner of the cloister is a marble lavabo incorporating a carved sarcophagus of the 2C AD.

From here we enter the ***Refectory**, an imposing vaulted hall of six bays, 30m long and 10m wide, near the NE of which is a staircase in the thickness of the wall, which ascends to the pulpit. A small rose window provides light from the E, while six windows on the N wall command a plunging view of the sea, and on a clear day, a distant view of the Turkish coast. The Cellarium and kitchens were situated to the W of the refectory and cloister, from the ruins of which steps descend to a *Crypt*. The ascent to the cloister roof is recommended for a view of the monastery itself and for the Kyrenia range rising abruptly to the S, and the Karpas peninsula to the E.

The *Treasury* is built over the N aisle of the church, the belfry of which can be seen to advantage from here.

An old track climbs S from Bellapais to the E of MOUNT ALONAGRA (or TRYPA VOUNO; 935m), descending the ridge to *Kato Dhikomo*: see Rte 20.

22 Kyrenia to Nicosia via Myrtou

57km (35 miles).

Drive due W from Kyrenia, leaving *Temblos*—probably a commandery of the Templars—on the left, near which, according to Gunnis, there was once a chapel much resorted to by women whose daughters remained unmarried, when suitable sons-in-law were named in dreams in response to prayers to the Virgin.

The road shortly passes GLYKIOTISSA (Snake) ISLAND and enters (5km) *Ayios Yeoryios*, immediately NW of which is the rock-cut chapel of *Ayios Phanourios*, dating from the Byzantine period, below which are numerous fossil remains of pygmy hippopotami, the bones of which (assumed by the villagers to be those of saints) were powdered and swallowed in a glass of water as a cure for most diseases. The beach here was known as 'Tiger Bay' by the British, while just to the W is FIVE MILE BEACH, on which the first Turkish forces landed at dawn on 20 July 1974. Within days some 40,000 troops had been concentrated in the bridgehead.

Trimithi lies to the SW, and below it stands the church of *Panayia Khrysotrimithiotis*, a Byzantine chapel now forming the apse of the present building, 'restored' c 1910, as was *Ayios Charalambos*, in which some Renaissance windows and doorways remain. Trimithi was the locale of slave-trafficking as late as 1910, when three motherless children were sold by their sister to a notorious caïque operator.—Uphill lies the delightfully situated village of **Karmi** (330m), from which a rough track ascends to *St. Hilarion*, see Rte 20.

6km **Karavas**, situated to the S of the old port, was founded in 1570 and largely settled from neighbouring Lapithos. It is also an important citrus centre: some of its lemon trees are at least 75 years old and produce as many as 5000 lemons each! To the S is *Ayios Yeoryios*, built in 1854 on the ruins of an earlier monastic church, with a charming iconostasis and women's gallery. *Ayia Irini* stands above the town and commands extensive views.

To the N of the town is *Ayios Evlalios* (15C), also built over an earlier structure. Picturesquely sited near AKHIROPIITOS POINT is **Akhiropiitos Monastery* ('built without hands'), founded in the 12C. It has two domes over the transept, but was rebuilt in the 14C, and has been much changed since with the addition of a huge apse, seven-sided externally but internally a semi-circle. It was surrounded by arcaded cells 'formerly inhabited by stray shepherds, farm animals and

English intellectuals', to quote the late Osbert Lancaster; it was converted by the Turkish invaders into a military warehouse and rest centre.

A short distance W is the Neolithic site of **Lambousa**.

It was a Greek settlement in the 12C BC and a Phoenician colony in the 10C BC, and was long an important trading centre, a major export of which was pottery. The town was walled, and had a lighthouse. From 295–27 BC it was the capital of one of four Ptolemaic Districts, and was later the site of Roman and Byzantine ports. A bishopric was established here in AD 61.

It was first attacked by Arab corsairs in 647, and virtually abandoned from 654, when much of its stone was also transported SW to build Lapithos. Quarrymen from the latter village had not infrequently unearthed artefacts from the older town, but the first scientific excavations were not made until 1913–17. The early 7C AD silver plates forming the famous 'Lambousa Treasure' were found near the chapel of *Ayios Evlambios* in c 1905, some of which remain in the Cyprus Museum, Nicosia (while others are in the British Museum and in the Metropolitan Museum, New York).

Among the hamlets to the SE of Karavas is that of *Paleosophos*, with its fields hedged by purple iris and wild pink antirrhinums; and *Elea*, where in the churchyard of *Ayios Nikolaos* is a tomb-slab depicting an armoured man, among other relics.

The main road W of Karavas by-passes (left) **Lapithos** (3500 inhab. in 1960), surrounded by lemon and orange groves.

Founded in AD 654 by settlers from coastal *Lambousa* (see above) after suffering from Arab raids, its Orthodox see was one of those suppressed by the Latins in 1222. In 1307 it was the estate of Echive d'Ibelin and from c 1464 of the Constable of Cyprus, Sor de Naves. Its citrus groves were famous even then. Cotton was also grown during the first Turkish occupation; and onions, sesame, and colocasi have been cultivated since. It is also noted for its pottery, woodcarving, and embroidery. The Easter celebrations here are well described in Patrick Balfour's 'The Orphaned Realm'.

Some 6km W of Lapithos we reach crossroads, just to the S of which, below MOUNT KORNOS (946m), the westernmost peak of the Kyrenia range, is *Vasilia*, with an Early Cypriot cemetery. To the N of the main road is the small fishing village of *Vavilas*.

After another 3km a right-hand fork continues to skirt the coast via *Orga* to (12km) *Liveras*, with the ruins of a Venetian watch-tower. Beyond this is CAPE KORMAKITI, with its lighthouse, and the closest point to Turkey—Cape Anamur being only 66km (41 miles) N across the Carmenian Straits. A Turkish ship which came to pillage the area in 1363 is said to lie wrecked off this point.

The main route can be regained to the SE near *Myrtou* via (7km) the village of **Kormakitis**, formerly largely inhabited by Maronites. The church of *Ayios Yeoryios* (completed 1940) is adjacent to another of the 15C, while just W of the village is the chapel of *Panayia*, retaining its barrel vaulting, and frescoes.

Turning inland, and traversing *Panagra*, the road now climbs to reach *Myrtou*, with the direct road SW via *Dhiorios* to *Morphou* (see below) veering right just before the village.

Myrtou is an ancient village, on the E outskirts of which are remains of the Byzantine village of *Margi*. Its principal monument is the Monastery of *Ayios Panteleimon* (closed in the 1950s), with a later church of c 1600. It was a residence of the Bishop of Kyrenia from 1571 to 1921. In the early part of this century it was too drastically 'restored', and retains only a few early relics of slight interest.—Just to the S is the Maronite village of *Karpasha*, with the rebuilt medieval church of *Stavros*.

Immediately W of Myrtou is *Dhiorios* (315m), providing good views of MORPHOU BAY and of the Troödos range to the S. An early 19C church has replaced a medieval building, parts of which can be seen at its W end.

FROM DHIORIOS TO MORPHOU (15km). Just SW of the village the main road bears left. The right-hand fork at this junction leads due W to (8km) *Ayia Irini*, the adjacent sand-dunes of which have been moored by re-afforestation. In a nearby ravine the fossilised bones of pygmy hippopotami may be seen. In the churchyard lies a carved Roman cippus. In 1930 a large number of terracotta statues, largely male, and other votive objects (now in the Cyprus Museum, Nicosia) were excavated from the temple site of *Paleokastro*, on a hillock overlooking the shore.—The main road leads S to (8km) *Kalokhorio*, with a 19C church, the S aisle of which is formed by a 16C building, with some murals remaining.—After c 4km a road leads right to adjacent *Toumba tou Skourou*, where in 1963 Late Cypriot artefacts were discovered. A hoard of Lusignan coins was found in 1904; and in 1973 the Harvard University Expedition excavated a range of materials including Minoan pottery, cylinder seals from Syria, African ostrich eggs, etc. and also uncovered a curious artificial mound of bricks, the only one known in Cyprus.—For *Morphou*, see Rte 19.

Leaving Myrtou we drive SE, passing near a Creto-Mycenaean site just to the W of the road, to (4km) *Asomatos*, a Maronite village. Nearby is the church of *Panayia Galoussa*, once a Latin chapel, but repaired in 1780, and with late 17C holy doors.—To the N lies *Kambyli*, with a derelict domed village church (15C). *Kondemenos* is by-passed prior to entering (8km) **Skylloura**, with a rebuilt medieval church preserving several Gothic details.

Some 6km E of Kondemenos lies the village of *Ayios Ermolaos*, named after a saint who was a bishop of Karpasia at the time of the Council of Chalcedon (451); it was apparently sacked in 1974 by the occupying army.—Further N, on the S flank of the Kyrenia range, lie the villages of *Sisklipos*, *Agridhaki*, and *Larnaka tis Lapithou*, the latter, once reputed for its gold- and silver-smiths and with a desecrated monastic church.

The road continues SE from Skylloura, passing through *Ayios Vasilios* (where 21 Turkish Cypriot bodies were found buried in January 1964), and then *Yerolakkos*, probably from the Venetian era but an unattractive village, beyond which the road veers E to **Nicosia**.

23 Kyrenia to Komi Kebir, for the Karpas

67km (42 miles); after the first 8km the road deteriorates and is often slow and winding.

This route follows the coast road E towards (left) *Karakoumi*, passing near the curious site of *Khryso Kava*, with ancient quarries, probably Roman, and the ruins of Byzantine *Ayia Ekaterina* and the 10C rock-cut church of *Ayia Mavra*, its paintings partially restored.

5km. **Ayios Epiktitos**, to the right, was once known for its local woodcarvers, and it is named after a 12C saint, possibly of German origin, who lived as a hermit in a cave below the church, a building of 1836 on an earlier site. N of the main road, near the shore, is the *Tékké Hazreti Ömer* (known as *Ayii Phanontes* by the Greek Cypriots), the reputed burial-place of seven Moslem saints; in 1968 the mosque was converted into a residence. A Late Neolithic site at

Ayios Epiktitos was the object of important excavations by E.J. Peltenburg in 1969–73.

FROM AYIOS EPIKTITOS TO ANTIPHONITIS VIA HALEVGA (27km). After c 2km we turn off the coast road and climb inland past (left) the village of *Klepini*, known for its local tradition that if more than 40 families live there death would inevitably level the numbers before the year's end. The much altered church of *Panayia* was Byzantine in origin; that of *Ayios Loukas* is largely 18C. The road bears SE and climbs towards the jagged peak of MOUNT PENTADAKTYLOS ('five-fingered'; 740m), shortly crossing the watershed before reaching a road junction. A minor mountain road leads W to a point below *Buffavento Castle* (see Rte 24); another follows the ridge directly E towards Halevga. The main road descends before forking left above *Kythrea* (see Rte 24; views), and after 3km ascends NE to *Halevga*, a forest station at an altitude of 620m.—A short distance NW is the so-called **Armenian Monastery** (or *Sourp Magar*), dedicated to St. Makarius of Alexandria (309–404), the hermit, and founded c 1000. Originally the property of the Copts, it was transferred to the Armenians 400 years later. The present church was erected in 1811.

From Halevga we follow the road along the N side of the crest to (10km) the rustic 12C church of *Antiphonitis, part of a monastery until 1965. It is octagonal in plan, its dome being supported by eight columns: four detached, and four abutting the side walls. Additions include a vaulted narthex (14C) and the open loggia on the S side (15C), with pointed arches. Note also its rare liquid amber or incense tree. The interior was once covered by frescoes of different periods from the late 12C onwards, with a Pantokrator in the dome, and formerly contained a superb carved 17C iconostasis, now dismantled. The paintings of the Tree of Jesse and of the Last Judgement have been wantonly destroyed by art-robbers, except for those out of reach in the dome. Murals on the lower parts of the walls had been mutilated previously by graffiti in Greek. Many of the icons were stolen.—Tracks descend SE to *Trypimeni*, and to *Knodhara* (see Rte 24); another continues to follow the main ridge, while the coast road can be regained 4km NE via *Kalogrea*.

Just beyond the junction from which the above sub-route commenced, and to the left, is the ancient site of *Vrysin*, with a cemetery dated 2300–2200 BC; relics from a temple uncovered here in 1932–35 may be seen in the Cyprus Museum, Nicosia.—Another site is passed (left) at *Alakati*, 6km further E; and 5km beyond, to the S, lies the village of *Kharcha*, its mid 19C church of *Arkhangelos* containing a good 16C icon, and a floor formed by rounded pebbles.

Some 2km beyond this turning is *Ayios Amvrosios*, an old village noted for its weaving, woodcarving, and apricots. Some of its houses still preserve tessellated floors of the Byzantine era. To the SE, towards *Antiphonitis* (see above), are the remains of the restored 16C church of the monastery of *Apati*; while to the NE, close to the shore, is *Panayia Pergaminiotissa* (repaired 1731, when buttresses were added) of the *Monastery of Melandryna*. On an adjacent hill is the site of a necropolis dating from 400 BC. In 1804 2000 Turkish troops led by Haji Georghakis Kornesios landed on the coast here to put down the Turkish revolt of that year.

The road continues to skirt the coast, after c 9km being joined by the main road N from Lefkoniko, and then veers NE.—2km S of the next junction lies *Akanthou*, below the peak of OLYMPOS (740m).

Akanthou is an old village dating from the 7–8C, and is near Early and Late Cypriot sites. It was known for its woodwork, cheese, and earlier for its embroidery. Ahmed Pasha landed here with a Turkish force to quell the revolt of 1684–90. The main church—at present used as a mosque—is an early 20C building replacing one of 1862.—4km NE is the church of *Panayia Pergaminio-tissa*, domed, and containing decaying 12C murals, which have been further damaged by thieves attempting to remove them; nearby is a rock-cut chapel. Some assume that the scattered ruins in the vicinity represent the ancient settlement of Pergamon (but compare above), but this is by no means proven.

The coastal road shortly passes (left) ruins, presumed to be those of *Aphrodisium* (or *Aphrodhosion*), capital of the Hittite kingdom of Cyprus c 700 BC, but this may have been 19km further E at *Galounia* (see below). The road continues E between the Kyrenia range and the coast, and after 9km by-passes the village of *Phlamoudhi*, and, 6km beyond, *Dhavlos*, the site of a Late Cypriot settlement.

To the SE, on a height, rises the **Castle of Kantara**, which may also be approached from here by a steep ascent to the village of *Kantara* (4km S: but see Rte 28). Our route bears inland at (4km) *Galounia*, where there are remains of an ancient aqueduct. Crossing a ridge, we climb down to (6km) **Komi Kebir**, where ancient *Ayios Auxentios*, restored in 1859, is named after a soldier-saint who lived in the seclusion of the cave of *Iotian*, near Dhavlos.

5km NE is *Ephtakomi*, where mid 18C *Ayios Loukas* has an exterior arcade and contemporary icons.

The main road from Famagusta to *Yialousa* can be reached 8km S, between *Patriki* and *Gastria*; see Rte 28.

24 Nicosia to Trikomo via Kythrea and Lefkoniko

53km (33 miles).

We drive NE on the main Famagusta road and after 4km fork left through *Mia Milea*, named after the fact that it was one Greek mile (3 statute miles) from the capital, leaving the road to *Buffavento Castle* on our left; see below.

FROM MIA MILEA TO BUFFAVENTO (c 11km). Turn due N, following a road climbing towards the Kyrenia range and the hamlet of *Koutsovendis* (325m), once a Maronite district.—Some 4km NW lies *Vouno*, with a monastery dedicated to St. Romanos (the son of Christian parents from Antioch, martyred in 310), founded c 1600. N of the village is a quarry, while in a cave (visited by Van Bruyn in 1683, among others) are quantities of fossil bones once supposed to be those of early martyrs.—Further NW lies *Sykhari*, N of which, at a height of 510m, are the remains of the monastery of *Panayia Absinthiotissa*, once known as the Abbey of Abscithi. The church, dating from the Byzantine period, was partly restored in the Gothic style in the 15C, and again in the 1960s. The 12C murals, which were in the narthex, have been looted.

N of Koutsovendis are the ruins of the large brick-built Byzantine church of *Panayia Koutsovendis* (also known as *Panayia Aphendrika*) in which some 12–14C murals are preserved, including a Pietà of the mid to late 12C. On an outer wall is an incomplete St. George (16–17C). It is at present in military occupation.

Beyond stands the 'White Monastery' of *Ayios Khrysostomos** (named after John Khrysostomos; 354–406), built in the 11C, and belonging to the Orthodox See of Jerusalem. It was one of the subjects painted by David Bomberg on his expedition to Cyprus in 1948.

Ayios Khrysostamos, near Koutsovendis

The main monastery contains an 11C Byzantine church with brick arcading round the central dome and an iconostasis of white marble columns from local quarries. It preserves late 11–12C frescoes restored in 1963 by Ernest Hawkins of Dumbarton Oaks. Notable among these are the heads of saints in roundels on the soffit of the NW recess. Some may still be visible and are now 'protected' after a fashion. The restored building preserves the geometrically designed marble floor of its apse, a marble door-frame (early 16C), and a remarkable wooden door; both the door and frame were copied for the Government House in Nicosia. The icon of Khrysostomos (1595) is now stored in the castle at Kyrenia. Note the immense cypress.

From the ridge above the monastery one may discern the *Castle of Buffavento, of yellower stone than the surrounding rocks. High up (954m) in the range, it was once a two-hour climb from the monastery, but is now partially approached by a road ascending NE and then turning NW towards the main ridge, where a minor road forks left, climbing to a point below the castle, reached by a stiff climb. The highest of the three great castle-eyries of the Kyrenia range, Buffavento is appropriately named after the gusts of wind it defies; indeed its precipitously perched position is more remarkable than either St. Hilarion or Kantara, although its tumbled remains do not compare with them in extent.

It was already known as an 'exceeding strong castle' in the 12C. It contains some Byzantine brickwork, which Gunnis suggests may have been an accidental survival of an earlier method of construction. It was here in 1368 that John Visconti was starved to death by Peter I for unwisely insinuating that his wife Eleanor of Aragón had been unfaithful to him during his absence abroad. During the last decade of the Venetian occupation the castle was dismantled and abandoned. It was visited by 'Ali Bey' in 1806, who called it 'the Palace of the Queen', probably referring to the fact that it was in the possession of the daughter of Isaac Comnenos when delivered to Richard I in 1191. A system of flares linked it at night with St. Hilarion, Nicosia, and Kantara.

After 6km—from Mia Milea—we reach crossroads, just N of which is Kythrea, the main village in the area. It was also the centre of a Neolithic settlement dating from c 3500 BC; the site—called *Ayios Dhimitrianos*—of ancient *Chytri*, colonised by the Greeks in c 1200 BC, lying E of the main road and N of the present village.

In 1928 a bronze statue of Septimius Severus (now in the Cyprus Museum, Nicosia) was discovered at *Voni*, an adjacent village to the SE, where a temple had been excavated in 1883.

Kythrea was the seat of an early Orthodox see, but it was destroyed by Arabs in c 800. The area, irrigated by a stream having its source at the *Spring of Kephalovryso* at the base of MOUNT PENTADAKTYLOS, which also supplied water via an aqueduct to Constantia (Salamis), was long famous for its flour-mills. It once had as many as 35 water-driven mills, and there were still 32 in 1879. This oasis in the Mesaorian plain is also well-known for its vegetables; its broccoli being exported to Europe as early as 1604, and its olives are also particularly fleshy.

Its women had a reputation both for their beauty and for their indiscretions: 'Ali Bey', curious to meet them, suggests that it was 'possibly the heat of the climate, the isolation of the houses which stand apart, the mulberry thickets, and the absence of the men, who are away during the day in the markets of Nicosia', which were the causes to which one might assign their character, 'for these are all circumstances favourable to debauch'. From the mid 17C it was also a Maronite enclave.

The principal churches are in the N part of the village. *Ayios Andronikos*, with early icons, is early 16C; *Ayia Marina* dates from 1734 and preserves an iconostasis of 1634, while in the centre of the floor is a Byzantine marble panel; the *Panayia Monastery* (16C; rebuilt in 1771) contains a Baroque iconostasis and early icons. Most of the other churches are modern, even if built on the sites of previous edifices.—To the N of the village a road ascends NE to *Halevga*, see Rte 23.

Immediately S of Kythrea are the villages and hamlets of *Khrysidha*, where the church of *Stavros* is a medieval building restored in 1836, but intermittent efforts to unearth a gold cross said to be buried deep in its foundations have proved abortive; and *Neokhorio*, founded at the turn of the 18C; while to the S, around the earlier medieval village of *Potanias*, are the ruins of a number of Roman tombs.

The road shortly traverses *Bey Keuy* (*Köy*), to the S of which is *Voni* (see above), and to the SE, *Epikho*, once owned by the Count of Tripoli, and more recently known for its large camel population.— 5km. To the left lies *Petra tou Dhiyeni*, where in 1426 'king' Alexis was captured by the Saracens.—Another 6km brings us to the crossroad for *Chatos*, to the N, with a mosque built on the site of a medieval church of which a doorway with dog-tooth moulding is preserved. To the S is *Marathovouno*.—The road (built in the 1870s) continues E, skirting *Knodhara* and traversing *Psilatos* to enter **Lefkoniko**, which was a centre of the unsuccessful 'Peasant Revolt' of 1427. Its natives have been unkindly denominated 'gaidhourofaes'— people who eat donkeys! It has a reputation for its striped hand-woven fabrics. The principal church, *Arkhangelos Michael*, is an ancient building remodelled in the early 19C and containing a late 17C diptych icon. The church of *Stavros* preserves holy doors dated 1680 and an icon of the Virgin of the same period.—There is a much-plundered temple site c 2km S.

A large *Air Base* has been constructed here.

FROM LEFKONIKO TO SALAMIS (18km). The road bears SE through *Milea*, an ancient village with evidence of Greek and Roman habitation. On the outskirts is the medieval church of *Ayios Yeorios*.—To the SW are *Piyi* and adjacent *Peristerona*, both with desecrated churches; in *Ayios Anastasios* (18C), in the latter village, is buried the saint. A Roman marble frieze has been built into a wall, while capitals and columns from an earlier building lie scattered around.

Some 3km beyond Milea we pass (left) near the monastery of *Panayia Avgasida* (NE of *Sandalaris*). The double-aisled church, which dates from the 17C, shows Gothic influence; the dome contains a painting of the Pantokrator. Into the buttresses of the N wall is built a medieval tombstone showing a man in contemporary costume. Fragments, including Byzantine capitals, from the earlier monastery lie around the site.

The Turkish Cypriot villagers of *Sandalaris*, *Maratha* (further W) and *Aloa*, which the road shortly traverses, were on 14 August 1974 slaughtered by EOKA-B terrorists and National Guards, buried in ditches and then bulldozed over. Sir Peter de Cassi was captured at **Ayios Seryios** (St. Sergius), by the Genoese in c 1375, and the Turks received a setback here before the siege of Famagusta in 1570. Its church of the same name, dating from the Byzantine era, has a number of marble columns from Salamis built into it. *Ayia Paraskevi* is 16C; the step into its S narthex is formed by part of a classical frieze.—*Salamis* (see Rte 27) lies to the SE.

The route from Lefkoniko continues due E through *Gypsos*, named after the gypsum found in the neighbouring hills. *Ayios Yeorios*, a double-aisled building (16C) in the village centre, with one apse rounded and the other hexagonal, contains an altar formed from a well-carved Byzantine plaque (12C), while outside is a large circular font.

Between here and (3km) *Lapathos* lies an extensive necropolis of the Iron Age. The church of *Ayios Ioannis* (early 18C) is double-aisled and divided by heavy squat columns.

Syngrasis, to the right of the road further E, has a large 13C church (*Ayios Prokopios*) with a coloured marble floor in its apse, where two Corinthian capitals and an inscription from the Byzantine period may be seen. Near the school are the ruins of *Ayios Nikolaos*, surrounded by interesting fragments, including carved corbels, a male figure, and part of the S door, with zigzag and dog-tooth moulding. On an adajcent hill stands the chapel of *Panayia Aphendrika* (early 18C), with two marble carved and floriated Byzantine crosses lying beside the S door. The oil from its lamps had the reputation of curing infectious diseases, sufferers changing into new clothes after smearing themselves, and leaving their discarded apparel by the W door.

Some 6km NW is the hamlet of *Ayios Iakovos*, N of which a wall surrounds its predecessor. Two sanctuaries, one dating from the Late Cypriot period, were discovered here in 1928. In them a collection of gold rings, a gold necklace, and other jewellery were found, together with a Babylonian cylinder with solid gold mountings.—To the N, nearer *Mandres*, is the monastery of *Panayia Tochni* (14C; the domed church restored), around which a number of Roman and Byzantine fragments are scattered.

4km. **Trikomo**, the birthplace of George Grivas Dhigenis (1898–1974), the EOKA leader and terrorist, is known for its production of pomegranates (said to have been introduced into Cyprus by Aphrodite). It was a centre of the 'Monks' Revolt' of 1832. The Dominican chapel of *Ayios Iakovos (St. James), standing in the village square, dating from the 12–15C and restored in 1804, is one of the most charming miniature churches on the island. Pointed arches support the tall drum, while internally its only decorations are acoustic plates in its vaulting. A replica of the building was erected on the Black Sea coast by Maria, Queen of Roumania, to serve as her private chapel. The main church, *Panayia Theotokos** (partly early 12C), with a N aisle clumsily added later, preserves some early 12C and late 15C paintings, and a Byzantine marble slab built into its belfry.

For the roads hence to the *Castle of Kantara* and the Karpas peninsula, see Rte 28.

25   Nicosia to Famagusta

A. Direct

55km (34 miles). The new road, although narrow, which follows the track of the former railway, by-passes all villages en route.

Driving NE from Nicosia, after 11km we leave on our left *Trakhoni*, with the 17C domed church of *Panayia*, and chapel of *Ayios Nikolaos* (15C or earlier), later transformed into a mosque, and then into a stable.—2km S is *Palekythro*, possibly the site of an early bishopric. Here, according to Drummond, who visited the place in 1750, the remains of a temple of Aphrodite was used by the local cadi to provide stone for a residence for his women. It was the site of the shooting of unarmed civilians during the Turkish invasion of 1974.

4km. To the left lies *Exometokhi*, in 1385 a fief of Sir John de Neuville.—6km. *Angastina*, to the right, was part of a feudal estate transferred from the Templars to the Hospitallers in 1308. The 18C church of *Ayios Therapon* (a 7C saint of German extraction) has been much restored. Its icons were stolen after the place was occupied by the Turkish Army, but recovered by British Customs and returned to Cyprus in 1975.—*Marathovouno* lies to the NE; see Rte 24.

The road continues to bear E across the MESAORIA, at 13km by-passing (left) *Pyrga*, where Ionnikos, a monk betrayed and hung here in 1832 during the Monks' Revolt at Trikomo, is said to have cursed the local peasants, above whom the cloud still hangs!—3km.

(right) *Prastio* on the main Larnaca–Lefkoniko road bisecting the Mesaoria from S to N, was once part of the feudal estate controlled by the castle of **Sygouris**, a moated fortress built some way to the S by James I in 1391, dismantled by the Venetians in 1530, and further destroyed when its stone was used in road construction in the late 19C, another inexcusable act of vandalism by the British administration (cf. Bellapais).

The road shortly leaves *Gaidhouras* to the right; its name meaning 'village of donkeys', but although no satisfactory reason for this is apparent, the disparaging name sticks (in spite of an attempt in 1930 to change it to Nea Sparti). We reach a road junction, the left-hand fork leading via *Styllos*, site of a battle in 1425 in which the Saracens were defeated by the Prince of Galilee, to *Engomi* and *Salamis*; see Rte 27. There are slight remains of the Roman aqueduct—from Kythrea to Salamis—in the area.—The right-hand fork bears SE to enter the NW outskirts of **Famagusta** 11km beyond; see Rte 26.

B. Via Vatili

61km (38 miles).

The 'old' main road leads due E from Nicosia, at 11km passing (right) *Tymbou Airfield*, a landing field laid out by the British during the Second World War, and revived and extended in 1975 by the Turkish Army to provide direct services with the Turkish mainland and elsewhere. It has been renamed *Ercan*.

The village of *Tymbou* may be reached by taking the next right-hand turning. Further S, across the river YIALIAS, lies the curious shrine known as the *Convent of the Forty* or *Kirklar Tékké*, a little mosque dated 1816, and supposed to contain the conventional 'forty' tombs, but whether they were of Christian or Moslem origin is uncertain.

Some 4km SW on the road to *Margo* stands the church of *Ayia Thekla,* of the late Byzantine period, abandoned, but in good repair and containing well-preserved frescoes; its icons were stolen by the Turks in 1974 but were recovered by the British Customs the following year and returned to Cyprus.—To the SE of the old village of *Margo* lies **Pyroi**, the birthplace of Kiamil Pasha (1833–1913), Grand Vizier of the Ottoman Empire. The Venetian bridge across the Yialias has been largely replaced by an iron structure. *Ayios Antipasios* is a pleasant Byzantine building, the W door of which has a Gothic rose window above it. The icon of the obscure saint to whom it is dedicated was once resorted to by those with the toothache. *Panayia Palouriotissa*, to the W, on the Attila Line, of the late Byzantine or early Latin era, contains fragments of frescoes.—Some 8km to the S is *Louroujina*, a Turkish-Cypriot enclave almost surrounded by the Greek-Cypriot sector.

A left-hand turning just beyond the airfield leads to (5km) *Mora*, built on the site of a Hellenistic necropolis. In the courtyards of two houses are seen the foundations of an ancient church and/or monastery.

We pass (right) the abandoned 15C church of *Ayios Artemios* at deserted *Ornithi*, before traversing *Aphania*, a Maronite village in the 16C, and enter **Asha**, once owned by the De Nores family and briefly the Venetian base of action after the fall of Nicosia in 1570. Just E of the village, known for the manufacture of bricks and nails, is the chapel of *Panayia* (15C or earlier), preserving remains of paintings above the apse.

8km due S of Asha lies **Tremetousha**, the site of ancient *Trimithos*, dating from the Hellenistic period. It was populated under the Romans and was later the seat of an Orthodox bishop. It was the birthplace of St. Spyridon, who attended the Council of Nicea in 325. In May 1191 Richard Coeur de Lion defeated Isaac Comnenos' forces near here in a sharp skirmish, the latter flying to Kantara. The neighbouring monastery of *Ayios Spyridhon* is one of the largest and oldest on the island, dating from possibly the 7C, but was rebuilt in the 18C. Gothic and Byzantine details have been incorporated into various parts of its dependencies. Four huge buttresses support the S wall. Three marble columns from the original structure have been built into the iconostasis of 1684, while above the sarcophagus of the saint hangs a Baroque lantern.

The body of St. Spyridon, after remaining here for some centuries, was sent to Constantinople for safe-keeping, until in 1460 it was carried to Corfu, where Spyridon became its patron saint, and (it is said) his intervention defeated the Turkish attack of that island in 1710!

To the W lies *Melousha*, possibly the site of the early see of *Chytri*, to the S of which, near the Attila Line, stand the ruins of *Ayios Photios*, of which the N and W walls survive, perhaps the 'cathedral' of the see.—2km E of Tremetousha (from which the main road may be regained at *Lysi*—see below), we traverse *Arsos*, where in 1913–17 a cornelian and gold necklace (7C BC) and a 3C limestone head were unearthed (now in the Cyprus Museum, Nicosia). Fragments of the Roman period may be seen in the area, while the small medieval chapel of *Ayios Phimios* contains slight remains of murals.—*Troulli*, in the Greek Cypriot-controlled zone, lies 6km S; see Rte 2.

Vatili, by-passed, once belonged to Sir Bartholomew de Montolif, being the dowry of Lady Margaret de Nores. Little remains of the original medieval church of *Ayios Yeoryios*, which was extensively restored in 1856. The ceiling of the iconostasis dates from the late 16C.

5km NE is *Sinda*, adjacent to which is a large stone enclosure of the Late Cypriot period, possibly a Mycenaean necropolis, with a doorway on the W side and a fort on the N, while to the NW is a smaller stone circle. Sinda was also the site of a battle in 1374, when the Genoese, resting with their plunder after the sack of Nicosia, were attacked by surprise and defeated by Jean de Lusignan, Constable of Cyprus, who rode thence from Kyrenia with 500 men-at-arms.

After 3km the main road by-passes (right) **Lysi** (3750 inhab. in 1960), largely devoted to market gardening, and inhabited since at least the 5C BC, as evidenced by the relief of a warrior dating from that era to be seen in the Cyprus Museum, Nicosia. Copper was also smelted here in ancient times. Lysi was the birthplace of the EOKA leader Gregoris Afxentiou, and it was here that part of Colonel Grivas's diary was discovered in 1955 by British troops. The huge church of *Panayia* dates from the end of the 19C.—14C *Ayios Ephimianos*, c 2km SW, although well preserved, has been robbed of its dome and apse paintings of the Virgin and Pantokrator, which are now held in trust by an American foundation in Houston, Texas; the walls had already been whitewashed.

3km to the E lies *Kondea*, which we traverse, and 3km beyond, after crossing the main Larnaca–Lefkoniko road, *Kouklia*, which in 1898–99 was briefly the camp of some 1125 Doukhobors who, expelled from Russia for refusing military service, passed through Cyprus on their way to Canada (others stayed at Pergamos—see below—and Athalassa); earlier this century it had a colony of Jews.

The reservoir of Kouklia, with its dam constructed in 1896, is to the N.

Pergamos lies 8km S of the crossroads just W of Kouklia, an enclave near the W end of the EASTERN BRITISH SOVEREIGN BASE AREA and on the road from Pyla; see Rte 2.

4km S of Kouklia lies *Makrasyka*, on the road to which are a number of medieval ruins, while in the village itself stand the remains of the double-aisled 16C church of *Ayios Yeoryios*; those of *Ayios Evstathios* and *Panayia* are also of interest.—*Athna*, beyond, and on the 'frontier', was the site of excavations in 1882, when c 1000 stone and terracotta figurines—many coloured and mostly female, and dating from the 3C BC—were discovered; a number of them are now in the British Museum. *Panayia Trasha* (16C) preserves its founder's tomb in the N wall.

At 4km *Kalopsidha* lies to the left, immediately to the W of which is the Middle Cypriot site first excavated in 1894, artefacts from which may be seen in the Ashmolean Museum, Oxford, and in the Cyprus Museum, Nicosia. The village was largely destroyed by the Saracens in 1426. The principal church, *Panayia*, is of medieval origin; the double-aisled chapel of *Ayios Ioannis* of the 17C.—In normal times the road shortly enters the *Eastern British Sovereign Base Area* and swings NE.

The next left-hand turning leads shortly to *Akhyritou*, once the property of Andronico Caridis, honorary Dragoman of the Apostolic Queen of Hungary. There are a number of early chapels in the vicinity, among them *Ayios Yeoryios* (13C); the monastery of *Ayios Kondeas* (5km S; 16C), with its holy well; while 3km N is the abandoned village of *Trapeza*, destroyed by the Saracens in 1426, with the barrel-vaulted church of *Panayia* with its two domes, a curious mixture of Byzantine and Gothic styles, probably restored in 1563.

We enter the E outskirts of **Famagusta** 6km NE of this turning; see below.

26 Famagusta

FAMAGUSTA (*Gazi Mağusa* in Turkish, but also referred to as *Magosa*), together with the suburb of **Varosha** (or *Maraş*), contiguous to the S, had a total population of 34,750 in 1960 (including 24,492 Greek Cypriots and 6120 Turkish Cypriots), ranking third in size after Nicosia and Limassol. Its present estimated population is 19,450. The walled town, one of the finest surviving examples of medieval military architecture, was almost entirely inhabited by Turkish Cypriots, while the modern commercial town facing the long beach was largely populated by Greek Cypriots until the Turkish military occupation of 1974. Since then it has been called *Maraş*, although the name Varosha was probably of Turkish origin.

The origin of the name Famagusta is generally considered to be a corruption of the Greek *Ammochostos* (buried in sand), but *Fami Augusti*, referring to a connection with the Roman Emperor, has also been suggested as an alternative. There is evidence, even if slight, of Roman habitation, but the town did not become in any way prominent until after the decline of Salamis, 8km to the N, in AD 648, when it was populated by its Greek refugees.

Count Wilbrand von Oldenburg, who visited the place in 1211, refers to it as having 'a good harbour, slightly fortified'. Hence

Frederick II Hohenstaufen set sail for Acre in September 1228. After the fall of Acre in 1291, Henry II of Cyprus offered it as an asylum to Christian refugees, and it grew considerably, soon becoming one of the main emporia of the Levant, superseding Limassol in importance. It was at that time largely inhabited by Syrians—notably after the fall of Acre. Coming from the mainland, they were Arabic-speaking Christian Melkites, Nestorians, Maronites, or Jacobites. The Greek population was in the minority. Ludolf von Suchen (1350) was more than impressed by this 'richest of all cities' where dwelt 'very many wealthy courtesans, some of whom possess more than one hundred thousand florins'. It was also one of four Dioceses of the Latin Church. By 1372, when occupied by the Genoese (until they were driven out by James II in 1464 after a sporadic four-year siege), it had already lost much of its prosperity, and according to Martoni, who landed there in 1394, almost a third was uninhabited, and the houses destroyed, even if it had finer walls—the earlier Lusignan walls—than he had seen in any town. He also remarked that because of a neighbouring marsh 'and the great number of courtesans, a bad air affects the men who dwell in that city'! James died suddenly in 1473, and through his widow, Caterina Cornaro, the island passed to Venice in 1489. This 'Sea-port in Cyprus' was presumably the scene of Shakespeare's 'Othello' (c 1604).

The Venetians set about rebuilding the walls on a massive scale, using stone excavated from part of the fosse, material removed from Salamis, and blocks quarried from Kakozonara. There is little indication that they were subjected to the intense bombardment of Turkish cannon from the end of September 1570 until the following August. During the famous *Siege of Famagusta* it has been estimated that of the 8000 Greek and Venetian troops defending the city, some 75 per cent perished, while perhaps as many as 50,000 Turks were slain, taking into account the usual exaggeration of the period. The latter drove deep trenches up to the outworks, and Armenian sappers systematically mined the Ravelin and the arsenal tower (later known as the Djamboulat Bastion). A breach made on 21 June was held, but with no Venetian fleet coming to their support, the besieged ran short of supplies—cats were eaten to stave off hunger—and on 1 August a truce was negotiated. Marcantonio Bragadino, the commander, met Mustapha Pasha on the 5th, but once in their hands, the Turk ordered him, after suffering sadistic indignities, to be flayed alive, and his skin, stuffed with straw, was paraded around the city, where barbarous atrocities were meanwhile perpetrated by the victorious and long-frustrated Turks. The stuffed skin was stolen from Constantinople in 1580 and conveyed to Venice, where it still survives in an urn at the church of Santi Giovanni e Paolo. A number of Turks, who had renamed the port *Magosa*, remained to colonise the island.

A traveller passing that way a century later observed that no stranger was allowed to set foot in the town, 'even the Greek inhabitants of the island dare not approach the ramparts, or if caught they run the risk of being forced to become Musalmans'. In more relaxed times, Richard Pococke, writing in 1738, remarked that only half the space within the walls was built over, and a great part of the houses were uninhabited. No longer did fountains of running water embellish all its street corners, as they once had. In 1751 Frederic Hasselquist, a Swedish physician and a pupil of Linnaeus, visited the town, of which the galley harbour had been 'wholly destroyed', while

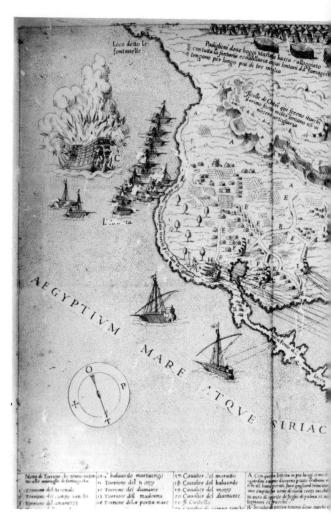

Engraving depicting the Turkish siege of Famagusta

he saw 'about two hundred cannon, not one of them serviceable', and 'never saw so many true aloes as on the ramparts', while the town was 'in far worse condition than the fort; all the houses built by the Venetians are utterly demolished or deserted. There are but three hundred inhabitants, chiefly Turks, who occupy the miserable remains of the famous city...'. The Christians in the area lived in a village to the SW of the Land Gate, and by the beginning of the 19C about one hundred houses stood there among orchards, orange

groves, and mulberry trees (to support the local silk industry). Later in the century the intervening space was built over, and during the early years of this century a new town was laid out overlooking the sandy strand stretching to the S.

By 1881 the combined population of the walled town (still described in a guide of 1890 as being a 'confused mass of ruins and filth') and the new, had risen to 2550 (1813 Greek Cypriots, 725 Turkish Cypriots), and by 1946 to 16,200.

Early photograph of Famagusta, with the mosque in the centre background, and St. George of the Latins to the right

When the British arrived in 1878 they found a number of State prisoners incarcerated there, including Subh-i-Ezel (died 1912), successor of Mirza Ali Mohammed, founder of the Babi sect in Persia. The harbour abutting the walls had been so silted up over the centuries that it was not until after 1906 that it was in any condition to thrive, later becoming the island's main port, further extended in 1962. Famagusta was also the E terminus for the island railway (commenced in 1905, running through Nicosia to Morphou and Evrykhou, which it reached in 1915), abandoned in 1951. The old railway bed was partly followed by a new highway between Famagusta and the capital, completed in 1962.

In August 1974 Famagusta and the then flourishing modern town of Varosha, with a sizeable tourist industry, fell to the advancing Turkish Army, who proceeded to appropriate some £20,000,000-worth of goods in the harbour warehouses. Until June the following year the new quarters were sealed off to civilians, and were also officially plundered, and private collections of antiquities (such as the Hadji-prodromos Collection, and the Marangos Library) were soon appearing on the European Black Market. The N part of Varosha was then resettled by Turks, and a ferry service to Mersin on the Turkish mainland was inaugurated.

The **Old City** is surrounded by a *Wall averaging 15m high and in some places as much as 8m thick, and defended by 15 bastions. Its E wall overlooks the Harbour; the other three sides rise from a fosse partly excavated in the rock, and on the SW embellished by gardens. There are now five entrances, the main sea-gate being adjacent to the

Citadel, or Othello's Tower, and the main land-gate at the SW corner of the rectangle, where the road from Nicosia enters the town, with a Turkish monument at the main roundabout.

Before entering at this point the various bastions will be described, starting at the Land Gate and working in a clockwise direction. Apart from a section near the N entrance, the exterior of the walls may be surveyed by road. The present walls date from the late 15–early 16C, and were constructed by the Venetians on the existing Lusignan fortifications.

The 9th edition of the 'Handbook of Cyprus' (1930) refers to the fact that golf was then played 'over the ramparts', requiring 'an accuracy of direction which makes up for the comparative shortness of the holes'. Thus Empire-builders relaxed: but admittedly it was only a nine-hole course.

The **Land Gate** is adjacent to the original gateway known by the Venetians as the *Porta de Limasso*, the arch of which, 9m high, may be seen. To the W rises the huge ****Rivettina Bastion** or *Ravelin* (1544), the scene of some of the fiercest fighting in the great Siege of 1570–71. The interior comprises a complex of dungeons and guardrooms.

The next four bastions, along the SW side of the enceinte, are the *Diocare*, *Moratto*, *Pulacazara* (originally *Podocataro*), and *San Luca* bastions.

In the counterscarp W of the first two, and also E of the Land Gate, a series of loopholes was revealed during road construction in 1982. From these the besiegers could fire on the Venetians attempting to remove the debris which the Turks were using to fill up the moat.

Beyond, jutting out like a broad arrow-head to the NW, is the immense ****Martinengo Bastion**, apparently so impregnable that the Turks did not attempt to assault it. Ventilation shafts for the escape of

The Land Gate, Famagusta; exterior view

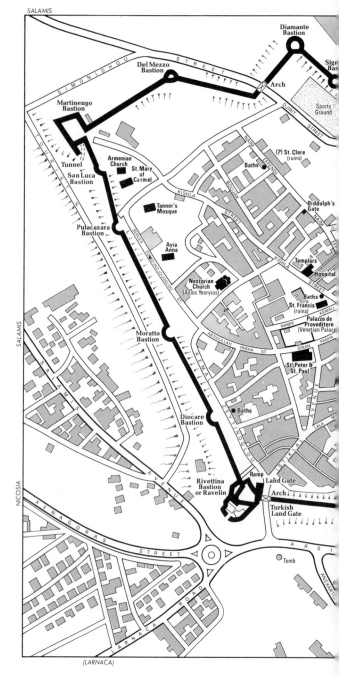

Famagusta

0   200 m
0   200 yds
N

Customs House

Citadel
(Othello's Tower)

Citadel Mole

Famagusta Harbour

KAPOU STREET

St George of the Latins

Arch

SHAKESPEARE

Tunnel

Sea Gate

Lion

ruins

Cathedral of St. Nicholas
(Lala Mustafa Pasha)

St. George of the Greeks

Ayios Symeon
(Byzantine Cath. ruins)

Ayios Nicolas

Ayia Zoni

Church of Stavros

Arch

Djamboulat Gate & Bastion
(or Arsenal)

Camposanto Bastion

Andruzzi Bastion

nta Napa Bastion

DELPHI ST.

AVENUE

GLADSTONE

gunpowder smoke may still be discerned in its vaulted casemates. The walls themselves are between 4 and 6m thick. It dates from c 1550 and is said to have been designed by Giovanni Girolamo Sanmicheli, nephew of the famous Veronese architect, and named after Hieronimo Martinengo, who died at Corfu on his way out to command Venetian troops in Cyprus in 1570.

The N sector is defended by the *Del Mozzo* (or *Mazzo*) *Bastion* and the *Diamante Bastion*, once washed by the sea, between which is an entrance to the city. Next comes the small *Signoria* (or *Signori*) *Bastion*, beyond which is the imposing **Citadel*, built in the 14C, with four round towers at its corners, and once almost surrounded by a sea moat. It was remodelled in 1492 by Nicolo Foscarini, who reduced the height of the towers. It contains an imposing *Great Hall*, 28m long. Note the Venetian winged lion over the entrance.

The citadel is also known as **'Othello's Tower'** from the fact that a certain Christophoro Moro, a Venetian Lieutenant-Governor of Cyprus in 1506–08, had a canting coat-of-arms of three mulberries sable, which gave rise to the story that he was a Moor (*moro* meaning both Moor and mulberry-tree), which eventually formed the plot for Shakespeare's tragedy. Others have conjectured that the moor may have been Francesco de Sessa, a professional soldier from southern Italy employed in the Venetian service in Cyprus, and known because of his dark complexion as 'Il Moro' or 'Il Capitano Moro', who in 1544 was put on trial for an unspecified offence and banished.

The Sea Gate, Famagusta; interior view

Beyond a modern entrance (after 1878) is the **Sea Gate**, the Venetian *Porta del Mare*, built in 1496 by Nicolo Prioli. Its iron portcullis is still visible; the iron-clad wooden doors date from the first Turkish occupation. The huge carved lion will be noted. The sea wall extends to the **Djamboulat* (or *Canbolat*) **Gate and Bastion** at the city's SE corner; see p 210. Between this point and the Land Gate extend the bastions of *Camposanto* (or *Composanto*), *Andruzzi*, and *Santa Napa*.

W front of the former cathedral of St. Nicholas, Famagusta; now the Lala Mustafa Pasha Mosque (from an old photograph)

Entering the enceinte by the *Land Gate* (see above) across a 19C bridge, we pass a ramp ascending through a Gothic arch in the ravelin, from which a good viewpoint is reached. Bearing half-left we may follow the interior wall towards the Martinengo Bastion. At the first main junction of streets a turning to the right leads shortly to the triple-apsed **Nestorian Church** or *Ayios Yeoryios Xorinos* ('St George the Exiler'), so called because it was believed that anyone wishing to rid himself of an enemy had only to collect some dust off the church floor and leave it in the enemy's house: the recipient would either conveniently die or leave the island within the year. A well-built edifice, it dates from c 1359, and was in use as an Orthodox church as recently as 1963, although in the past it had served as stables for camels.—Since 1974 many churches have been put to secular use by the Muslim citizens occupying the old city.

Returning to the main street circling the inner wall we shortly pass *Ayia Anna*, with its heavy belfry; some murals are visible, below which are Latin inscriptions.—To the right at the next corner is the so-called *Tanners' Mosque*, originally a 16C church.

We next pass (right)—in an area of the town under military occupation—the **Carmelites' Church**, or *St. Mary's*. Its monastery has disappeared; the church dates from the mid 14C. It is said that the body of the Latin Patriarch of Constantinople, Blessed Peter de Thomas, who died of wounds received at the siege of Alexandria in 1366, was buried at the entrance of the choir, 'so that all, even goats and dogs, might walk over it'. The interior preserves on its N wall some 14–15C Italian frescoes and coats of arms.

Almost adjacent is the *Armenian Church*, probably a chapel of the same monastery, containing some acoustic vases built into the ceiling; fragments of murals are seen on the walls. The Armenian community reached Famagusta in the 1330s and 40s, and the building dates from soon after their arrival.

Further NW is the *Martinengo Bastion* (see above), and two huge subterranean chambers (discovered in 1966), and provided with ventilation shafts. It could accommodate 2000 people and may well have been a place of refuge during the great siege.

Bearing NE, the wall is reached near the N entrance, where veering right we approach the ruins of **St. George of the Latins**, an attractive late 13C structure, once fortified, which might lead one to presume that it antedated the city walls. Note the capital of one of the wall shafts in the form of cluster of bats.

Passing near the entrance of the **Citadel** and the *Sea Gate* (for both see p 206), just beyond which are slight ruins of a church, turn right down Liman Yolu Street to the former *Cathedral of St. Nicholas, a remarkable example of early 14C French Gothic and the most important individual monument in Famagusta.

It was previously known as *St. Sophia* or *Aysofya*, until its name was changed in 1954 to the **Lala Mustafa Pasha Mosque**.

The building (55m long and 23m wide), possibly after the design of a Frenchman named Jean Langlois, was consecrated in 1326, and the only additions to the original structure are the two chapels on its S side and one on the N. Here, until 1372, the Lusignan kings of Cyprus (already crowned at Nicosia) came to be crowned 'King of Jerusalem', an empty honour; and here James II (the Bastard) and his infant son, James III, the last two sovereigns of that house, were buried (in 1473 and 1474 respectively). Caterina Cornaro, widow of the former, here renounced her royal rights in 1489, ceding the kingdom to Agostino Barberigo, Doge of Venice, before retiring to Asolo, N of Venice. (For her life, readers are referred to 'Caterina Cornaro: Queen of Cyprus', edited by David and Iro Hunt, and published by Trigraph in 1989).

It was much damaged during the bombardment of 1571, and on its conversion to a mosque any representation of the human figure in its decoration, furnishings, stained glass, and ornaments, etc. was destroyed, and its frescoes whitewashed, and altars demolished, although some medieval tombstones survive in the N aisle. Having been spared the usual Baroque embellishments and 19C 'restorations' which have destroyed the unity of many European cathedrals, it remains an unusual example of Gothic architecture at its most uncluttered. It was also considerably damaged by earthquake in 1735.

Bragadino (see Famagusta, History) was flayed alive between the two granite columns on the Parvis, probably from Salamis, once surmounted by a Venetian Lion and a statue of St. Theodore, respectively.

The PARVIS, shaded by an ancient *Ficus sycomorus*, was once more extensive. Here St. Bridget of Sweden is said to have preached against profligacy. It provides a good view of the West Front, with its three shallow porches (the centre one wider than the others), each surmounted by richly carved straight-sided gabled canopies. Over the centre porch is a superb six-light window, above which is a rose window (which may be compared to the more ornate W window at Lichfield). Above the side doors are tall blind double-light windows. The glass in the rose is an unfortunate 'restoration' of the turn of this century. The twin towers, of which only the lower parts survive, have been compared to those at Reims. The slender Minaret on the N tower is not too conspicuous.

Opposite the N wall are the ruins of the *Archbishop's Palace*, while from this wall projects what may be a sacristy. Much Gothic detail may be seen in the apse.

S of the Parvis is a *Loggia* in the Venetian style, of which the upper storey has been removed. It now contains a fountain for ritual Moslem ablution. The central doorway is flanked by two circular windows above which are Venetian coats of arms sculptured in marble. Below the window nearest the cathedral is a fragmentary marble frieze, probably from the cornice of a Roman temple, representing animals chasing each other through foliage.

On the W side of the square stands the imposing façade of the Venetian **Palazzo del Proveditore**, consisting of three arches supported by four columns, presumably from Salamis, and masking the earlier Lusignan palace. Over the central arch are the arms of Giovanni Renier, Captain of Cyprus in 1552. It was used as a prison during the first Turkish occupation, while among later prisoners was Mehmed Namik Kemal (1840–88), one of the most famous of Ottoman poets, exiled for his defiance of the sultan; his bust now embellishes the square. The imposing walls of the palace are now seen to advantage further W, since the site has been cleared.

To the NW is the ruined church of *St. Francis* (13C), almost all that remains of the monastery (described by Martoni in 1394 as 'a fair cloister, a dormitory, many cells and other rooms, with a fine garden and a quantity of conduits, and cisterns'). Its S chapel contains a number of tombstones dating from 1314 to 1474. Further down the same street is a 15C chapel; and adjacent are domed *Baths*.

Almost opposite St. Francis are the twin abutting churches of the *Templars* and the *Hospitallers* (14C), restored earlier this century, the latter with sockets in the gables for flagstaffs.

On the left-hand side of Naim Effendi St, leading N from the cathedral, survives a house in the Italian Renaissance style. A short distance beyond is an elaborate doorway known as '*Biddulph's Gate*', after the British High Commissioner who saved it from destruction in 1879.

Continuing down the street flanking the Venetian palace, we reach (left) the church of **St. Peter and St. Paul**, a heavy building of c 1360 with a Gothic N door, perhaps moved here from another church, and clumsy flying buttresses supporting the nave vaulting. Its reasonably good state of preservation owes much to the fact that it was used as a mosque and later as a storehouse, for it had been damaged in the earthquakes of 1546 and 1548. It is now a library.

The street leading S from the Cathedral square approaches, in the next left-hand turning, the curious church of *St. George of the Greeks*, a large Gothic building restored early this century, to the S of which lie the ruins of the original Byzantine Cathedral (*Ayios Symeon*), a smaller

structure, of which two apses survived the Turkish bombardment of
1571. It is claimed (but see p 213) that St. Epiphanios (310–406),
Archbishop of Salamis, was buried here, although his body was taken to
Constantinople in c 900. Fragments of paintings remain in the arches,
and founders' tombs are preserved on the side wall.

A short distance SW stands the barrel-vaulted church of *Stavros*
(16C), with a well-carved W doorway. It was long used as a mosque, and
more recently as a store.

Between St. George of the Greeks and the Djamboulat Gate to the SE
are two small ruined churches; *Ayios Nicolaos*, of which two semi-
circular apses remain and part of the S nave, once covered with murals;
and nearby to the S, *Ayia Zoni*, a 14–15C building in the Byzantine style
dedicated to the 'Holy Girdle', likewise once decorated with paintings
of which slight traces of an Archangel Michael survive.

Hence we may make our way to the ***Djamboulat Gate and Bastion**,
formerly the *Arsenal*, where the Turkish hero of the Siege of 1571 was
buried where he died. The vaulted hall of the bastion now contains a
small *Museum*, largely devoted to Turkish costume, including a bride's
dress, purses, etc.; also arms, and Venetian pottery (15C) and Ottoman
pottery (17C). The ascent to the tower is locked.

The *Land Gate* may be regained by following Arsinoë Av. to the W.

In the S sector of Famagusta (or **Varosha**)—at present (1990) out of
bounds—is the *Police Station* towards the N end of Anexartisias Av.
(leading SE from the Land Gate), where railway enthusiasts may
inspect the steam engine which from 1905–51 operated on the
Famagusta–Nicosia line, made by the Hunslet Engine Co. Ltd, Leeds,
and restored in 1972 by Major B.S. Turner and A.E. Fletcher. The
District Museum, situated further S in 28th October St, housed a
collection of local antiquities, largely from Salamis, and from the Royal
Tombs: see Rte 27.—Delphi St and its continuation lead SE from the
Djamboulat Bastion to the promenade flanking FAMAGUSTA BAY,
providing a view towards the extensive *'Golden Sands'* to the S.

27   Salamis and Enkomi-Alasia

The sites are approached by driving N from the *Land Gate* of Walled
Famagusta (see Rte 26), after c 6km crossing the estuary of the river
PEDIEOS, some distance beyond which the entrance to the main site of
SALAMIS is sign-posted on the right adjacent to the Custodian's
lodge.

Its traditional founder was Teucer, the banished son of Telamon, king of the
Greek island of Salamis. Artefacts of the 11C BC recently excavated lend
support to the claim, although there is evidence of some earlier settlement. It
replaced adjacent Alasia or Enkomi (see below) after c 1050 BC, when the more
ancient site was destroyed by fire and earthquake. Salamis was evidently the
first Cypriot city with its own coinage, c 560 BC. In c 400 Evagoras, its king,
indicated an Hellenic revival against Phoenician encroachments, but later the
island was obliged to pay tribute to the Persians, and in 306 its walls were
destroyed by Demetrius Poliorcetes ('the besieger').

Until 27 BC the island was under Ptolemaic rule, but Salamis had been
superseded meanwhile as the capital, and remained subordinate to Paphos until
c AD 350, when it was rebuilt after its port (famous for its shipyards) had been
destroyed by a tidal wave. It was renamed *Constantia* after its builder, the
Byzantine Emperor Constantine II. St. Barnabas was a native of Salamis (cf.
Paphos), which had a considerable Jewish population in the 1C, and here he,

Salamis

and probably St. Paul, suffered martyrdom at their hands. In 116–17 the Jews revolted and were suppressed throughout the island, and later expelled. It was the seat of an early Orthodox see, and provided one of three Cypriot bishops who in 325 attended the Council of Nicea.

The town was severely damaged by earthquakes in AD 76 or 77 and in the 4C, and in c 647–49 was sacked and largely razed by the Arabs under Muawiya, the first Ommayad caliph; it was on this expedition that Lady Umm Harām (maternal aunt of the Prophet Mohammed) accompanied her husband; see p 82. The town was abandoned by its inhabitants, who fled to nearby Famagusta, the walls of which were partly constructed from masonry quarried from the ruins of Constantia. These were occasionally visited and described in later centuries, Martin von Baumgarten (in 1508), among others, referring to them. The first of a number of modern expeditions to excavate the site took place in 1880; the most recent (University of Lyon) was interrupted by the Turkish invasion of 1974.

Soon after turning off the main road we bear left past (left) remains of the *City Wall*, and the site of *Thermae*, to reach a car park.

To the NW are the imposing ruins of the **Gymnasium*, the porticoed palaestra of which is entered from the S between the two pillars of a triple opening. Most of the marble columns re-erected here in 1952–55 are from the ruins of the adjacent theatre, and had already been transferred here during the Byzantine reconstruction. An annexe in the SW corner contains a semi-circular range of latrines, with seating for 44. The columns of the wider E portico (also from another ruined building) are taller, and fluted. Beyond each end of this portico are annexes containing rectangular pools, the northern one once embellished with statues, but some of these have been removed to the Cyprus Museum, Nicosia. Off each end of the portico are two *frigidaria* containing octagonal tanks, between which is the so-called *West Hall* (or *sudatorium*, the hot air room, heated by hypocausts), at either end of which are two small semi-circular niches, the southernmost preserving crude frescoes in its semi-dome.

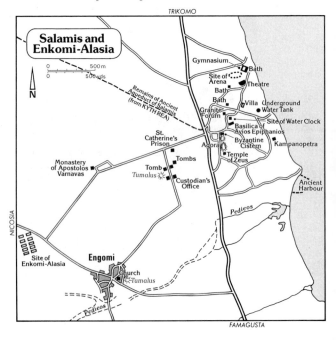

Hence we enter the *Main Building* of the **Baths**, the *caldarium*, its water heated from underground furnaces off the adjacent *North Hall*. The E end has been reconstructed in the form of an apse similar to that in the North Hall, the latter being entered via two tunnels in the thickness of the walls, between which is a mosaic. Another mosaic is preserved in the N wall of the North Hall, its outer wall sustained by three buttresses. We may return through the Main Building to enter the *South Hall*, in which parts of restored mosaics are visible. It is probable that both the North and South Halls were also *sudatoria*. Abutting the latter is a vaulted area, with stepped seats to the S.

A short distance S of the Gymnasium is the site of an *Amphitheatre* (yet to be excavated), and further S is the partially restored *Theatre, only discovered in 1959. It probably originated in the reign of Augustus Caesar, although remodelled during the 1–2Cs AD. It was destroyed during the earthquakes of the 4C, and later used as a quarry for the reconstruction of other buildings, most of the columns decorating the *frons scenae* being removed to the Gymnasium. The semi-circular auditorium consisted of about 50 rows of seats, with a capacity of 15,000 or more. They were dressed with white limestone, which is preserved on some of the lower rows.

The other sites of Salamis are spread over a wide area, partly hidden among low scrub and trees, but most of them may be visited with ease by foot or car. Turning due S just behind the theatre, we shortly pass (left) the slight remains of a Roman *villa*, before reaching a junction of tracks.

The left-hand turning leads to an underground Byzantine *Cistern* (6C), preserving paintings and inscriptions, but kept locked (apply in advance to the Custodian), beyond which we reach the shore. We may bear S here to approach the remains of the ancient *Harbour*, first passing (left) the site—yet to be thoroughly excavated—known as the **Kampanopetra**, with a large Early Christian *Basilica*, with two forecourts. A pavement with a design of concentric circles has been exposed to view, and five columns are standing.

Bearing half-right at the above junction, we shortly pass the so-called *Granite Forum*, preserving a number of columns of Egyptian granite from Aswan, c 5·5m in length. A short distance beyond, to the left, are the foundations of another **Basilica**, thought to be that of *Ayios Epiphanios*, measuring 58m long and 42m wide, and dating from the 4C. It consists of a central nave divided by columns from two side aisles. The semi-circular apse of the nave was probably provided with a synthronon, or raised benches for the clergy, in the 6C. At the E end of the S aisle is a marble-lined tomb, presumably that of St. Epiphanios, whose remains were transferred to Constantinople at the beginning of the 10C (see also p 210). By then the edifice had been largely devastated in Arab raids, and a new church was built c 698, extending E from the tomb, and comprising a nave and two side aisles separated by square piers which probably sustained a wooden roof; this in turn was reconstructed in the 9C, and the roof over the central nave replaced by three domes. This annexe to the ruined basilica continued in use until the 14C, but was later abandoned.

Continuing S, we soon veer to the right past (left) the 7C reservoir, known as the *Vouta* from its vaulting, built to receive water carried by the *Aqueduct* from Kythrea, c 56km away. Parts of the aqueduct are seen bearing NW away from the main road just beyond the Custodian's lodge.

Immediately S of the reservoir is the *Agora*, also known as the *Stone Forum*, the remains of which survive from its restoration prior to 22 BC, and which covered an area c 230m long and 55m wide. At the far end are the slight remains of a *Temple of Zeus*.

Continuing on our track, we shortly turn right and then left to regain the Custodian's lodge, and the main road.

Just S of this point we bear W, shortly reaching (left) a lane in which is the entrance to the ***Royal Tombs**, with a small *Museum* adjacent to the Custodian's lodge, containing some of the bronze horse-furniture found on the site, and some isometric drawings of interest.

The most easterly of the tombs is that long known as *St. Catherine's Prison* (Tomb 50), constructed of huge blocks of stone in the Roman period, and probably once used as a chapel dedicated to that Alexandrian martyr. However, excavations carried out in 1964–65 confirmed that the structure had been superimposed on tombs similar to others in this necropolis, dating from the 7C BC, and it had two yoked horses buried near the entrance.

Among other tombs, first excavated in 1962, which may be inspected, are those known as Nos 47 and 79, both containing the skeletons of horses ritually sacrificed after drawing the hearse of the 'king' to the *dromos*, the broad entrance passage to his tomb, where he would have been cremated. Remains of their harness, chariots, and other funerary objects were also found, while the burial chambers themselves had remained undisturbed.

Regaining the road, we turn left to approach (right) the **Monastery of Apostolos Varnavas** (St. Barnabas), first passing a small restored mausoleum covering an empty rock-cut tomb, claimed to have once contained the remains of that saint, said to have been killed by the Jews of Salamis. These relics were opportunely revealed in 477/8, and a monastery was erected adjacent, which was destroyed later in Saracen raids. The present *Church*, incorporating remains of its 15C predecessor, and including a green spirally-fluted column adjacent to the bema, was built in the traditional style in 1756, but was damaged by an earthquake in 1941. Several capitals, presumably from Salamis, have been re-used. Other relics lie adjacent to the building, including what appear to be two female statues, which deserve preservation. It has drum domes replacing the original wooden roof, a cloister to the W, and a bell-tower added in 1958.

Bearing SW, we shortly reach the *Site* of **Enkomi-Alasia**, the name *Alasia* being added in 1952, although the debate continues as to whether it was the ancient capital of Cyprus (c 1600–1050 BC).

The name Alasia occurs on eight of the El Amarna Tablets found in Egypt and recording letters from foreign rulers to Pharaohs Amenophis III and Akhenaten (18th Dynasty). Many scholars argue that Enkomi or Cyprus was the place called Alasia in the El Amarna letters.

The earliest finds so far discovered date from the Middle Cypriot era (2000–1700 BC), but its period of prosperity commenced c 1550 BC when it became a copper-processing centre, with mines probably at Khalkovouni, near Lysi, c 19km SW. It continued to flourish as an emporium for the export of minerals and had close trading contacts with Ugarit (modern Ras Shamra), 145km across the sea near Latakia, in Syria. In the following two centuries it was ravaged by the Anatolians and Greeks. Consumed by fire, what remained of the partly rebuilt town was razed in an earthquake later in the 12C BC. It was finally abandoned in c 1050 BC, and its inhabitants moved to nearby Salamis. It was later partially submerged by silt from neighbouring rivers.

Plundered over the centuries, the necropolis was first systematic-ally excavated in 1934, when Professor Claude Schaeffer uncovered a number of buildings, although in 1896, 1913 and 1930 various tombs had been opened to reveal important artefacts, including Mycenaean pottery. In 1946–47 a stretch of its outer fortifications was discovered, since when—until 1974—further expeditions have continued work on the site. Although of paramount importance, for the layman the site, laid out on a rough grid, is somewhat confusing, for comparatively little survives above ground.

The main buildings so far excavated are—from N to S—a fortress-like structure abutting the *North Gate*; the *Sanctuary of the Horned God* (where the famous statue, now in the Cyprus Museum, Nicosia, was found: see below); the so-called *Building 18*, of fine ashlar stone construction; the *House of the Pillar*; and the *House of the Bronzes*, named after the quantity of bronze objects unearthed there.

The adjacent village of **Enkomi** or *Engomi* (its name probably derived from *Neo Gomi*) was not resettled until comparatively recently, and the site was not excavated until 1896 (British Museum Expedition). Subsequent excavations revealed the buildings of ancient Alasia, and a number of important finds, including (in 1948–51) the remarkable 'Horned God' (12C BC), and a fragmentary baked clay tablet inscribed on one face with Cypro-Minoan script, as yet undeciphered, but with similarities with Linear A. Artefacts from Enkomi-Alasia in private collections in Famagusta have since the Turkish Occupation of 1974 been appearing on the European Black Market in antiquities.

The church at *Engomi*, a short distance E, which we pass to regain the main Famagusta road, was rebuilt in 1736, while further E is the so-called *Cenotaph of Nicocreon* (late 4C BC), a tumulus covering a stone platform erected for a funeral pyre. When excavated in 1965–66 this revealed a number of gold ornaments, clay statues, etc., but no human remains, suggesting that the funeral may have been merely symbolic, and perhaps commemorating the death of Nicocreon, the last king of Salamis, and of his family.

28 Famagusta to the Apostolos Andreas Monastery: the Karpas Peninsula

98km (61 miles).

We drive N, parallel to FAMAGUSTA BAY, after 5km crossing the river YIALIAS, immediately beyond which the left-hand turning leads to *Enkomi-Alasia* (see above); and a short distance further N, on the right, is the entrance to the site of *Salamis*: see Rte 27. *Ayios Seryios* (see Rte 24) lies NW of the latter turning.

5km. *Spathariko* lies to the W, probably populated during the Byzantine era, while Roman tombs have also been found in the village.

3km SW is the abandoned village of *Paradiso*, once the site of a residence of King Aimery, whose wife and children were kidnapped from here by Greek pirates and eventually ransomed and restored by King Leo of Armenia. Built into the S narthex of the 16C church are columns and capitals removed from Salamis.

After 4km a left-hand fork off the coast road leads shortly to *Trikomo*, see Rte 24.

A road leads N hence through *Ardhana* to (c 15km) *Kantara*; but see below. After c 10km this road circles the N side of the peak of KANTARA (724m), otherwise known as *Sino Oros* (with a TV relay station), to approach the hamlet of *Kantara*

At 6km we enter the coastal village of *Boghaz*.

FROM BOGHAZ TO THE CASTLE OF KANTARA (c 16km). After traversing adjacent *Monarga*, we follow an attractive road via *Ayios Elias* (where we fork right) and *Yerani*. The road then climbs steeply to the hamlet of *Kantara*. The *CASTLE OF KANTARA lies some 4km further NE, rising to a height of 630m. The road ascends to within a few minutes' walk from the main E entrance.

Its name is probably derived from the Arabic for a bridge. The original castle—the most easterly of the three great fortresses of the Kyrenia range— was built towards the end of the 9C, although improved during the Lusignan era, and was first referred to as that in which Isaac Comnenos took refuge after his skirmish with Richard I at Tremetousha, before his eventual surrender, when he was apparently fettered in chains of silver.

In 1229–30 it was held by supporters of Frederick II Hohenstaufen, and held out until the death of Gauvain de Chenichy, who had sought refuge there; it was likewise briefly in the hands of Sir Aimery Barlais. It was also a pocket of resistance during the Genoese occupation, and Prince John of Antioch escaped here later. In 1391 James I re-fortified the place, which remained an important defensive outpost of the island until dismantled and abandoned by the Venetians in 1525 and left to the mercy of the elements. Its ruins were apparently occupied by a hermit called Simeon between 1815 and c 1875. A system of flares at night linked it with Buffavento and Nicosia.

An impressive *View may be gained by the less energetic from a point a short distance E of the E bastion.

We scramble up a winding path to enter through an imposing but ruined barbican protected by towers, and cross the outer bailey to reach the main enceinte and Custodian's lodge in a vaulted room to the left. Continuing the circuit in a clockwise direction, we pass a range of three vaulted chambers provided with loopholes, and used as barracks, abutted by a medieval latrine. Further on is a horseshoe-shaped cistern, some distance beyond which, at the SW corner of the fortifications, are three more vaulted chambers, a sally port, and cisterns. From here we may climb to the *Summit Tower*, providing panoramic *Views, and preserving a Gothic window. Descending to the NE we may visit the *NE Tower*, approached through a loopholed passage, from the upper floor of which a projecting loopholed parapet is reached. Hence, by making our way along the E wall, we regain the entrance.

At 4km NE of Boghaz the road by-passes (right) *Gastria* (ancient *Alaas*), with a Byzantine church now a school, and by the shore the ruined chapel of *Ayios Ioannis*. Gunnis suggests that a more important church once stood here, owing to the evidence of the numerous glass mosaic cubes to be found. A gypsum and cement factory has been established here. By the shore rise the slight remains of the twin Templar castles of *Kastros* and *Strongylos* (c 1101), below which King Henry II, sent into exile by the usurper Amaury, Prince of Tyre, set sail for Armenia in 1310; in 1229 Jean d'Ibelin landed here to assist his relatives in the revolt of that year.

Not far N of Gastria is the village of *Patriki*, of little interest, but the site of what was a curious local custom. On Easter Monday all the married peasants gathered in the churchyard where stood a large stone with a hole in it, through which the men, coatless, had to crawl. Any unable to do so were considered cuckolded, his horns preventing him! According to Gunnis, even as recently as 1935, when one man stuck, he beat up his wife on his return home and started divorce proceedings, his inability to pass through being considered ample evidence (cf. *Spitali*).

For *Komi Kebir*, 8km N of the main road, see Rte 23.

5km. *Ayios Theodhoros*, also the site of a Mid and Late Cypriot settlement, had the first cable office in Cyprus (1871; from Latakia on the Syrian coast; this cable was soon after extended to Larnaca). Its village church is much restored.

5km S, near CAPE ELEA, lie the ruins of the Phoenician settlement of *Cnidus*, destroyed by the Ptolemites c 250 BC, but having a natural harbour, still survived until the 2C AD. It was the birthplace of Ctesias (late 5C BC), author of a History of Persia, etc.

Some 5km N of Ayios Theodhoros, and beyond the village of *Livadhia*, is the early Byzantine church of *Panayia tis Kyras* or *Kyriotissa* (?7C), with a S porch and narthex added later. The superstition that a mosaic cube carried in the pocket would prevent pimples, etc., was largely responsible for the disappearance of the mosaic of the Virgin, and now little remains. Damp-stained relics of 13C murals survive.

The main road continues NE to (6km) *Tavros*, a pleasant village also approached by a more southerly road via *Vokolidha*, surrounded by a number of old tombs of varying periods, while near the beach the wreck may still be seen of an Austrian steamer carrying Circassian colonists to Cyprus in the early 1860s; most of the passengers perished.

Galatia, said to have been founded c 300 BC by Greek immigrants, lies c 2km N of Tavros, but is of little interest in itself. The church of *Ayia Marina* was converted into a mosque in the 17C.

6km. **Koma tou Yialou**, an ancient village apparently much larger in the Middle Ages, was the site of the burial of Margaret d'Ibelin (1323). Above the village stands *Ayia Solomoni*, a well-preserved building of the 15C or earlier, covering a tomb dating from the Classical era; a necropolis of this period surrounds the church, in which some crude 9 or 10C murals were to be seen. Other churches and chapels of interest are those of *Panayia* (17C, with wall-paintings), *Ayia Nikolaos* (16C), and *Nikoloudhi* (to the W; also 16C). To the E is the *Kakozonara quarry*, source of much of the stone for the rebuilding of the walls of Famagusta.

The main road now bears N to (5km) **Leonarisso**, with the church of *Ayios Dhimitrios*. A Late Cypriot site was excavated here in 1914, while Gunnis reported that he was responsible for the re-erection here of two 3C BC statues that had long lain prone in the village.

FROM LEONARISSO TO GALINOPORNI (c 16km). This minor road leads parallel to the S shore of the **Karpas Peninsula** via **Lythrangomi**, N of which stands the ancient and admirably composed church of **Kanakaria** (11–12C). Until recently it preserved mosaics from its 6C predecessor. That of the Virgin and Child, of which a fragment survived in the conch of the apse, and more primitive than that at Kiti, was removed by art-thieves in 1974–79. These appeared on the art market in Indianapolis (USA) in the summer of 1989, and were reclaimed by the Government of Cyprus. The church consists of three barrel-vaulted naves supporting a tall domed drum at the crossing, and has semi-circular apses. A domed narthex was later added. The whole was restored in 1779, and badly handled in 1920, after which it was again restored.

Adjacent *Vathylakkas* has a 17C church (*Ayios Yeoryios*), with an open colonnade and old plates decorating its vault; to the S is that of *Ayios Theodhoros* (14C), ruined and surrounded by a thicket of trees, local superstition assuming that illness or death will strike down those who attempt to cut wood here.—3km SE, near the coast, is the village of *Neta*, to the E of which are the ruins of a large temple, and walls, while to the S of this site a quantity of terracotta figurines has been unearthed. Below the 18C church of *Panayia* is a subterranean vaulted chamber and holy well.—Further E is domed *Ayios Seryios* (14C), its interior once covered with frescoes, now destroyed.

Continuing E from Vathylakkas, we traverse (3km) *Ayios Symeon*, near which is a curious and important *Cave Tomb* (access difficult), cut some 26m into the precipice, and best visited with a guide. Near by is the former settlement of *Elissu*, also with rock-cut tombs, probably Phoenician in origin.

7km. *Korovia*, near which, at *Nitovikla* (or *Nektovikla*; 4km S on the coast), a Middle Cypriot fortress was excavated in 1929.—3km beyond Korovia, we reach **Galinoporni**, on the outskirts of which, near ruined *Ayia Anna*, is another remarkable cave tomb 21m long, and similar to that near Ayios Symeon (see above). Numerous other rock-cut tombs, assumed to be Phoenician, are scattered over the slope on which the semi-troglodyte village lies. The road—or rather, track—continues NE towards (13km) *Rizokarpaso*, see below. There is a ruined Romanesque church (*Panayia Aphendrika*; 12C) 3km NE of Galinoporni.

Continuing NE from Leonarisso, and by-passing *Kilanemos*, N of which is a domed Byzantine church, its interior garishly restored, we traverse (5km) **Ayios Andronikos**, with a large late 18C church. *Ayia Photeini* (reportedly looted) is of slight interest. In the vicinity is a small medieval chapel.

4km. **Yialousa**, a large and ancient village, contains several churches; the principal one (*Arkhangelos Michael*), a small 13C building with an arcaded apse, and an 18C church added, is the only one of interest.

Hence the main road approaches the N coast of the **Karpas Peninsula**, traversing olive and carob groves near (right) the church of **Ayia Trias** (1730), on the site of a recently excavated Early Christian *Basilica, of which three aisles, a baptistry, and a quantity of mosaic paving survive. After 7km we reach the church of *Ayios Thyrsos* (15C) and 3km beyond, that of *Ayios Photios tis Selinias* (?10C), badly restored c 1930 and later abandoned.

About 2km from the former are two large female statues of the Roman period, cut from the limestone, and lying where their sculptor left them over 1600 years ago. Remains of a medieval watchtower may also be seen.

Some 8km beyond Ayios Thyrsos—near the S end of RONNAS BAY— is the monastery of *Panaya Eleousa*: the church is early 16C, with a richly decorated S door. The interior has been whitewashed and its frescoes hidden.

We bear E to (4km) **Rizokarpaso**, the seat of one of the 12 Lusignan provinces of the island. It belonged to a number of important families, among them the De Nores, La Roche, and Verny, and from 1222 to c 1600 it was the residence of the Orthodox Bishop of Famagusta. Some of the houses date from the mid 18C, but the more modern parts of the town are unappealing. Much tobacco is grown here.

Its inhabitants had a reputation for the prevalence of blue (or green) eyes, but be that as it may, Sir Samuel Baker, when he visited the place over a century ago, was not so thrilled by its womenfolk, whom he ungallantly condemned as 'the ugliest, dirtiest, shortest and most repulsive lot' he ever saw, reinforcing Alexander Drummond's opinion (1750), who also reported that he 'did not see one handsome woman in the place, which hath been always famed for its beauties'.

The principal church (*Ayios Synesios*) dates from the 12C, and was originally a cathedral; two apses retain their Byzantine arcading. The building was drastically modernised and enlarged in the 18C, but is of little architectural note and the interior contains nothing of interest, although recently restored after a fashion.—There are, however, a number of churches and chapels in the vicinity, among them *Ayia Mavra* (to the N), of the 13C or earlier, preserving some decayed murals, and mosaic pavements, the whole restored; likewise neighbouring *Ayia Marina*, lit only by small arrow-slits, and roofed with large stone slabs.

Some 3km due N of the town, near the sea, by the imposing ruins of ancient *Karpasia*, is the church of ***Ayios Philon** (10C), immediately S of which is the marble mosaic floor of a basilica some 500 years earlier in date, which it superseded. Regrettably, it has been the object of pilfering tourists. Karpasia was possibly the landing-place of Demetrius in 306 BC, and the two moles of large square blocks clamped together with metal rivets may be seen, perhaps Phoenician in origin. The place was burned by the Arabs in 802.

Some 6km NE is the ancient settlement of **Aphendrika**, which according to Strabo was in c 200 BC one of the six great cities of Cyprus, but only three ruined churches and a citadel remain to remind us of its former prosperity: *Panayia Khrysiotissa*, the largest, is a cruciform structure of the 12C in the ruins of which a smaller church was constructed in the 14C. To the S are the ruins of a domed Byzantine church (*Ayios Yeoryios*), containing narrow arched passages connecting the central apse to those on either side.—Further N is the harbour of the ancient city, largely silted up; to the W is the necropolis, with numerous rock-cut tombs, and beyond, the site of a temple. E of the churches is the interesting citadel, the plan of which is determined by the fact that many of its rooms were cut into the rock itself. The site is entered from the SE.

Some 3km SE of Rizokarpaso is the ruined Byzantine church of *Ayios Pappos*, only of interest because of its dedication to the first bishop of the see of Chytri, who forcibly consecrated Epiphanios as Bishop of Salamis.

The main road from Rizokarpaso crosses a ridge and then descends past the settlement of *Khelones* and skirts the S shore of the peninsula to (c 16km) the Monastery of **Apostolos Andreas**, a building of 1867 which particularly since 1895 has been the occasional goal of pilgrimage, as it is said to be the site where St. Andrew put in for water during a voyage. The large church is without much interest, although it contains several chandeliers and an iconostasis. Below, nearer the rocky shore, is a 14–15C chapel vaulted from a central pillar. The area is one of the many where it is claimed Isaac Comnenos surrendered to Richard I in 1191.

A track continues N to (4km) the CAPE OF APOSTOLOS ANDREAS, the far NE point of Cyprus, where stood a temple of Aphrodite Akraia, beyond which the chain of the *Klidhes Islands* runs out to sea, on one of which is a lighthouse. On the tip of the cape is the Neolithic settlement of *Kastros*, the earliest yet found in Cyprus, excavated in 1971–73. The islands are the habitat of the rare Audouin's Gull (Larus Audouini).

Richard Pococke made the expedition to this NE promontory in 1738, when it was 'almost uninhabited, except that there are a few Turkish herdsmen on the south side'. He remarked that he could 'very plainly' see Mount Cassius near Antioch (to the NE) 'and the mountain of *Rhossus*, now called cape *Hog*, which is between *Kepsé* and *Scanderoon*'.

INDEX

Topographical names are printed in roman or **bold** type, the names of persons in *italics*; subjects are in CAPITALS. Towns and the main sites have subordinate indexes. Some of the more isolated churches and monasteries are included. When more than one place name is listed, the district (or nearest town or village) is indicated in brackets: (Fam)agusta; (Kry)enia; (Lar)nica; (Lim)assol; (Nic)osia; and (Paphos). For the various archaeological periods, see the Chronological table on p 33; note also the paragraph on Place-names on p 12.

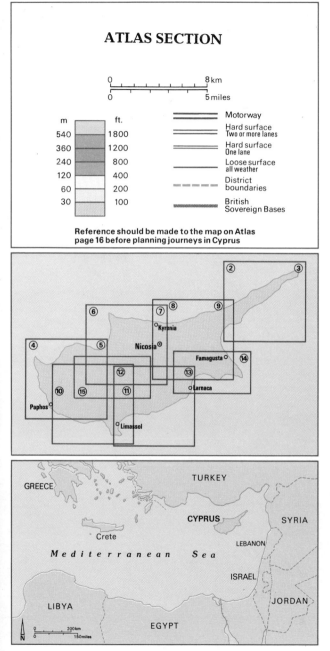

ATLAS SECTION

m		ft.
540		1800
360		1200
240		800
120		400
60		200
30		100

Motorway

Hard surface
Two or more lanes

Hard surface
One lane

Loose surface
all weather

District
boundaries

British
Sovereign Bases

**Reference should be made to the map on Atlas
page 16 before planning journeys in Cyprus**

Kyrenia
Nicosia
Famagusta
Larnaca
Paphos
Limassol

GREECE
TURKEY
CYPRUS
SYRIA
Crete
LEBANON
Mediterranean Sea
ISRAEL
LIBYA
JORDAN
EGYPT

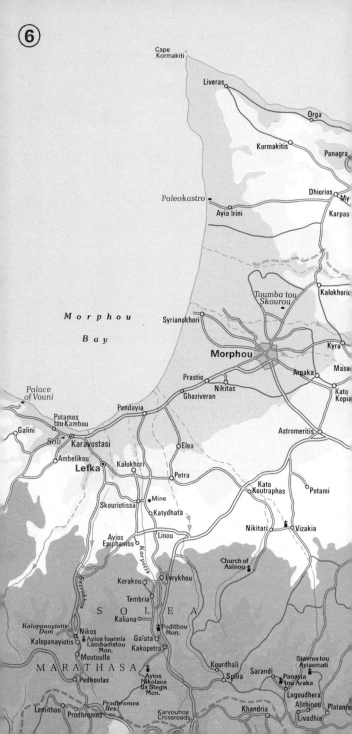

Vavilas

Margi

Akhropiitos Point
Lambousa

Akhiropiitos Mon.
Glykiotissa Island (Snake Island)

Kyrenia

Vasilla
Lapithos
Karavas
Elea
Ayios Yeoryios
Temblos
Karakoumi

Mt. Kornos 946m
Paleosophos
Trimithi
St. Hilarion Castle
Thermia Kazaphani
Ayios Epiktitos

Larnaka tis Lapithou
Karmi Prophitis
Abbey
Bellapais

Agridhaki
Elias 888m
Aghirda
Mt. Alonagra 935m
Panayia Absinthiotissa

Sisklipos
Pileri
Pano Dhikomo
Sykhari Vouno

ambyll
Asomatos
Kondemenos
Krini
Ayios Ermolaos
Kato Dhikomo

Photta

Prophitis Elias Mon.
Skylloura
Ayia Marina

yios eoryios igatos on.

Philia

Ayios Vasilios
Geunyeli
Orta Keuy
Pedieos
Trakhonas

Yerolakkos
Nicosia

Avlona
Mammari

Kokkino Trimithia
NICOSIA AIRPORT
Engomi
Strovolos

Akaki
Paleometokho
Arkhangelos Gabriel Mon.

Meniko
Laxia

Orounda ios olaos
Ayii Trimithias

Eliophotes
ato oni
Ayios Panteleimon Mon.
Anayia
Panayia Khrysospiliotissa
Kato Dhftera

Agrokipia
Aredhiou
Argates
Psomolophou

Mitsero
Malounda
Ayios Mnason Mon. (ruin)
Episkopio
Pera
Tamassos
Ayios Eftykios
Nisou
Ayii Apostoli

Klirou
Pollitiko
Ayios Heracleidios Mon.
Margi
Kochati
Perakhorio

Ayios Epiphanios
Kalokhorio
Kambia
Analiondas
Ayia Paraskevi
Ayia Varvara

Pedieos
Kalaliondas
Panayia Khrysogalatousa
Mine
Alambra

Gourri
Phikardhou
Kapedhes
Mathiati
Sha

Lazania
Lythrodhonda

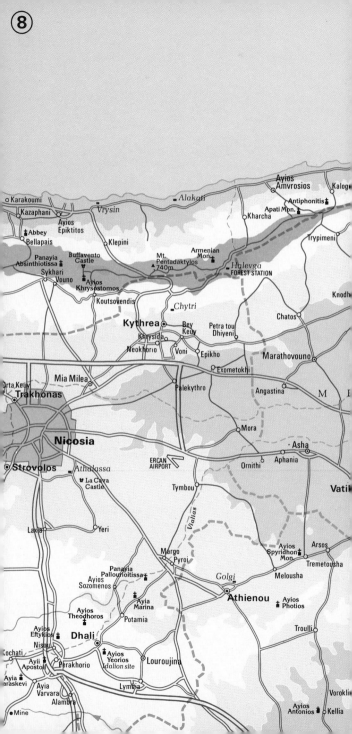

Karakoumi
Kazaphani
Abbey
Bellapais
Ayios
Epiktitos
Klepini
Vrysin
Alakati
Ayios
Amvrosios
Antiphonitis
Kalog
Apati Mon.
Kharcha
Trypimeni

Panayia
Absinthiotissa
Sykhari
Vouno
Buffavento
Castle
Ayios
Khrysostomos
Koutsovendis
Mt.
Pentadaktylos
740m
Armenian
Mon.
Halevga
FOREST STATION
Knodh

Chytri
Kythrea
Bey
Keuy
Petra tou
Dhiyeni
Chatos

Khrysida
Neokhorio
Voni
Epikho
Exometokhi
Marathovouno

Orta Keuy
Mia Milea
Trakhonas
Palekythro
Angastina
M

Nicosia
Mora
Asha

Strovolos
Athalassa
ERCAN
AIRPORT
Ornithi
Aphania

La Cava
Castle
Tymbou
Vati

Laxia
Yeri
Vialias

Mergo
Pyroi
Ayios
Spyridhon
Mon.
Arsos
Tremetousha

Panayia
Pallouroitissa
Ayios
Sozomenos
Golgi
Melousha

Ayios
Theodhoros
Ayia
Marina
Potamia
Athienou
Ayios
Photios

Ayios
Eftykios
Nisou
Dhali
Troulli

Kochati
Ayii
Apostol
Perakhorio
Ayios
Yeorios
Idalion site
Louroujina

Ayia
araskevi
Ayia
Varvara
Alambra
Lymbia
Vorokli

Mine
Ayios
Antonios
Kellia

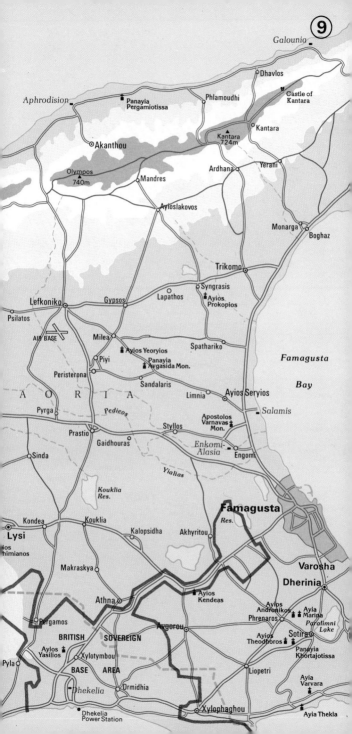

Galounia

Dhavlos

Aphrodision

Panayia
Pergamiotissa

Phlamoudhi

Castle of
Kantara

Kantara

○Akanthou

Kantara
724m

Ardhana

Yerani

Olympos
740m

○Mandres

Monarga

Boghaz

Ayioslakovos

Trikomo

Lefkoniko

Gypsos

Lapathos

Syngrasis

Ayios
Prokopios

Psilatos

AIR BASE

Milea

Spathariko

Famagusta

Piyi

Ayios Yeoryios

Panayia
Avgasida Mon.

Bay

Peristerona

Sandalaris

A O R I A

Limnia

Ayios Seryios

Salamis

Pyrga

Pedieos

Prastio

Styllos

Apostolos
Varnavas
Mon.

*Enkomi-
Alasia*

Gaidhouras

Engomi

○Sinda

Yialias

*Kouklia
Res.*

Kondea

Kouklia

Kalopsidha

Akhyritou

Famagusta

Res.

●**Lysi**

ios
himianos

Makraskya

Varosha

Dherinia

Athna

Ayios
Kendeas

Ayios
Andronikos

Ayia
Marina

*Paralimni
Lake*

○Pergamos

BRITISH

SOVEREIGN

Avgorou

Phrenaros

Ayios
Theodhoros

Sotira

Ayios Yasilios

Xylotymbou

BASE

AREA

Panayia
Khortajotissa

Pyla

Dhekelia

Ormidhia

Liopetri

Ayia
Varvara

Dhekelia
Power Station

Xylophaghou

Ayia Thekla

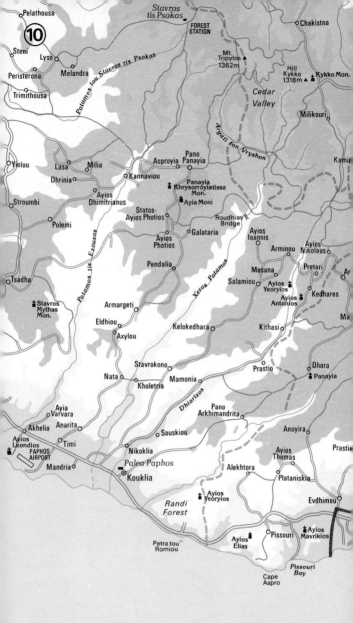

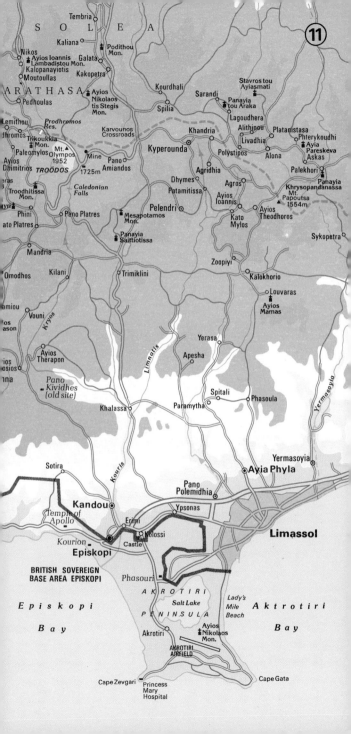

S O L E A

Tembria
Kaliana
Podithou Mon.
Nikos
Ayios Ioannis
Galata
Lambadistou Mon.
Kalopanayiotis
Kakopetra
Moutoullas
Kourdhali
Stavros tou Ayiasmati
A R A T H A S A
Ayios Nikolaos tis Stegis Mon.
Sarandi
Panayia tou Araka
Pedhoulas
Spilia
Lagoudhera
Lemithou
Prodhromos Res.
Karvounos Crossroads
Khandria
Alithinou
Livadhia
Platanistasa
Phterykoudhi
thromos
Trikoukkia Mon.
Pano Amiandos
Kyperounda
Polystipos
Alona
Ayia Pareskeva
Paleomylos
Mt. Olympos 1952
Mine
Askas
Ayios Dhimitrios
1725m
Agridhia
Agros
Palekhori
TROODOS
Dhymes
Ayios Ioannis
Panayia Khrysopandanassa
Troodhitissa Mon.
Caledonian Falls
Potamitissa
Pelendri
Ayios Theodhoros
Mt. Papoutsa 1554m
Phini
Pano Platres
Mesapotamos Mon.
Kato Mylos
Sykopetra
ato Platres
Panayia Saittiotissa
Zoopiyi
Kalokhorio
Mandria
Kilani
Trimiklini
Louvaras
Omodhos
Ayios Mamas
amiou
Vouni
Yerasa
os ason
Apesha
Ayios Therapon
Spitali
Phasoula
ios osios
Pano Kividhes (old site)
Paramytha
Yermasoyia
nna
Khalassa
Yermasoyia
Sotira
Ayia Phyla
Pano Polemidhia
Kandou
Ypsonas
Temple of Apollo
Erimi
Limassol
Kourion
Kolossi Castle
Episkopi
BRITISH SOVEREIGN BASE AREA EPISKOPI
Phasouri
A K R O T I R I
E p i s k o p i
Salt Lake
Lady's Mile Beach
A k r o t i r i
P E N I N S U L A
Bay
Akrotiri
Ayios Nikolaos Mon.
Bay
AKROTIRI AIRFIELD
Cape Zevgari
Princess Mary Hospital
Cape Gata

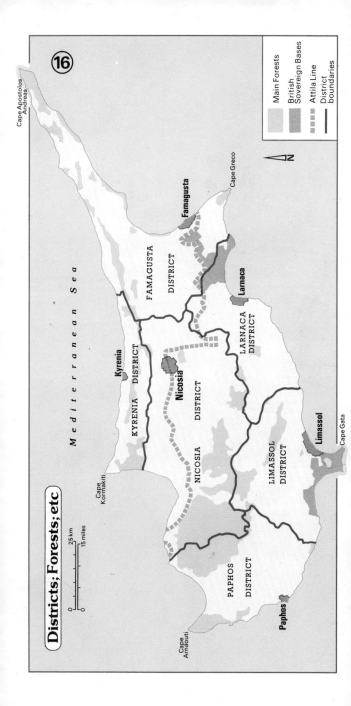

Districts; Forests; etc

Legend:
- Main Forests
- British Sovereign Bases
- Attila Line
- District boundaries

⑯

N

Mediterranean Sea

Cape Apostolos Andreas

Cape Kormakiti

Cape Arnaouti

Cape Greco

Cape Gata

Kyrenia

Famagusta

Larnaca

Nicosia

Limassol

Paphos

KYRENIA DISTRICT

FAMAGUSTA DISTRICT

LARNACA DISTRICT

NICOSIA DISTRICT

LIMASSOL DISTRICT

PAPHOS DISTRICT

0 25 km
0 15 miles